IMAGES
*of America*

# MARSHALL COUNTY

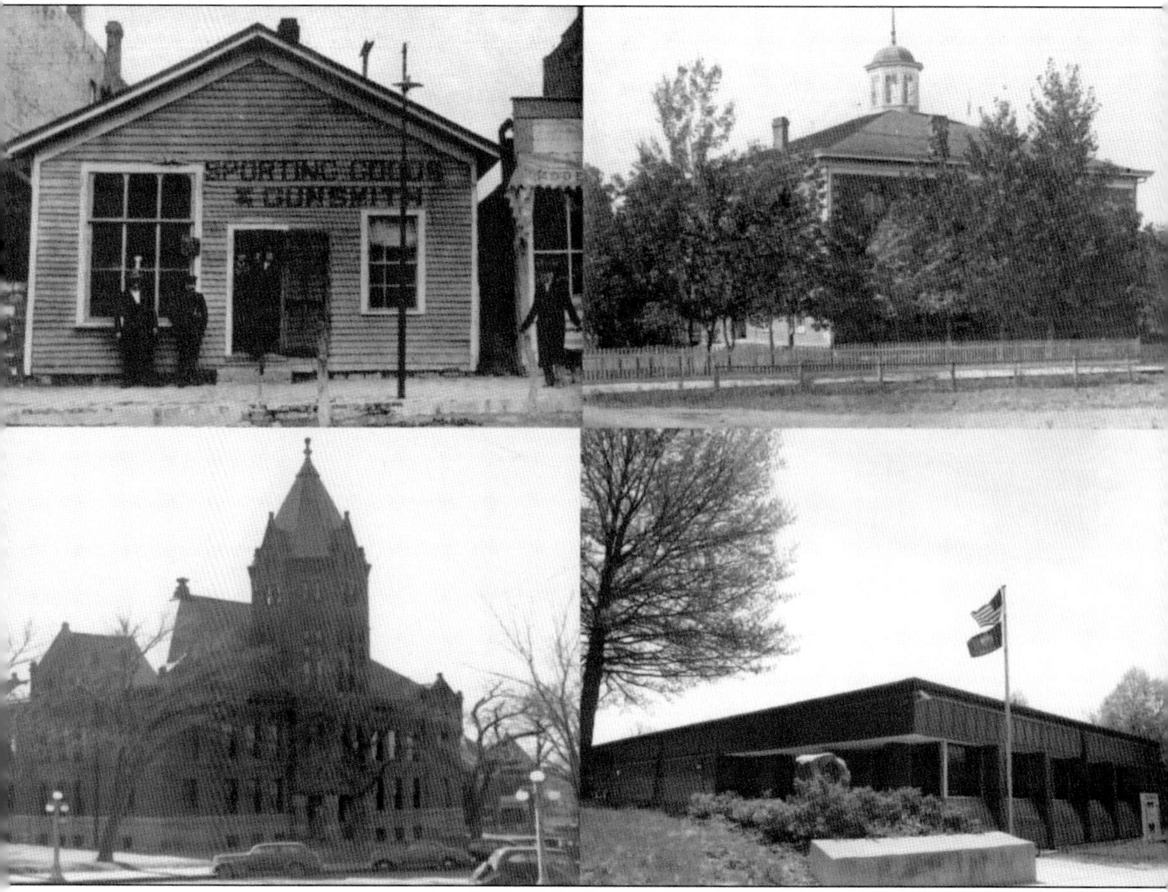


Marshall County has had four courthouses since 1862. Between the county's formation in 1855 and its first designated courthouse building in 1862, meetings were held wherever convenient. The first courthouse, upper left, was in use from 1862 to 1874. This frame building was originally a church and later a stable in Palmetto, a town immediately north of Marysville. In 1862, the building was moved by a team of oxen to 810 Broadway and became the first county courthouse. The photograph was taken in the 1890s, when the building was a gun shop. The second courthouse, upper right, was built on Broadway at Thirteenth Street in 1874. It was destroyed on New Year's Eve 1890 in a fire of suspicious origin. The third courthouse, lower left, was built in 1891 at the same location as the previous courthouse. The total cost of this stately brick Richardsonian Romanesque building was $43,000. This courthouse was saved from demolition in the 1970s through the efforts of the Marshall County Historical Society and many county citizens, and is currently a museum and research library. The county's current courthouse, lower right, was built in 1979 and is located directly west of the 1891 courthouse. (Photographs of the 1862, 1874, and 1891 courthouses, courtesy of the Marshall County Historical Society; photograph of the 1979 courthouse, courtesy of Raoul Delmare.)

**On the Cover:** In the 1920s and 1930s, the Marysville Labor Day parade down Broadway was an extravaganza. Most businesses participated, often with floats covered with flowers or crepe paper. Bands and other marching units, like the Turnverein and the Modern Woodmen of America, entertained throngs of adults and children gathered along the route. Harry Bair, a Kansas Power and Light lineman, was the announcer for a clown band in 1930. Here, he entertains children before the parade begins. (Courtesy of the Marshall County Historical Society.)

IMAGES
*of America*

# MARSHALL COUNTY

Sherrill Wadham Sparks
with the Marshall County Historical Society

ARCADIA
PUBLISHING

ISBN 978-1-4671-1301-4

Published by Arcadia Publishing
Charleston, South Carolina

Printed in the United States of America

Library of Congress Control Number: 2014940113

For all general information, please contact Arcadia Publishing:
Telephone 843-853-2070
Fax 843-853-0044
E-mail sales@arcadiapublishing.com
For customer service and orders:
Toll-Free 1-888-313-2665

Visit us on the Internet at www.arcadiapublishing.com

*In memory of my great-grandparents Mathias and Christina Mentgen, grandparents Percy and Clara Wadham, and parents, Ambrose and Shirley Wadham. They gave me roots in Marshall County.*

# Contents

# Acknowledgments

I am indebted to the Marshall County Historical Society for entrusting me, an out-of-state stranger, with this project. I have always loved this part of Kansas, but Marshall County is roughly 900 square miles, and during my childhood visits I had never been more than six blocks from my grandmother's house by the city park. I had a lot to learn!

I am immensely grateful to Julie and Frank Popejoy, who opened their home and included me as family during all of my trips for research and writing. I truly treasure their friendship, support, and genuine interest in this project.

I sincerely thank Carol Achterkirch for 45 years of friendship and for hospitality and good company midway in my trips to and from Kansas.

The book could not have been completed without my committee from the historical society. Barb Fenstermacher has been the research librarian at MCHS for nearly 25 years. With her help, research took a fraction of the time it might have. Volunteer Luann Kongs has catalogued more than 3,500 of the seemingly endless collection of photographs, and she enthusiastically prepared all the photographs for this book. Dennis Richardson has an extensive collection of early photographs and remarkable knowledge about county landmarks and railroads; he generously shared both. Elizabeth Skinner has a reverence of language that has been invaluable, and she has tamed my literary excesses to ensure an articulate narrative. I have enjoyed their company and I value their contributions. A simple thank-you is not enough.

I wish to acknowledge the contributions of those who have died but whose photographs, histories, journals, and memoirs have been left for succeeding generations to ponder, research, and enjoy: Emma Forter, John Ellenbecker, Omar Hawkins, Olin Deibert, Byron and Eulalia Guise, Oretha Ruetti, my aunt Geraldine Wadham Holle, and my father, Ambrose Wadham.

I offer special thanks to my husband, Russell Sparks, who has his own fond memories of small-town life. He has been supportive throughout this project, especially in my belief that a frequent 1,000-mile commute was perfectly reasonable.

With only a few exceptions, the photographs used in this volume are the property of the Marshall County Historical Society. The choice of chapter topics, photographs, and stories was mine alone. Any errors belong solely to me.

# INTRODUCTION

*Reveries of the Past—Scribbling in albums is not my forte, although I believe I understand their import. For my part I shall not attempt here to call up particularly any of the events of the past ten years of our acquaintance. Our life on these boundless prairies of the far West has perhaps been as varied as the seasons have made the landscape that surrounds us. I can only express the sincere wish here that your future life may be more Summer than Winter – more Sunshine than Clouds – that Friendship may smile upon you, as the bright sun smiles upon the beauteous and variegated plains of Kansas, and that the flowers of thought that will gather here may form a smiling wreath on which Memory may often linger to dispel the gloom of life's winter.*

*Truly, Your old friend, P.H. Peters, "Marysville Enterprise"*

—from the autograph book of Emma McDougal
June 28, 1868

When P.H. Peters, former editor of the *Marysville Enterprise*, penned his reveries, Marshall County was 13 years old. Thousands of hopeful, weary, westward-bound emigrants, on foot and in prairie schooners, had crossed the Big Blue River by ford or ferry. The tense local proslavery and free state sparring of the 1850s was over, and in 1861 Kansas had entered the union as a free state. The prospect of free land had increased the population from 34 in 1855 to 2,280 in 1860; by 1870, that population would more than triple.

But long before the pioneers began moving across the prairie, the Marshall County land was home to Native Americans. Early settlers tell stories of Sioux, Pawnee, Missouri, Kaw, Otoe, Wichita, and Potawatomi, but it was the Otoe who were at home in Marshall County. In an 1854 treaty with the United States, the Otoe ceded much of their land, retaining only a small reservation along the Big Blue River in northern Marshall County and southern Nebraska; in 1881, Congress forced the Otoe to move to Oklahoma. Oketo, a northern Marshall County town, is named for Otoe chief Arkaketah.

Jim Bridger, John C. Fremont, and other scouts passed through the area, blazing trails for the US Army and more than 100,000 pioneers who traveled the Mormon, California, Oregon, and Parallel Trails, the Pony Express, stage routes, and the Military Road.

Missouri entrepreneur Frank Marshall built a ferry and store on the Big Blue in 1852, and made a fortune through fees and sales to emigrants. His post office, Marysville, was established in 1854. Although there is no evidence that he brought slaves to Kansas, Marshall was a slave owner in Missouri and was a proslavery advocate who wanted Kansas to enter the union as a slave state.

He was the proslavery candidate for territorial governor in 1857, but was defeated. In June 1861, just six months after Kansas became a state, Marshall and his family left for Colorado.

By 1880, Marshall County had 16,136 residents. Wooed in large part by the Homestead Act, the early settlers came from other states and other countries, looking for a new life in a place where they could prosper. They were Irish, German, Swedish, English, Czech, Canadian, and Danish. After the Civil War, Exodusters—blacks from Kentucky and Tennessee—settled in communities near the center of the county. The settlers' architecture and businesses often reflected their heritage. Their churches, and occasionally their schools, were conducted in languages that were familiar and probably comforting in this place that was so different and so far from the places they had previously called home.

Settlers brought with them the industries they had known. They built sawmills, flour mills, breweries, hatcheries, and cigar factories, and they invented better farming implements. They quarried limestone and mined gypsum. They made sunbonnets, vinegar, pottery, soap, paper, car curtains, brooms, ice cream, aprons, rifle stocks, ice, barrel staves, and "soda water in sterilized bottles." Over the years, mills and factories turned out Perfection flour, Sincerity cigars, Honey Dew pig meal, Easiespin lawn mowers, and Ful-O-Pep animal feed. Today, a gypsum mine and a limestone quarry are still active. The mills and early factories are gone, but locally produced stock trailers and equipment for farming and construction are sold nationally and internationally.

Farming is a way of life in Marshall County. Nearly 200 farms have been owned by successive generations of one family for 100 years or more. During the county's first 50 years, there were fruit orchards, milo, sorghum, and other grains like hops and alfalfa. Chickens and turkeys were nearly as plentiful as beef and dairy cattle. Sheep and race horses and mules were also raised here. Farms are fewer now, and larger, but the dedication of the farming families remains. Today, the primary crops are corn, wheat, and soybeans, and in livestock, beef cattle and hogs predominate.

The county's towns grew up along the Missouri Pacific and Union Pacific Railroads and their branch lines. In 1917, Marysville became a Union Pacific division headquarters, with repair yards, roundhouse, and an enormous feed-in-transit stockyard. Silk trains passed through at night with their precious, heavily-guarded cargo. Hundreds of passenger trains and thousands of freight trains used county tracks every year. The last passenger train departed in 1955 and freight trains are fewer, but Marysville is still an important Union Pacific crew change point.

In 1900, a one-cylinder Oldsmobile, an Orient Buckboard, and an early Stanley Steamer were the first three automobiles in Marshall County. Cars turned out not to be a passing fad, and federal highways were constructed to meet the need of the new leisure travelers and a burgeoning trucking industry. Two major highways—US 36 from Ohio to Colorado and US 77 from Iowa through Texas to the Mexican border—intersect in Marysville.

The tribulations of war and the challenges of weather were met with resilience here. Towns and farms alike were affected by the tornadoes, floods, and droughts that periodically visited. The CCC, WPA, PWA, and NYA were among the federal "alphabet agencies" that helped put Marshall County residents to work in the 1930s. Most of the structures built then are still in use. During wartime, county women made bandages and set up canteens. Scrap iron and milkweed silk were collected, and bond drives held. During World War II, classified military work was done in a factory in Marysville and a Japanese balloon traveled more than 6,000 miles to land in a Bigelow farm field. "Use it up, wear it out, make it do or do without" was a familiar slogan during that war and the ethic is still a part of county culture.

Modern town schools have replaced the 125 rural schools that dotted the prairie between 1858 and 1969. Gone too are nearly 50 towns and post offices, some of which had a full life, while others were merely the speck of some settler's dream.

The "boundless prairies" of 1868 have disappeared, but the meadows, bluffs, rivers, and undulating farmland are still "beauteous and variegated." From whitewashed depots to family farms, vestiges of the early days remain, but the county is sustained—in "Summer" and "Winter"—because residents embrace 21st-century technology and farming methods. They cherish the past, but look to the future.

# One

# Establishing a County

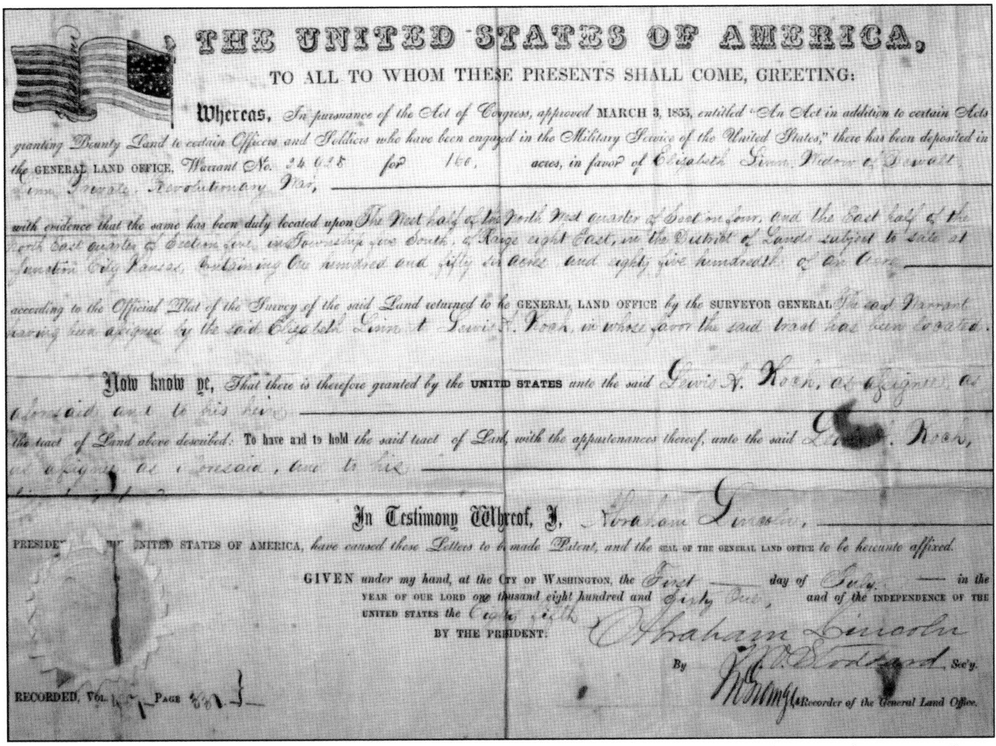

THE UNITED STATES OF AMERICA,

TO ALL TO WHOM THESE PRESENTS SHALL COME, GREETING:

Whereas, In pursuance of the Act of Congress, approved MARCH 3, 1855, entitled "An Act in addition to certain Acts granting Bounty Land to certain Officers and Soldiers who have been engaged in the Military Service of the United States," there has been deposited in the GENERAL LAND OFFICE, Warrant No. [illegible] for 160, acres, in favor of Elizabeth Linn, Widow of [illegible] Revolutionary War,

with evidence that the same has been duly located upon The West half of the North West quarter of Section four, and the East half of the North East quarter of Section five, in Township five South, of Range eight East, in the District of Lands subject to sale at Junction City Kansas, containing One hundred and fifty six acres and eighty five hundredths of an acre

according to the Official Plat of the Survey of the said Land returned to the GENERAL LAND OFFICE by the SURVEYOR GENERAL, The said Warrant having been assigned by the said Elizabeth Linn to Lewis A. Koch, in whose favor the said tract has been located.

Now know ye, That there is therefore granted by the UNITED STATES unto the said Lewis A. Koch, as assignee as aforesaid and to his heirs, the tract of Land above described: To have and to hold the said tract of Land, with the appurtenances thereof, unto the said Lewis A. Koch, as assignee as aforesaid, and to his heirs [illegible]

In Testimony Whereof, I, Abraham Lincoln, PRESIDENT OF THE UNITED STATES OF AMERICA, have caused these Letters to be made Patent, and the SEAL OF THE GENERAL LAND OFFICE to be hereunto affixed.

GIVEN under my hand, at the CITY OF WASHINGTON, the First day of July, in the YEAR OF OUR LORD one thousand eight hundred and Sixty One, and of the INDEPENDENCE OF THE UNITED STATES the Eighty fifth.

BY THE PRESIDENT: Abraham Lincoln

By W. O. Stoddard, Sec'y.

[illegible], Recorder of the General Land Office.

RECORDED, Vol. [illegible] Page [illegible]

The Kansas-Nebraska Act, passed by Congress in 1854, opened the Great Plains to homesteading. Of the roughly 50 million acres open in Kansas Territory, 576,000 were in what is now Marshall County. This early land grant, assigned in 1861, gives title to 160 acres of that land. A territorial census from 1855 shows the population in this area to be 34. By 1860, the population had swelled to 2,280; in 1870, 6,901; and in 1880 it was 16,136. With an influx of homesteaders, merchants, industries, and railroads, the county reached a population high of 24,355 in 1900. In 2010, the population was 10,117. (Courtesy of Raoul Delmare.)

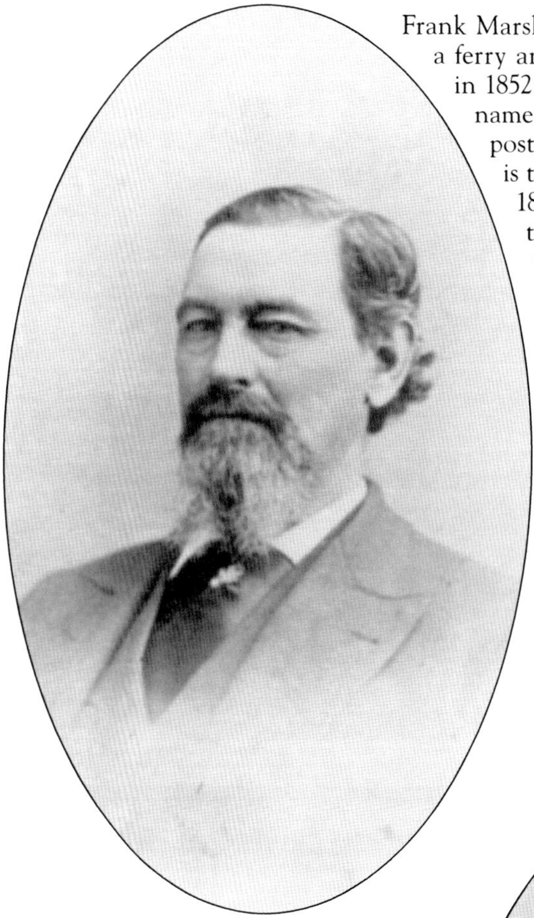

Frank Marshall, a pro-slaver from Missouri, operated a ferry and trading post along the Big Blue River in 1852. In 1854, he was granted a post office and named it Marysville for his wife. It was the first post office in Kansas named for a woman and is the oldest civilian post office in the state. In 1855, Marshall County was established by the territorial legislature and Marysville became the county seat. Marshall was nominated as the proslavery candidate for territorial governor in 1857. He was defeated by the free staters despite documented proslavery voter fraud in Marysville. Kansas entered the nation as a free state in January 1861. Southern states seceded that same month, and when the Civil War—often referred to here as the "War of the Rebellion"—began in April, Southern sympathizers began leaving the county. The Marshalls left in June for Colorado, where he made a fortune in silver mining.

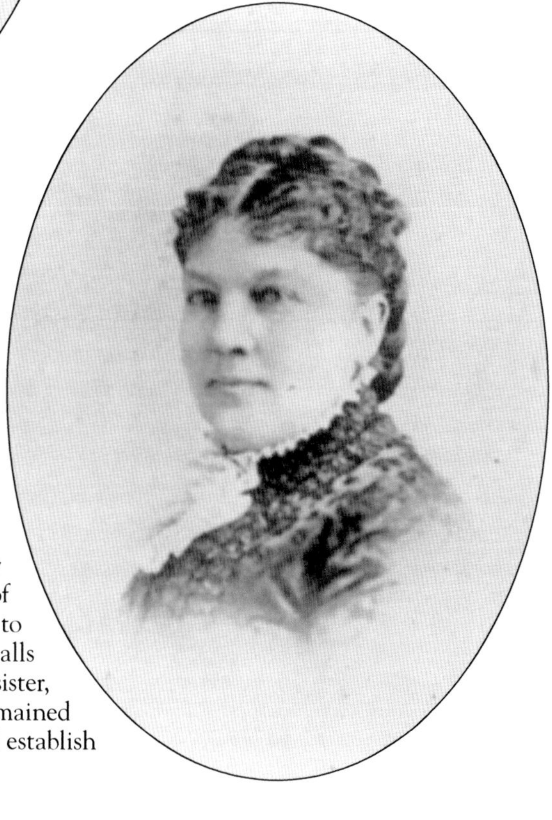

Mary Williams married Frank Marshall shortly before her 16th birthday and they lived in Weston, Missouri, where he owned a hotel. During Marshall's first years of operating the ferry in Marysville, Mary and their two children remained in Weston and he returned there each winter. In 1854 or 1855, Marshall brought his family to live in what was to become the town of Marysville. Two more children were born to the couple in Marysville. When the Marshalls left for Colorado in 1861, Mary's younger sister, Emma, and her husband, John Watson, remained in Marshall County. The Watsons helped establish the town of Frankfort.

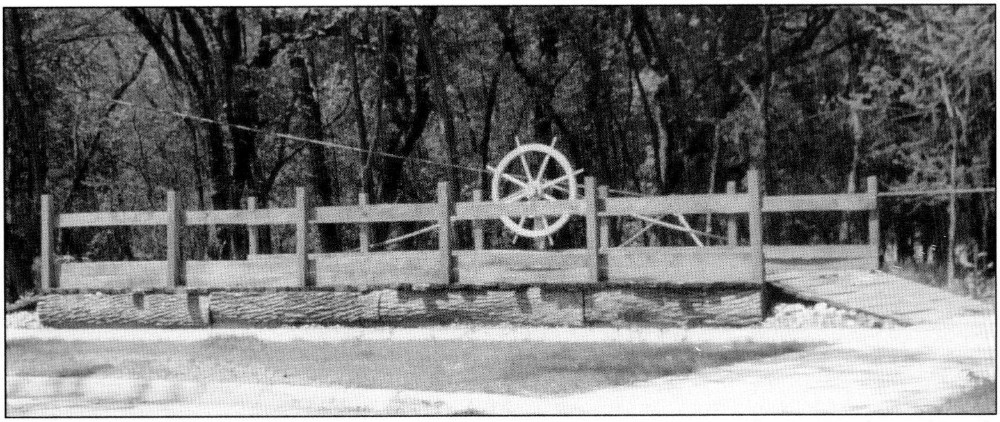

This reaction ferry, located in Historic Trails Park just west of Marysville, is a replica of Frank Marshall's ferry used by pioneers and other travelers to cross the Big Blue River. Emigrants were charged up to $5 per wagon and 25¢ per head of livestock. The original ferry operated from 1852 to 1864, when a bridge was built. The rope-and-pulley system allowed the ferryman to turn the wheel so the ferry was carried to the opposite bank by the current.

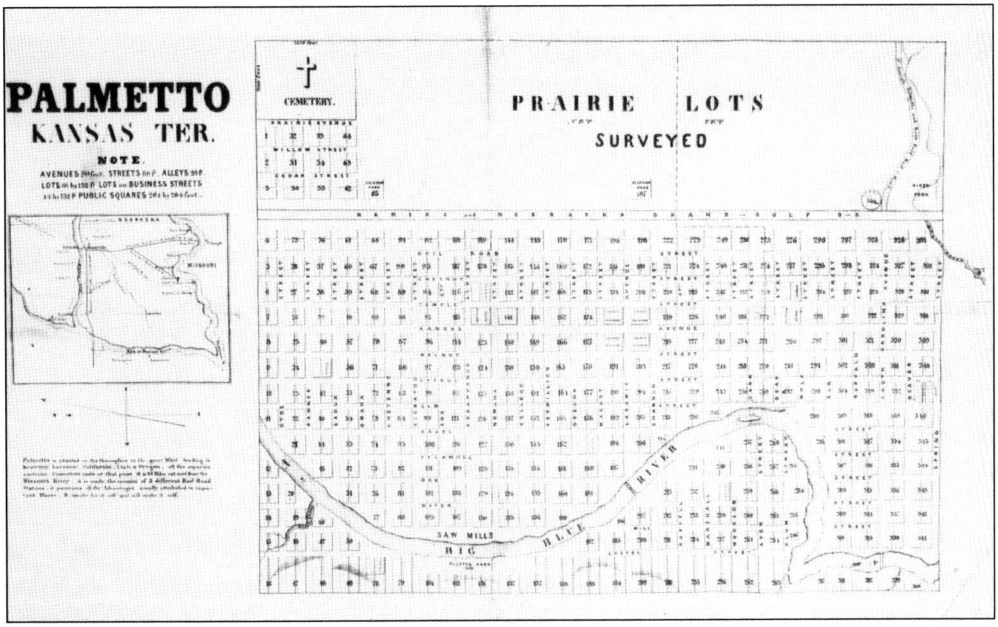


In 1856, a small group of young proslavery advocates from South Carolina formed the Palmetto Town Company (named for their state tree), intending to swell the voting rolls to help ensure that Kansas would enter the union as a slave state. This plat map, from 1857, bears little resemblance to the actual layout of the 320 acres that became known as Palmetto. In any event, the town failed for lack of interest and the Southerners sold their town shares to Marshall and the Marysville Town Company. Only one home was built in Palmetto during its very short existence.

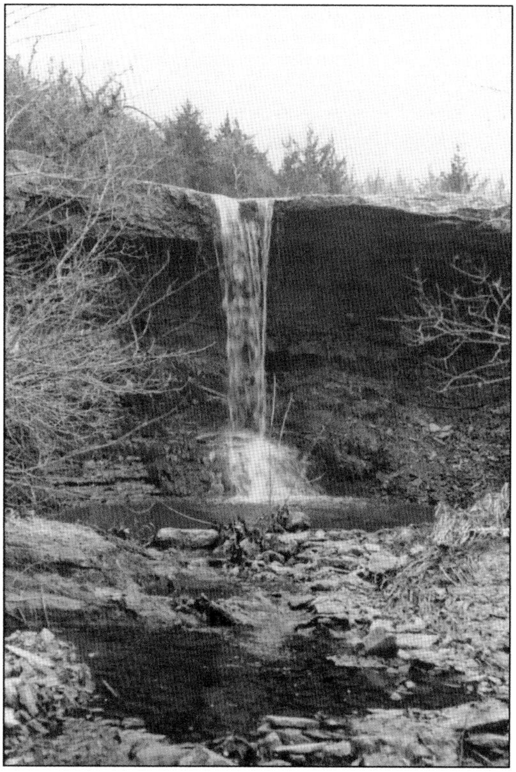

Alcove Spring was discovered and named in 1846 by Edwin Bryant, a member of the ill-fated Donner Party, when they camped in the area on their way to California. Sarah Keyes, another member of the party, died here and was buried nearby. The spring and its waterfall, named Naomi Pike Falls for a child in the Donner Party, became a familiar landmark on the Oregon and California Trails. It was placed in the National Register of Historic Places in 1972, and in 2013 the National Park Service began work with the Alcove Spring Preservation Association to develop trails and interpretive signage.

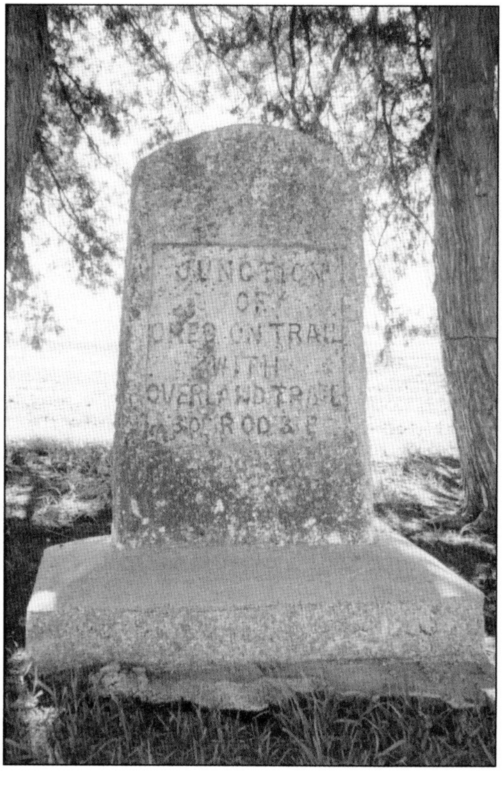


Trail markers dot the landscape in Marshall County. This one, southwest of Bremen, marks the junction of the main Oregon-California Trail and a connector route from St. Joseph, Missouri. In 1849, a traveler on the main trail wrote that at this junction "for an indefinite number of miles there seemed to be an unending stream of emigrant [wagon] trains. . . It seemed as if the whole family of man had set its face westward." Early in 2014, a trail remnant near this marker, known as the Pacha Ruts, was placed in the National Register of Historic Places.

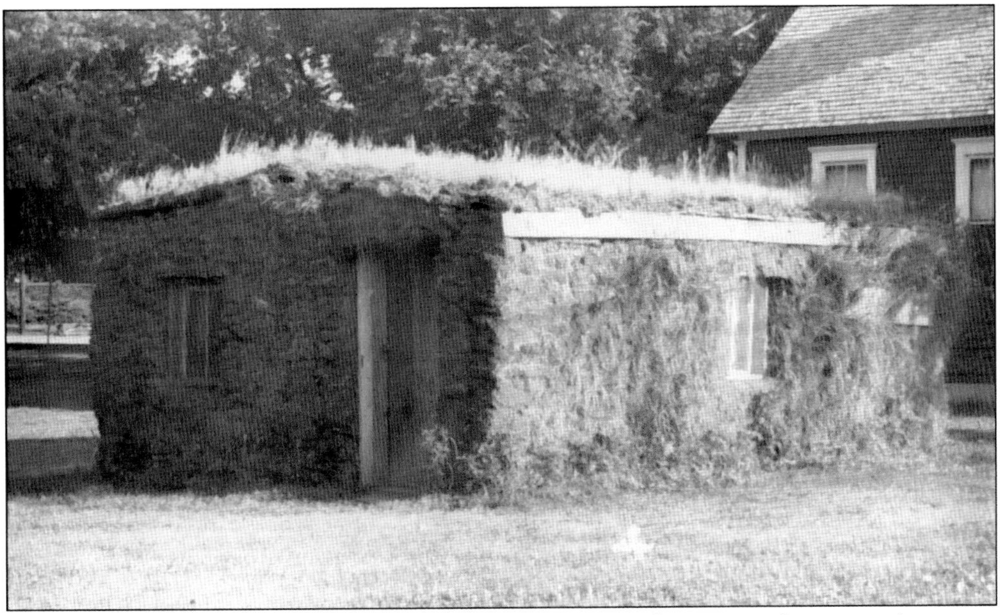

Although no original sod houses remain, there are many references to them in early county documents. This sod house was constructed by members of the Marysville Kiwanis Club in the city park in 1968. It was built with 30,000 pieces of sod. With only occasional repair, it is still on display in the park. Prairie sod houses generally had blocks that measured one foot wide, two feet long, and four inches thick, and weighed about 50 pounds apiece.

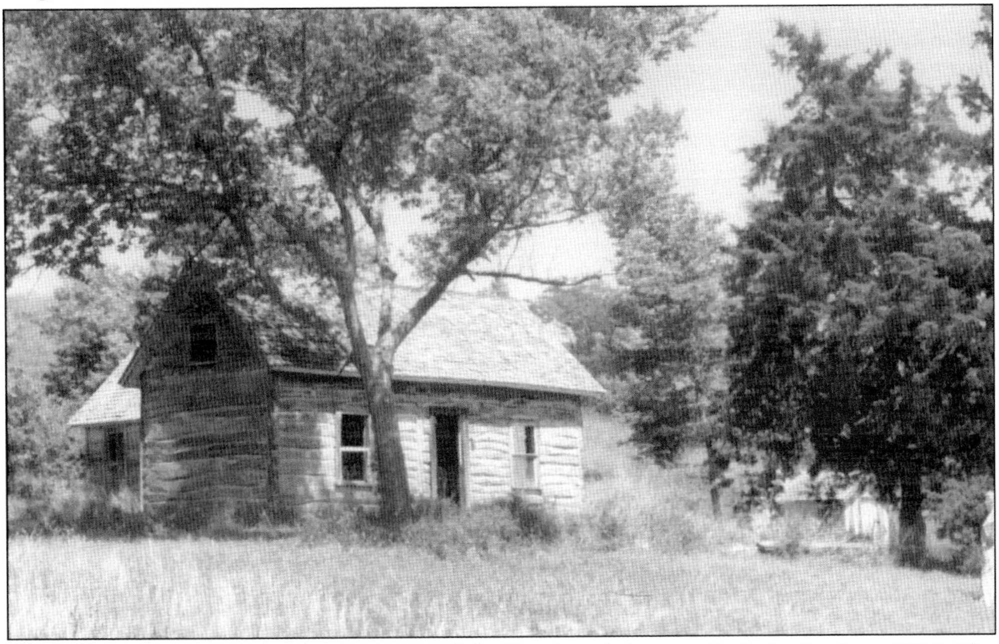

This log cabin was built south of Blue Rapids by Frank and Augusta Sjoholm in about 1886. The Sjoholms, originally from Sweden, shortened their name to Holm to ease American pronunciation. The cabin—12 feet by 26 feet, with a sleeping loft—housed the Holms and their seven children. When the photograph was taken in 1987, the land belonged to grandson Melton Holm, who was born in the cabin in 1921. The cabin was moved to the Blue Rapids square in 1996.

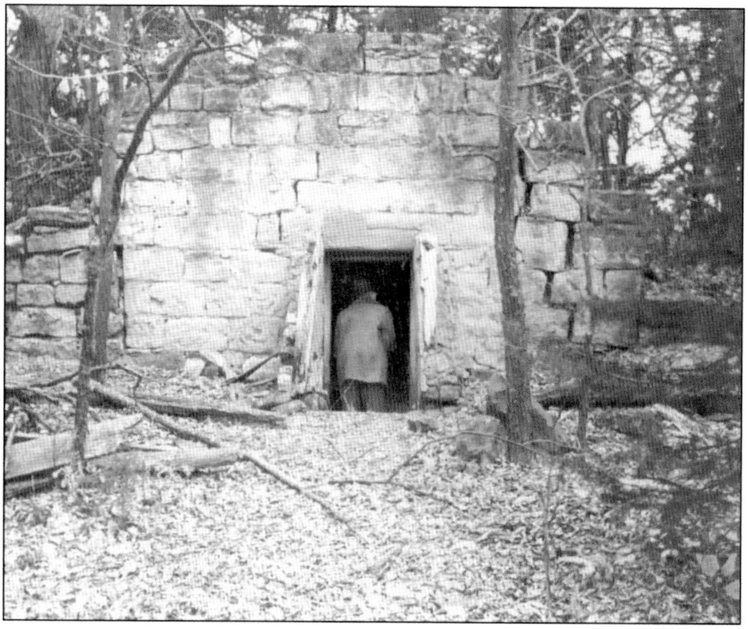

Located in Elm Creek Township, this root cellar/tornado shelter was built into the hill at the site of a log cabin built in 1859 by John Reiter, a German immigrant. The cabin was covered with clapboard siding and rooms were added as Reiter's family grew. When the siding began to decay in the 1970s, the cabin was rediscovered. It, too, has decayed, but the root cellar remains.

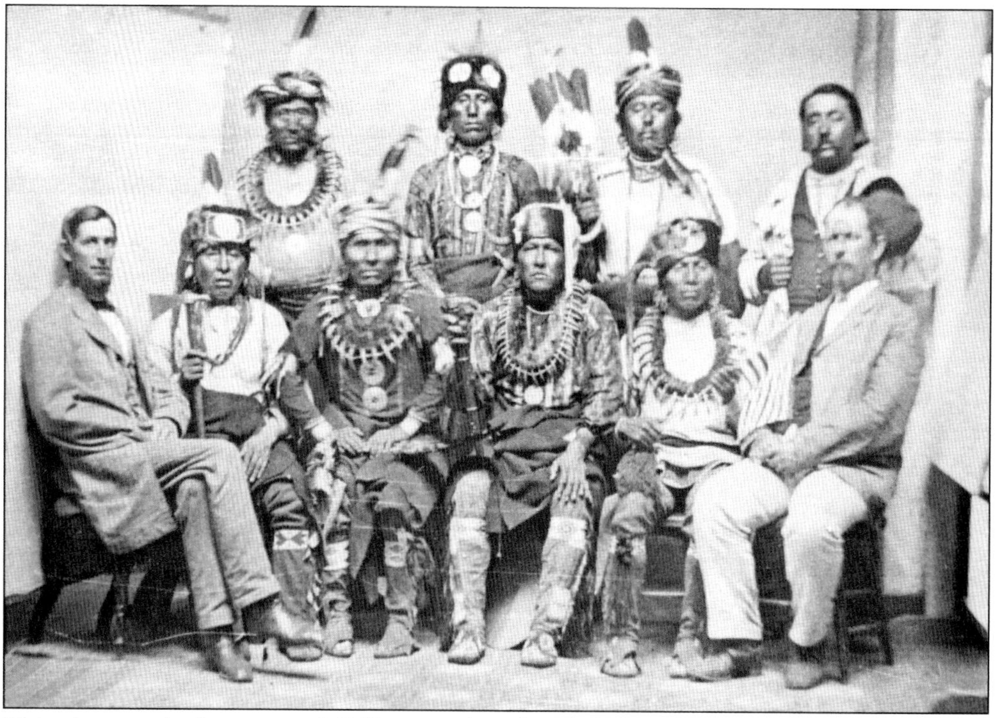

This photograph, from around 1880, was taken shortly before the Otoe tribe moved from its reservation in northern Marshall County to Oklahoma. Pictured, from left to right, are (back row) Howdy-Howdy, White-Horse, Joe-John, and interpreter Baptiste DeRoin; (front row) Indian agent Jesse W. Griest, Otoe chief Arkaketah, Pawnee Cuchee, Wahanyi, Toehee, and US Army captain and paymaster Pearman. The Marshall County town of Oketo was named for Chief Arkaketah.

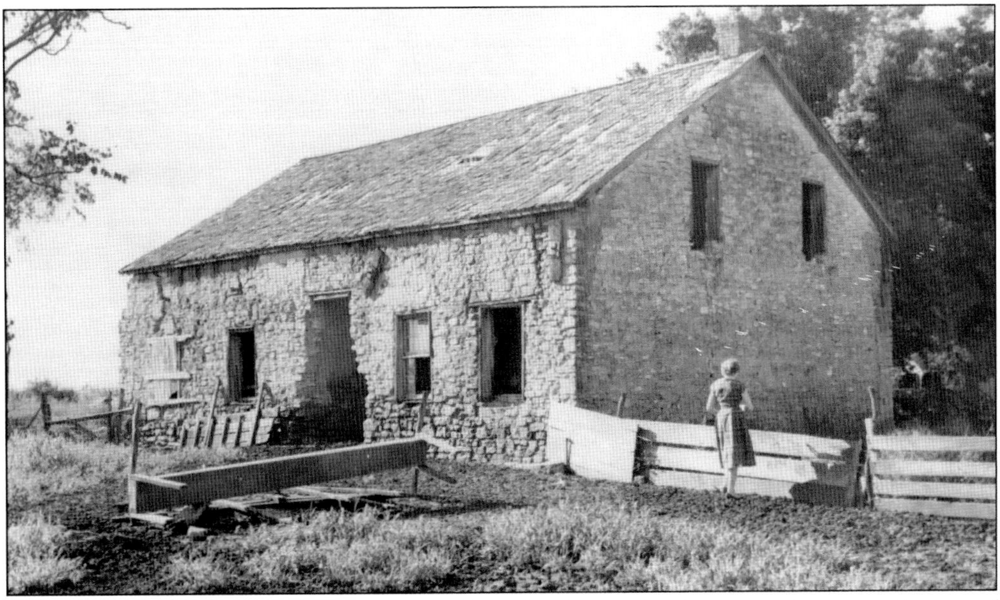

This is a mission school built in Balderson Township by the Presbyterian Missionary Society of New York City for use by the Otoe Indians. It was opened by Rev. C. Murdock in 1857, but closed soon after. Originally, the building had three stories. After a tornado tore off the third floor, the building was repaired and used as the Stolzenbach Post Office, founded in 1875 and named for a settlement in Germany from which immigrants in this area came.

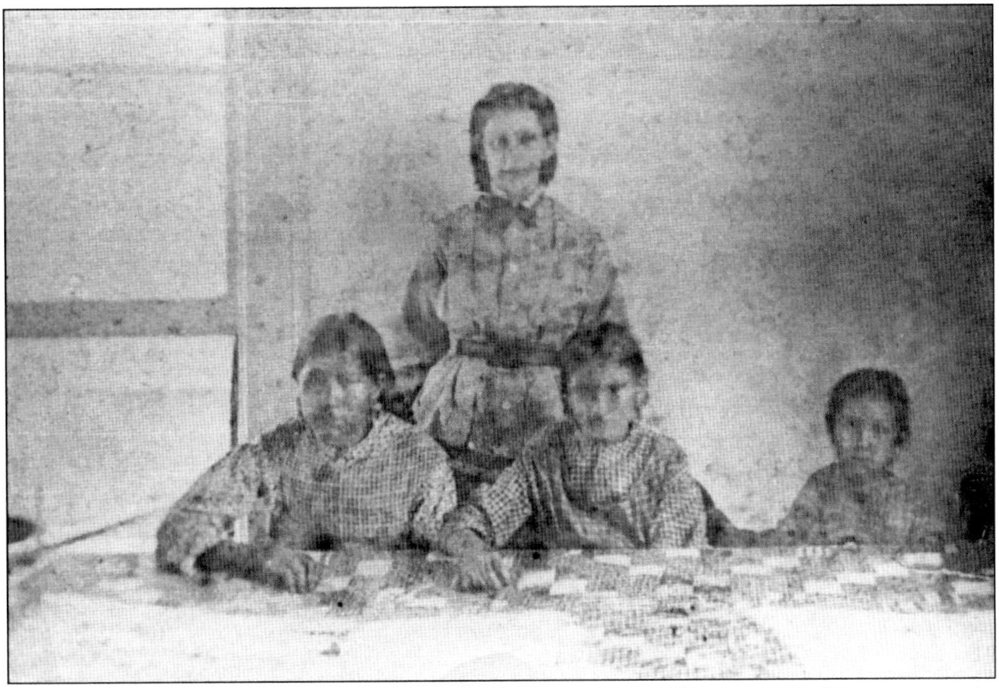

Only a handful of photographs, most grainy with age, remain to document the Otoe presence in Marshall County. In this photograph, from around 1880, Lavinia Moore is with her students at the mission school. Her uncle Jesse Griest was the Otoe Indian agent. Moore later became mayor of Oketo, the first woman mayor of a Marshall County town.

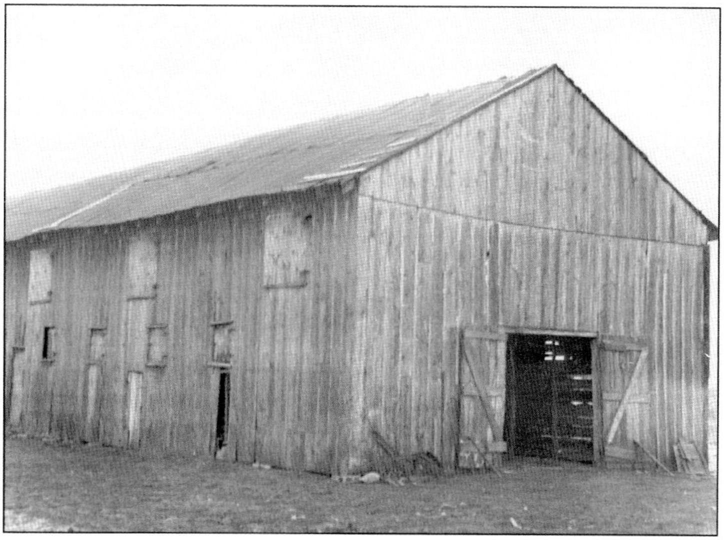

Guittard Station, northeast of Marysville near the present town of Beattie, was a stop on the Pony Express and the Overland Stage roads, and was on the St. Joe Road of the Oregon Trail. It was a post office from March 1861 to October 1900.

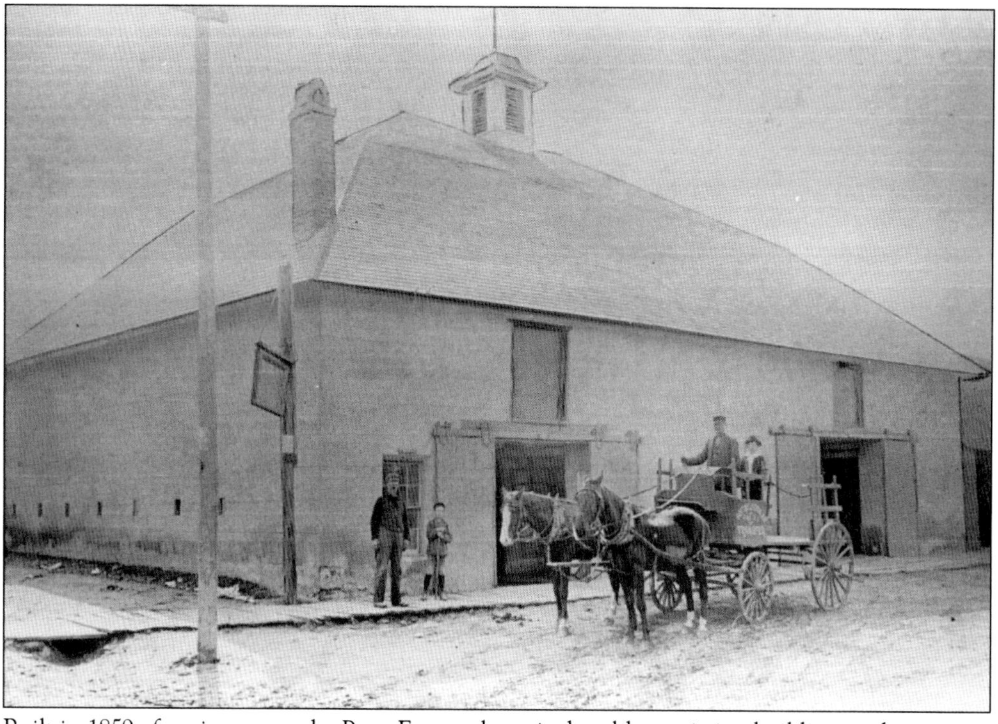

Built in 1859 of native stone, the Pony Express barn is the oldest existing building in the county. When the Pony Express began service in April 1860, there were 40 home stations—stops along the route where both riders and horses were changed—between St. Joseph, Missouri, and Sacramento, California. Marysville was Home Station No. 1, providing temporary stabling for the horses and lodging for riders next door at the Barrett Hotel. After the Pony Express ceased business on October 27, 1861, the barn housed a number of businesses and is now a museum. It is the only original barn remaining along the Pony Express route and was placed in the National Register of Historic Places in 1973. This photograph was taken in the early 1890s, after the walls were raised and the roof redesigned following a fire in 1876. The National Pony Express Association holds a 10-day Re-Ride over the entire 1,966-mile route each summer.

# *Two*

# Rails and Roads

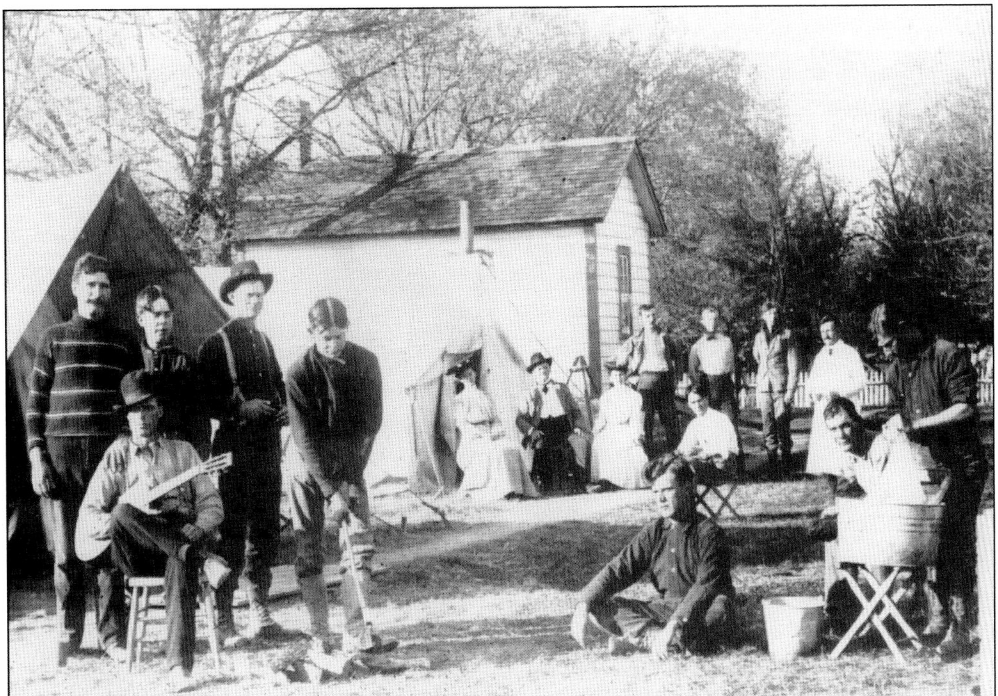

Sunday afternoon in this railroad camp near Marysville was a time for weekly chores and relaxation. These workers were building the Topeka and Northwestern Railroad line between Upland (three miles east of Marysville) and Topeka in 1909.

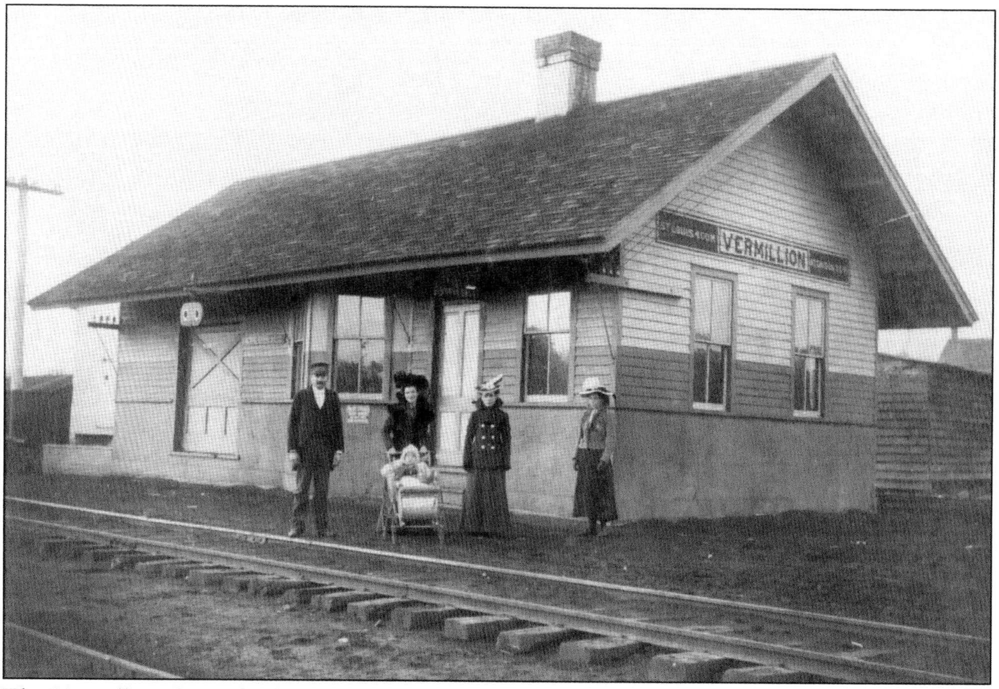


The Vermillion depot, built in 1869 for what was then the Central Branch of the Union Pacific Railroad, was the first depot in Marshall County. Depot agent John Neuman, his wife and baby, and two sisters are standing on the depot platform around 1910. After more than a century of service, the Missouri Pacific closed the depot in the 1970s. It was moved to city property and is now part of the Vermillion History Rooms.

In 1868, the first train rolled into what was soon to become Waterville. Located 100 miles west of Atchison on the Central Branch of the Missouri Pacific Railroad, this town became the terminus for livestock and freight. Cattle drives from Texas and elsewhere brought herds to be transported by trains from Waterville east. No photographs exist, but documentation indicates that at least one "turkey drive" herded hundreds of birds to Waterville on their way to market.

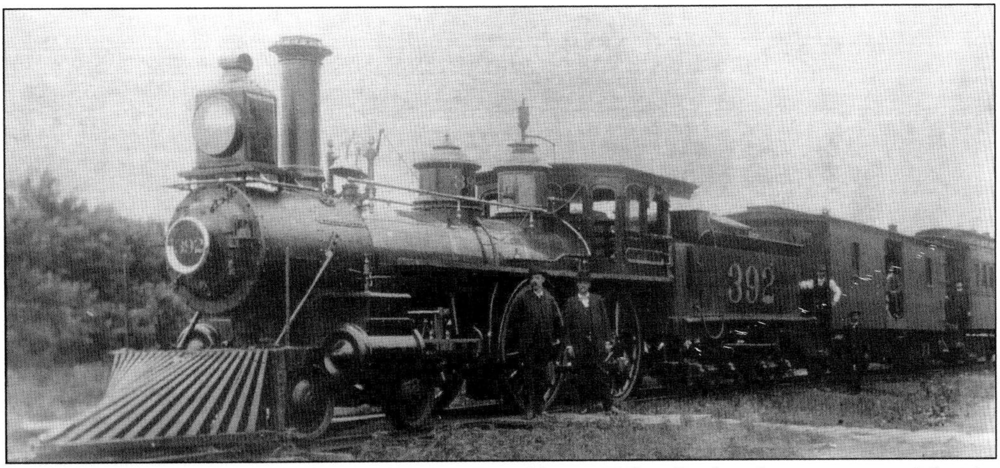

This 1882 photograph shows an Omaha & Republican Valley Railroad passenger and freight train at Seventh and Elm Streets in Marysville. This railroad was one of the Union Pacific's first branch line subsidiaries.

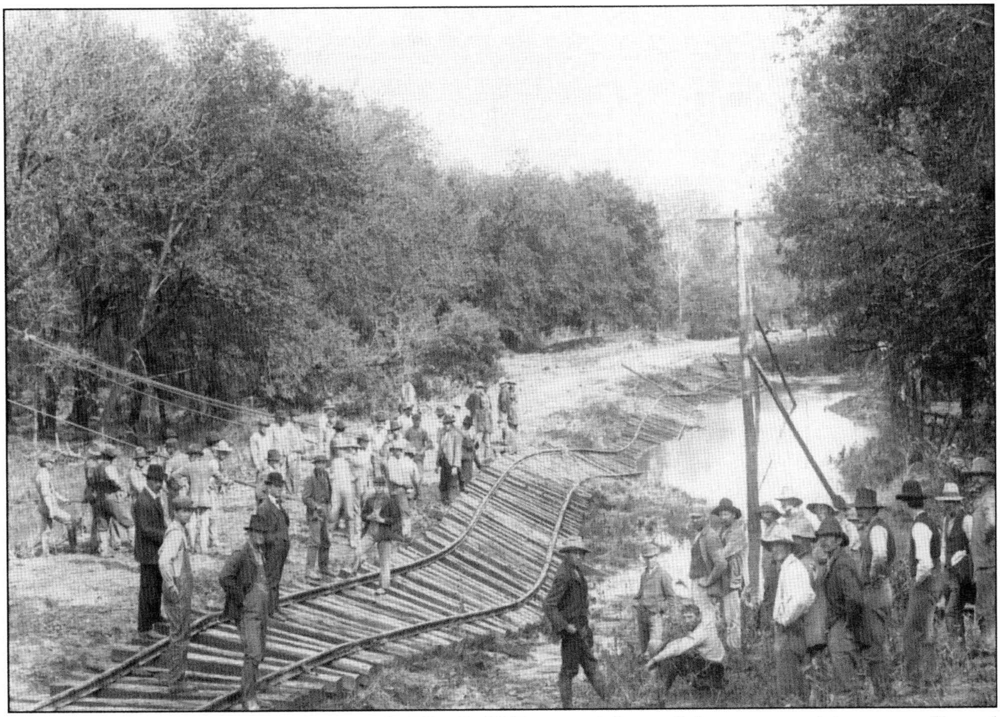
Floods were a frequent menace in early Marshall County. Many of the communities were affected by the rains of spring 1903. At Coon Creek, west of Waterville, flooding washed out the Missouri Pacific Railroad tracks.

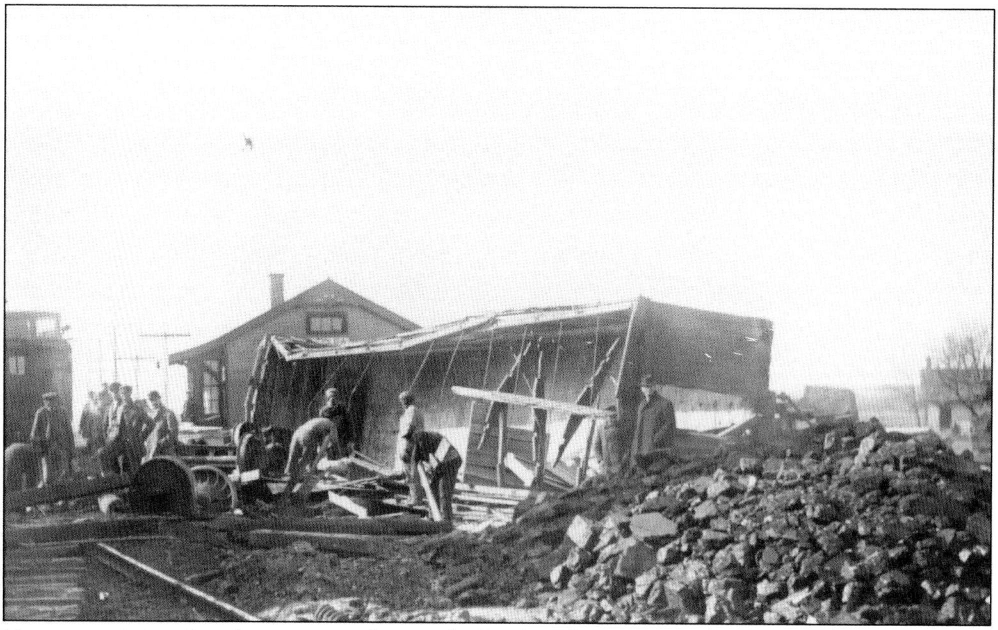

No one was injured in this train wreck near the Bigelow depot in 1910, but railcars were overturned and coal, potatoes, and lumber were strewn over the Zebre homesite. In small towns, residents as well as railroad workers were called upon to salvage and clean up following accidents.

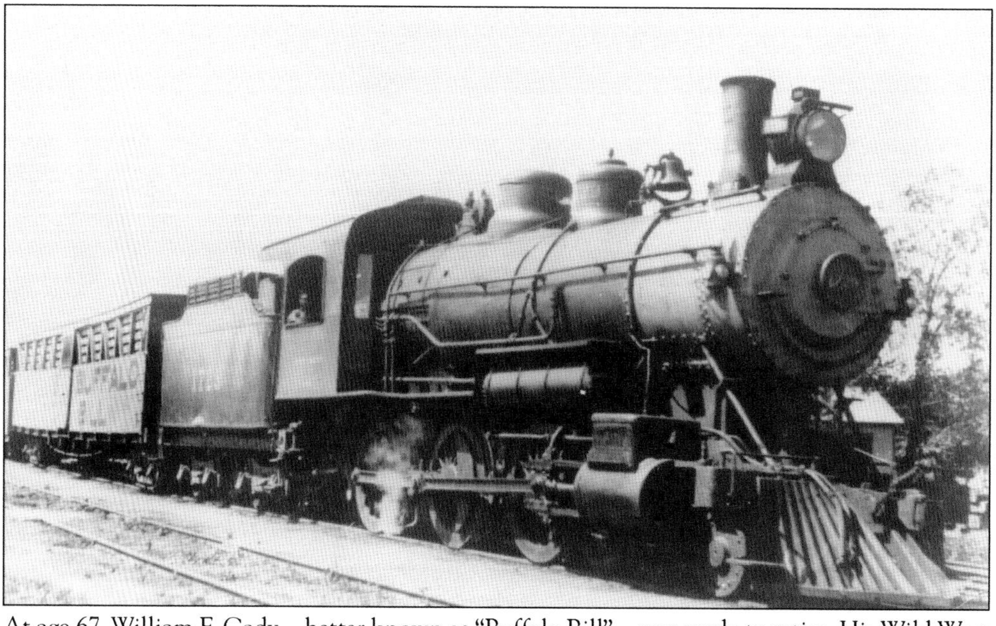

At age 67, William F. Cody—better known as "Buffalo Bill"—was ready to retire. His Wild West Show had traveled the world for 25 years and he was making his Farewell Tour. On Saturday, September 14, 1912, Buffalo Bill's train rolled into Marysville for the last time. Despite heavy rain, a crowd estimated to be between 7,000 and 9,000 attended. General admission was 50¢; grandstand seating was $1. In his youth, Cody had ridden through Marysville as a Pony Express rider. He died just five years after his final tour.

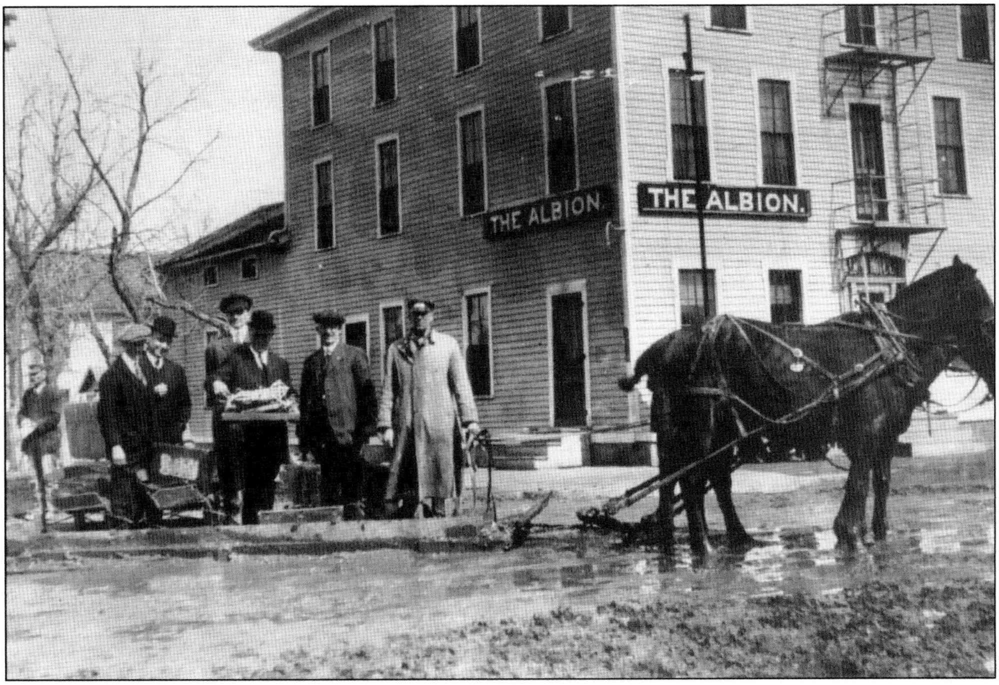


The "mudboat" in this 1915 photograph was an early form of taxi service in Marshall County. It conveyed Blue Rapids travelers from the Union Pacific depot northeast of town to the Albion Hotel, located on the north side of the square east of Main Street. The horses' tails were knotted to keep them from getting muddy and, in turn, flicking mud on the passengers.

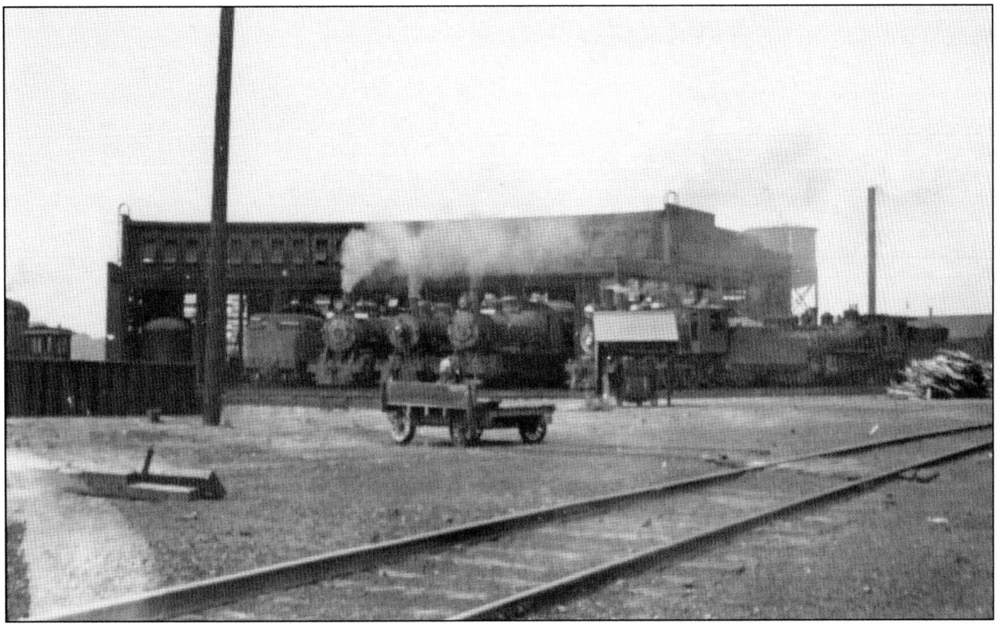

The first section of the Marysville Union Pacific roundhouse was built in 1917. Ten more stalls were added in 1925. This photograph, taken about 1920, shows three steam engines in the roundhouse. The little shack with the white roof, known as the "doghouse," contained the turntable controls.

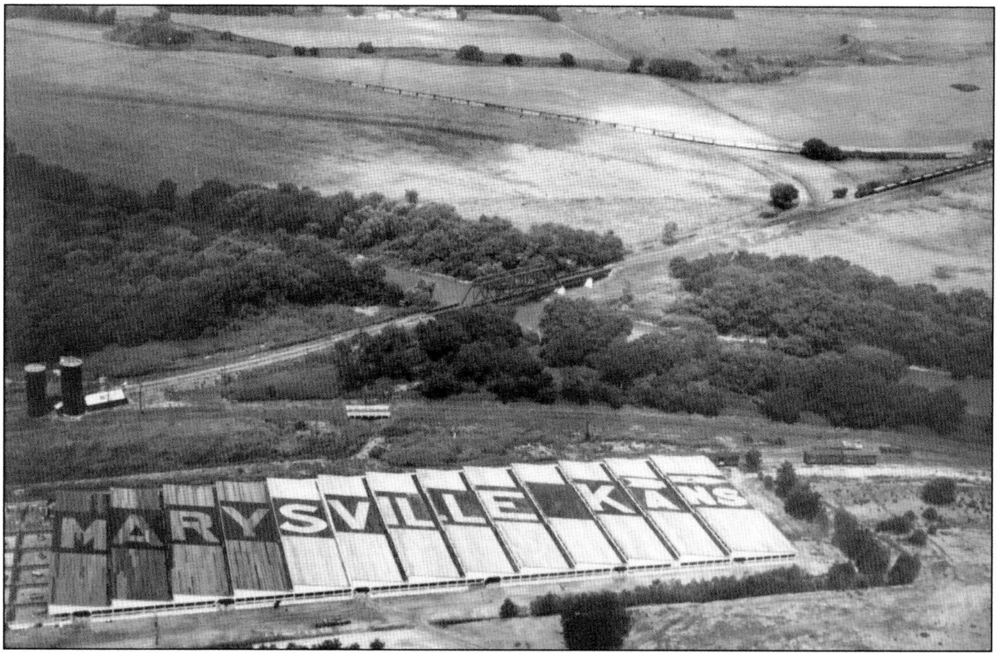


In 1917, the Union Pacific and the St. Joseph and Grand Island railroads moved their division headquarters to Marysville. Soon after, a feed-in-transit stockyard was built northwest of town to meet a law that livestock be unloaded, fed, and watered while in transit from western ranches to slaughterhouses in Chicago and the Midwest. This was the largest completely roofed stockyard in the United States. The sign—600 feet long and 75 feet wide—was painted in 1929, but lasted only a few years as the paint weathered into the roofing. After World War II, use of the stockyards slowly declined, and they are now only a memory.

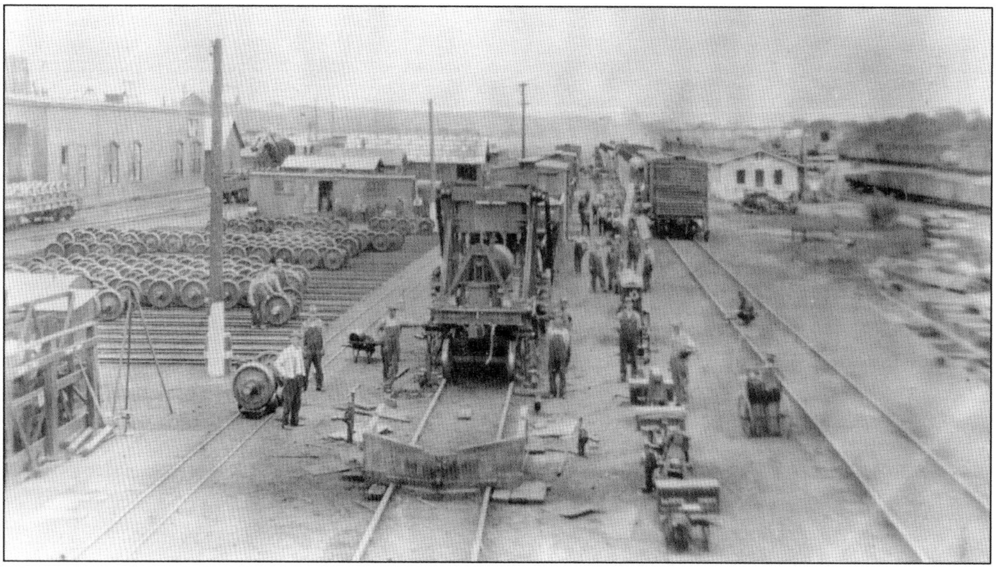

The Union Pacific repair track in Marysville was a busy place in 1926. The wheels on the flatcars were on their way to be stored along the track, and worn wheels were replaced on the repair track at the right. The men are working on a spreader, used to lay gravel along the ties. Ploughs like the one in lower center could be used to spread gravel evenly along the railbed.

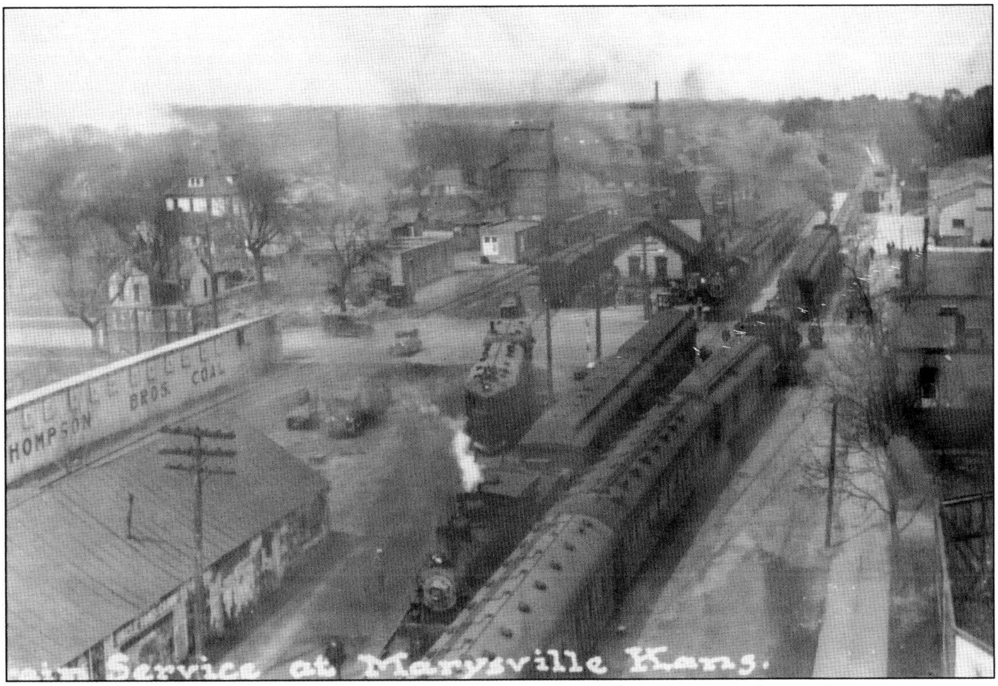


This photograph, taken around noon on a winter weekday in 1930, shows four trains—two eastbound and two westbound—and the "motor" (a one-car passenger train), all in Marysville at the same time. The third depot, built in 1880, is at the center of the various trains. The fourth depot, built in 1929, is partially visible at upper right.

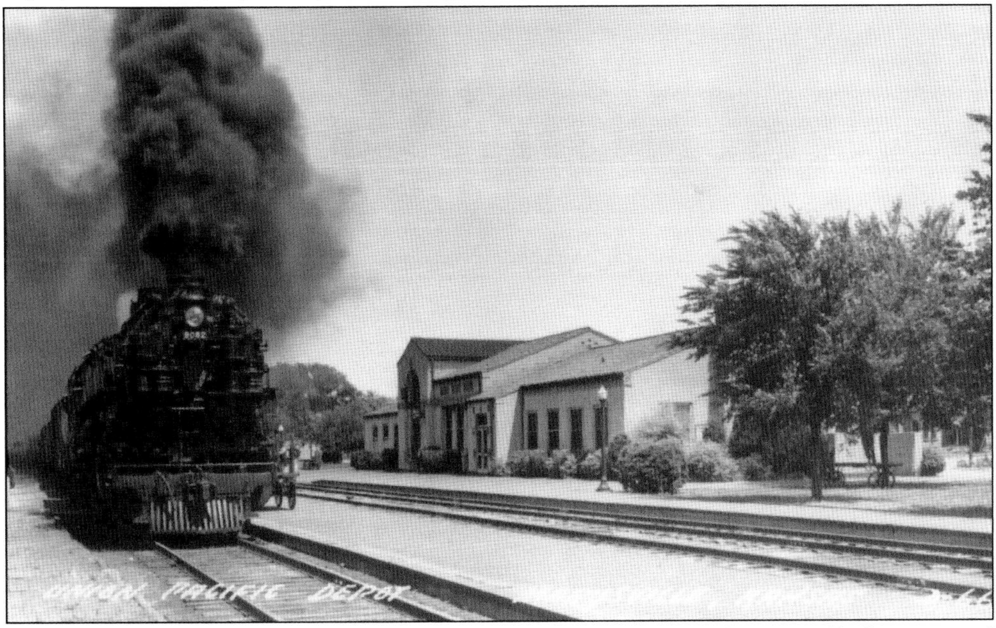


The 9082 Union Pacific locomotive is eastbound in front of the fourth Marysville depot around 1939. More than a dozen passenger trains passed through this station daily in its heyday. Train travel dwindled as travelers began to favor automobile and plane travel. The last passenger motor train left this station on February 12, 1955.

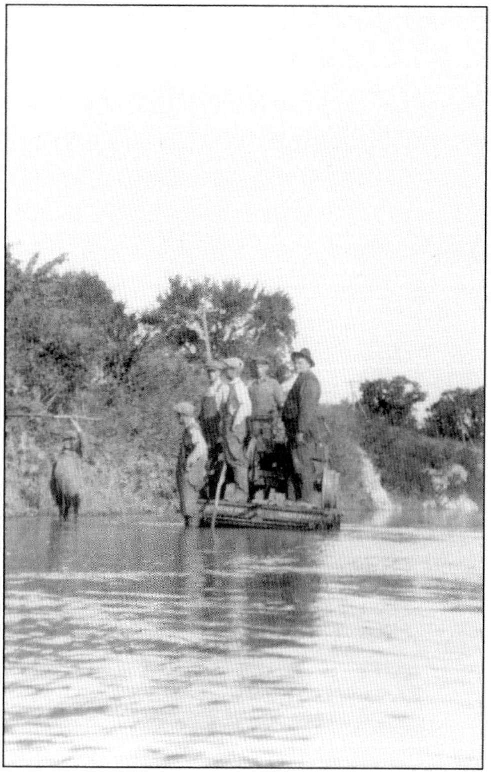

Railroad workers are aboard this handcar that is travelling along a submerged track during flooding in August 1941. The original print of this negative was reversed, adding to the irony of the slogan on the front of the handcar: "Safety First, Union Pacific."

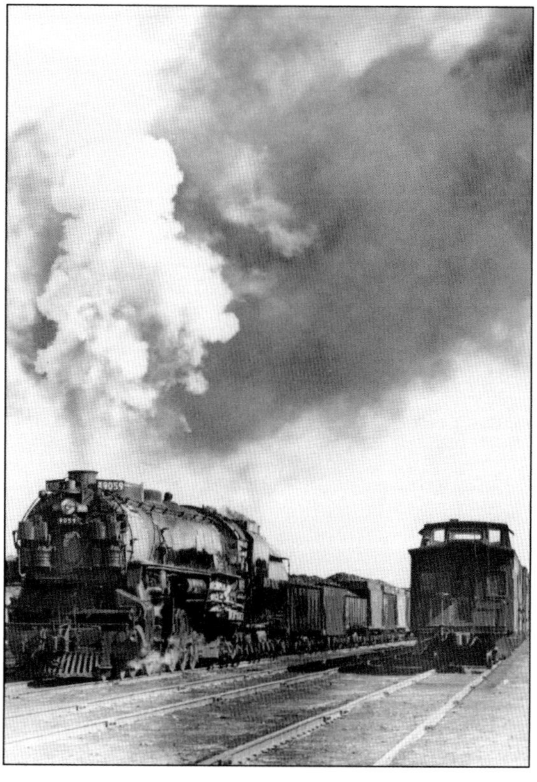

On April 1, 1946, John L. Lewis, president of the United Mine Workers of America from 1920 to 1960, called 340,000 coal miners out on strike, affecting not only the mining of coal, but also its movement by truck and rail. This and other strikes in the Strike Wave of 1946 affected 4.3 million workers and threatened the postwar economy. On May 29, Lewis and the government reached a compromise and the mine strike was over. This coal train, heading west from Marysville on May 30, 1946, is the first after the strike.

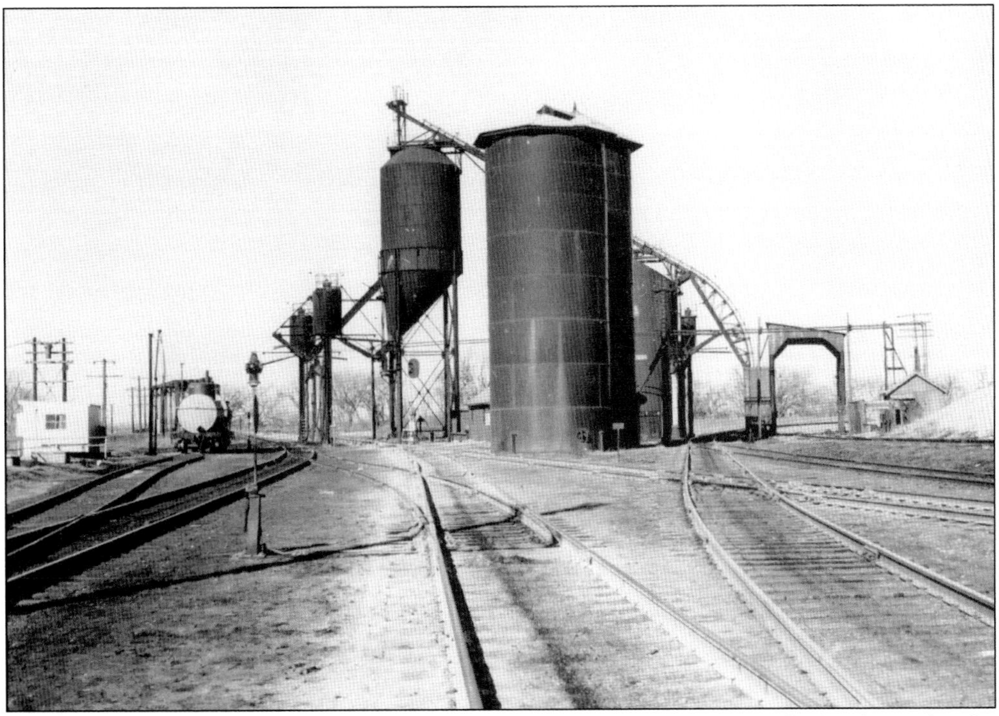

The Union Pacific coaling station was built in late fall 1931 in the Marysville freight yards. The coal and sand chutes are shown here in 1957, shortly before the coaling station was torn down.

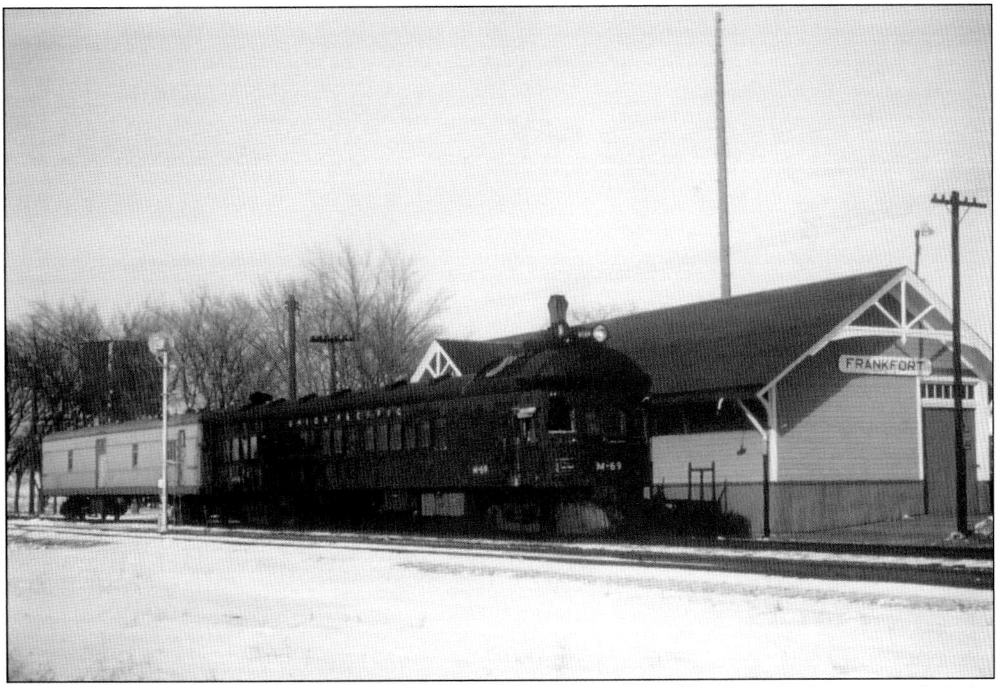


Passenger service in Marshall County ended on February 12, 1955, when the last motor left the Frankfort depot for Topeka. (Courtesy of Steve Slupianek.)

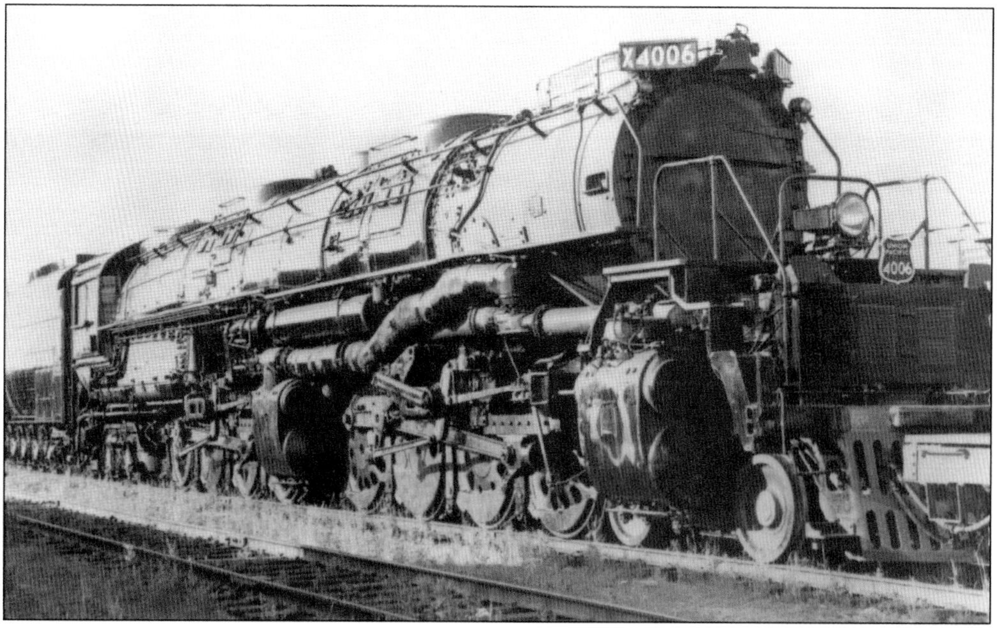


This 4000-class Union Pacific "Big Boy" engine (the largest engine in the world) is in the yards in Marysville in 1963. Of the 25 of these engines built, only seven still exist, and they are on permanent display in various locations. The engine in this photograph is now in Dallas, Texas.

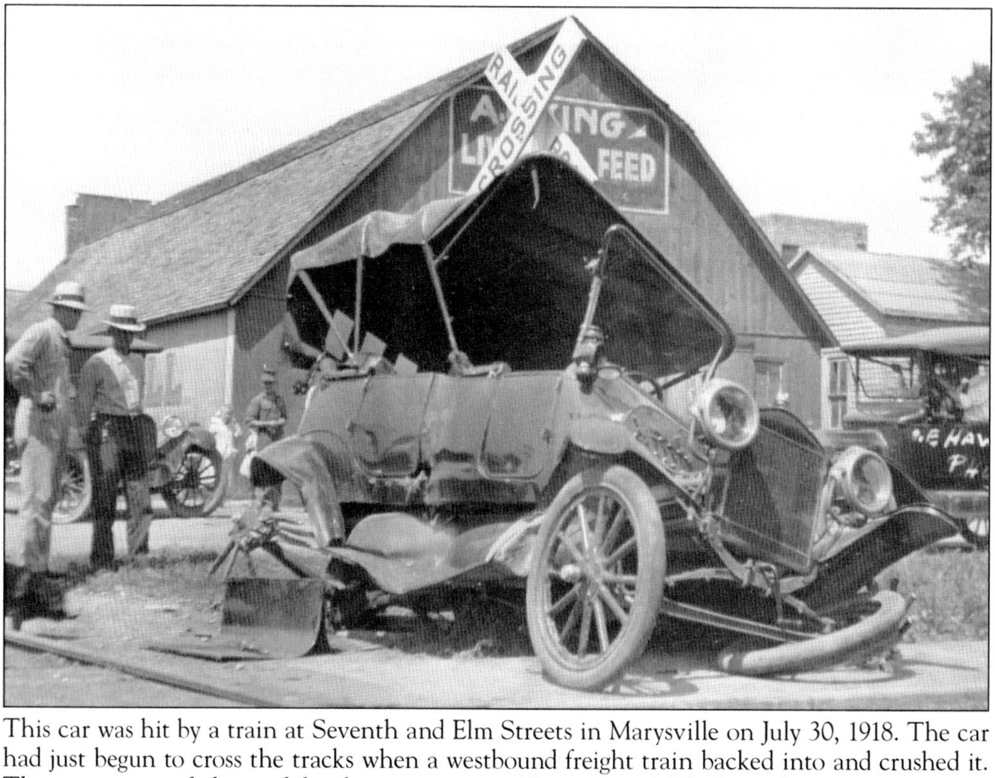


This car was hit by a train at Seventh and Elm Streets in Marysville on July 30, 1918. The car had just begun to cross the tracks when a westbound freight train backed into and crushed it. The passengers, a father and daughter, were injured but survived. The livery barn near the tracks made it difficult to see approaching trains until cars were already nearly on the tracks.

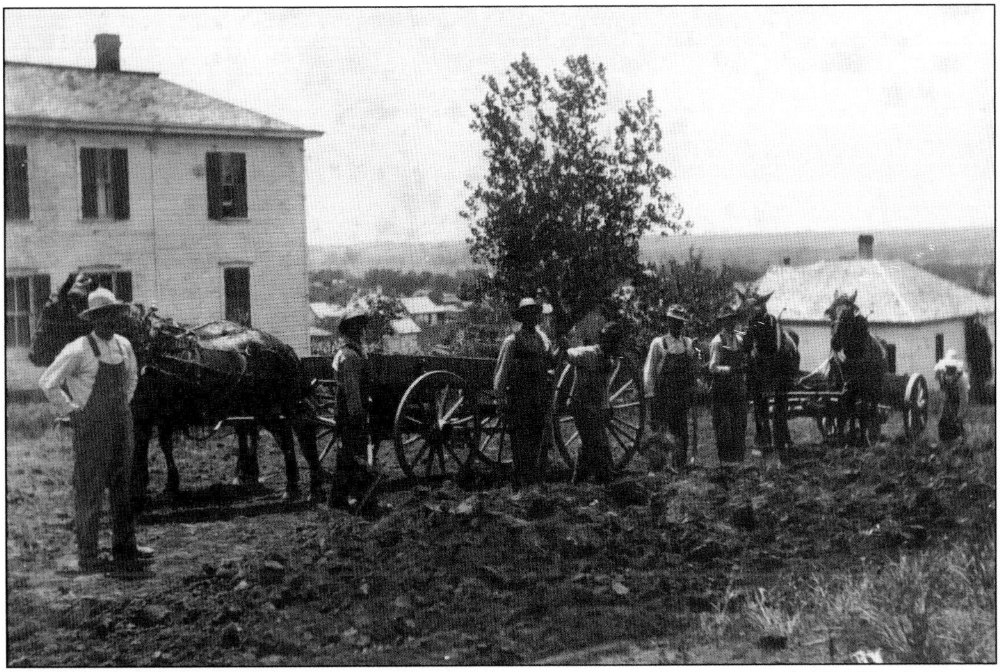

This Marysville city street crew is working on Laramie Street between Ninth and Tenth Streets in 1914. The men would have used hand tools to turn and grade the ground for a new street.

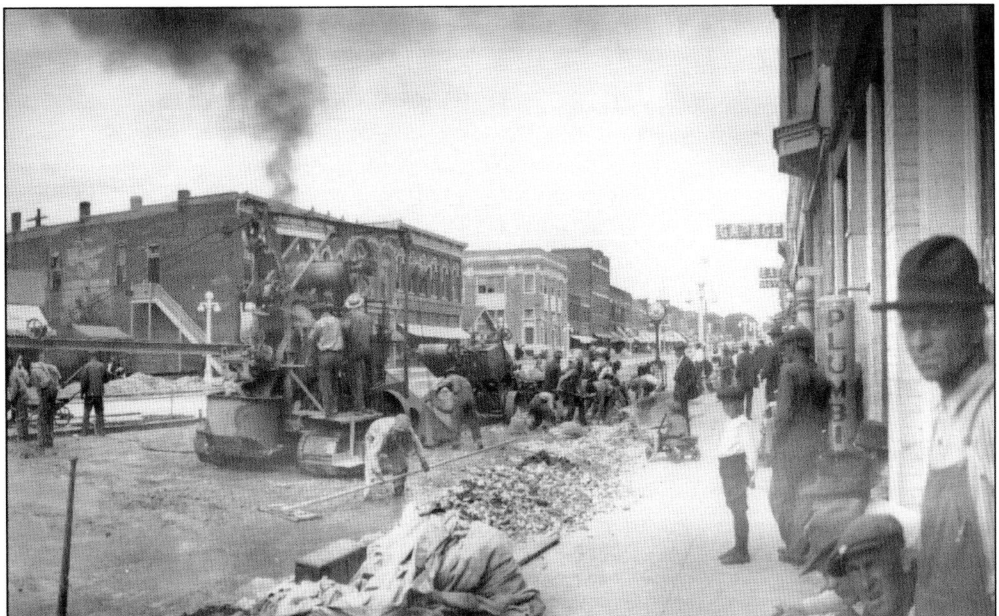


City workers are beginning the work of paving (bricking) Marysville city streets. They are shown here working on Broadway at Seventh Street in the mid-1920s. Businesses long gone are visible along the street; the Pacific Hotel is at left, and the Model Clothing Store was in the hotel. Leader Cigars is on the awning of the building at the right and Bralyer Plumbing at the right on the corner. There are still 6.184 miles of brick streets in Marysville, including the 10-block length of Broadway.

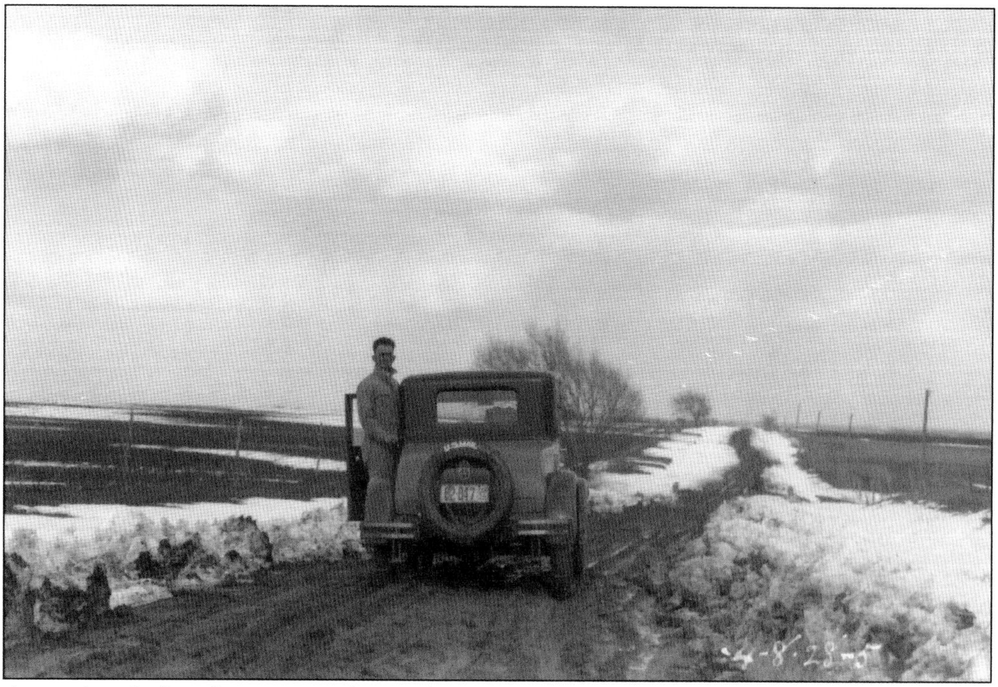

An unidentified mail carrier travels west through gummy spring mud on old Highway 36 on April 8, 1928. At this time, US 36 ran west along Calhoun Street in Marysville, about a quarter mile north of its current route straight through town on Center Street.

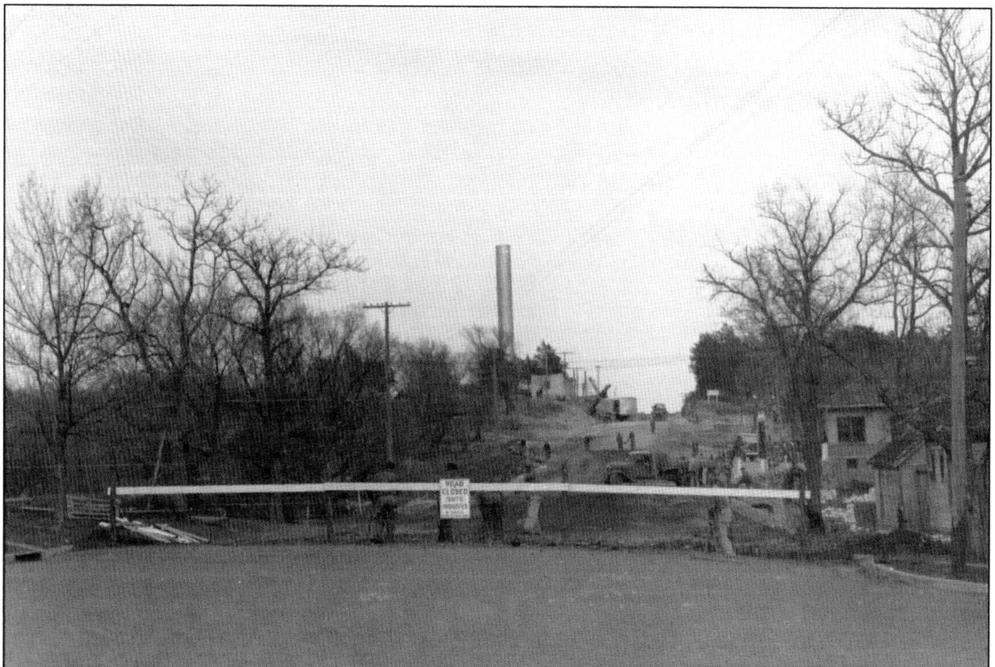

On April 2, 1936, US Highway 36 was being straightened and the hill lowered to prepare for paving. The tree at the lower right edge is at the corner of Fourteenth Street in this view looking east along US 36 (Center Street). The city water tower standpipe is in the distance.

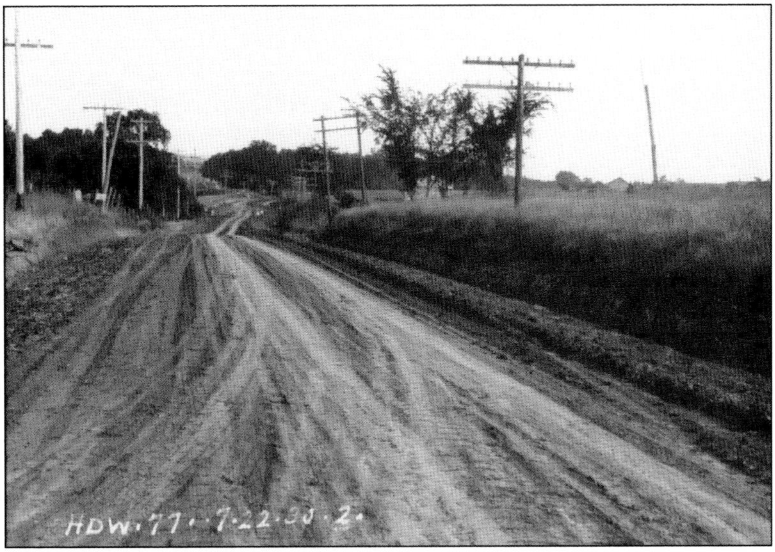


US Highway 77 north of Marysville was little more than a country lane in July 1930. This view near the Perry Hutchinson house shows the state of the road as it wends its way toward Nebraska, about 10 miles to the north.

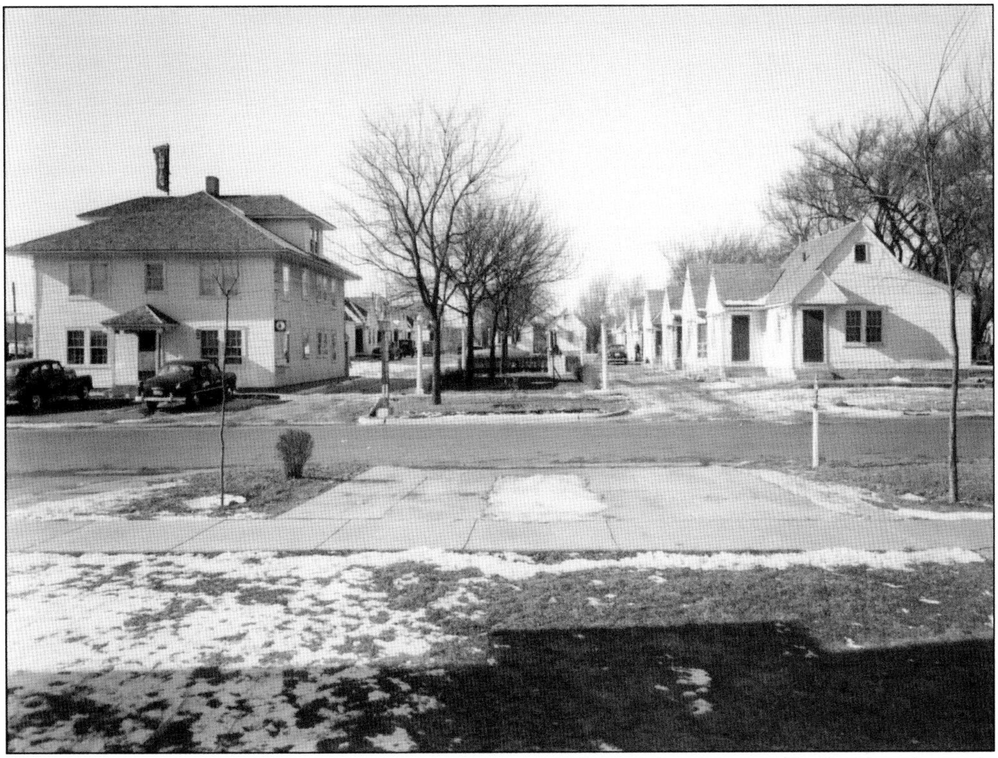

The West Side Court was an early tourist court, one of several in Marysville, built in the early 1940s. The cabins were models of cleanliness and comfort for travelers just beginning to enjoy the novelty of seeing America on the new cross-county highways. Local servicemen returned from World War II, got married, and established their first home in one of these cabins—living room with kitchen and eating area, bathroom, and one or two bedrooms—for about $12 a month. West Side Court closed in the 1960s, but some cabins are still standing near the US 36 bridge at the west edge of town. Once a welcome sight for weary travelers or home to young families, the remaining cabins are now empty and being demolished.

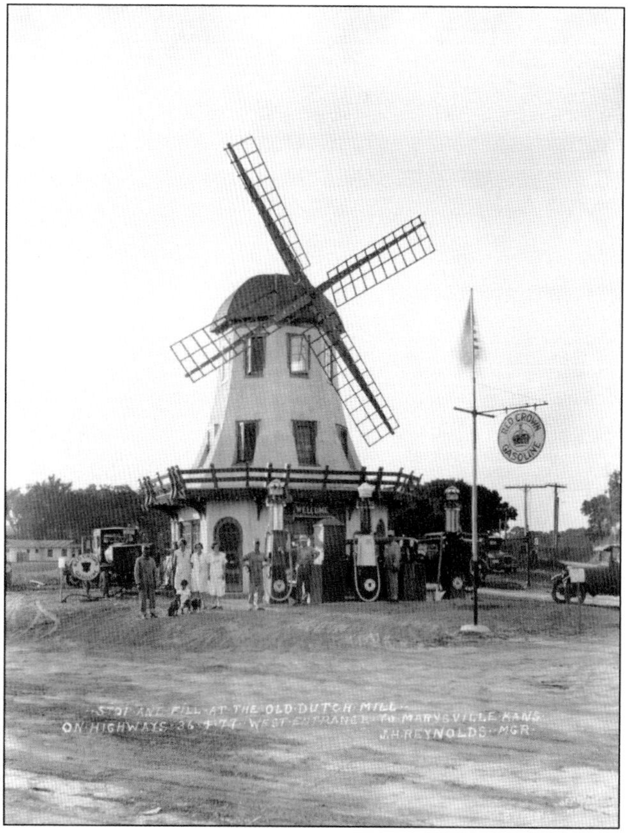


The Dutch Mill three-pump Red Crown gasoline station was at the southeast corner of Cahan's amusement park on US 36 and US 77 at the old bridge over the Big Blue River. It was erected in the 1920s. This photograph was taken August 19, 1928. The Dutch Mill included a lunch counter, tourist cabins and a wash house (forerunner of a Laundromat). The Dutch Mill went out of business when the old bridge was removed and the highway rerouted in the early 1930s.

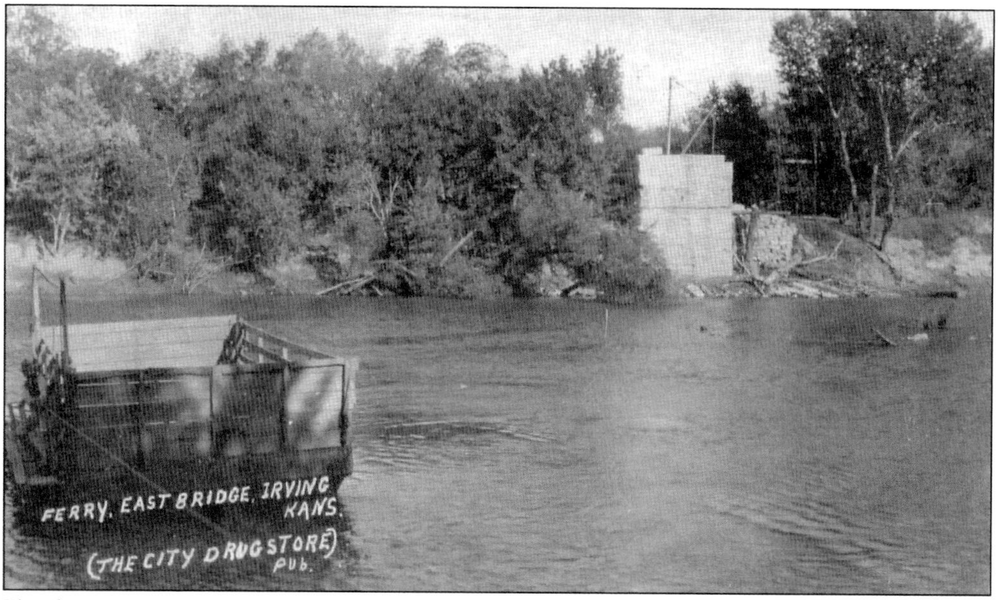


Floods were such a normal occurrence that county residents were necessarily creative in dealing with short- or long-term inconveniences. This temporary ferry operated in 1908 after the bridge over the Big Blue east of Irving was washed out. It was located on the south side of the west approach and was operated by Harry Huffmeir.

# *Three*

# LIVING ON THE LAND

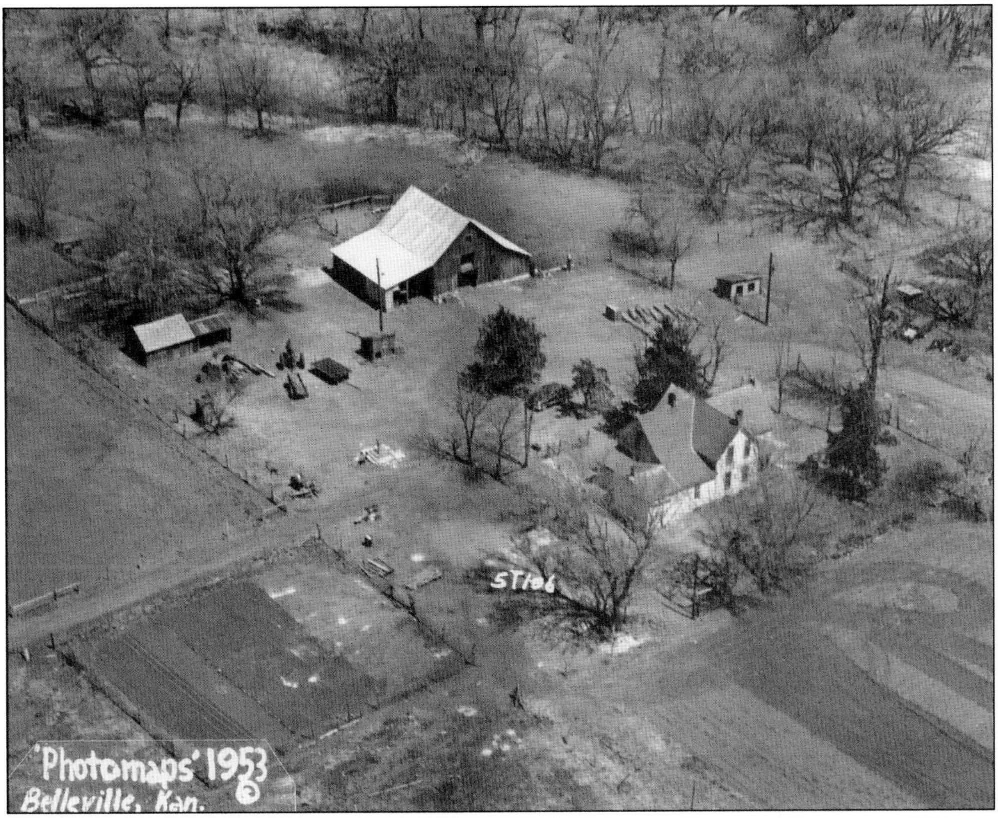


The Hazen farm is the first to be honored by the Marshall County Historical Society as a 150-year family farm. More than 180 farms have operated in the same family for 100 years, but this is the first to be able to trace its roots back 150 years. Gwynn and Marilyn Hazen own and operate a farm purchased in 1864 by Gwynn's great-grandfather. Sterling Hazen, the original owner, was a New York attorney who enlisted in the Union army during the Civil War. After suffering a gunshot wound to his neck and shoulder in 1863, he was discharged and moved to Marshall County the following year. The barn and house in this 1953 aerial view are the original structures. The house was replaced a few years ago with a modern home, but the original barn is still in use.

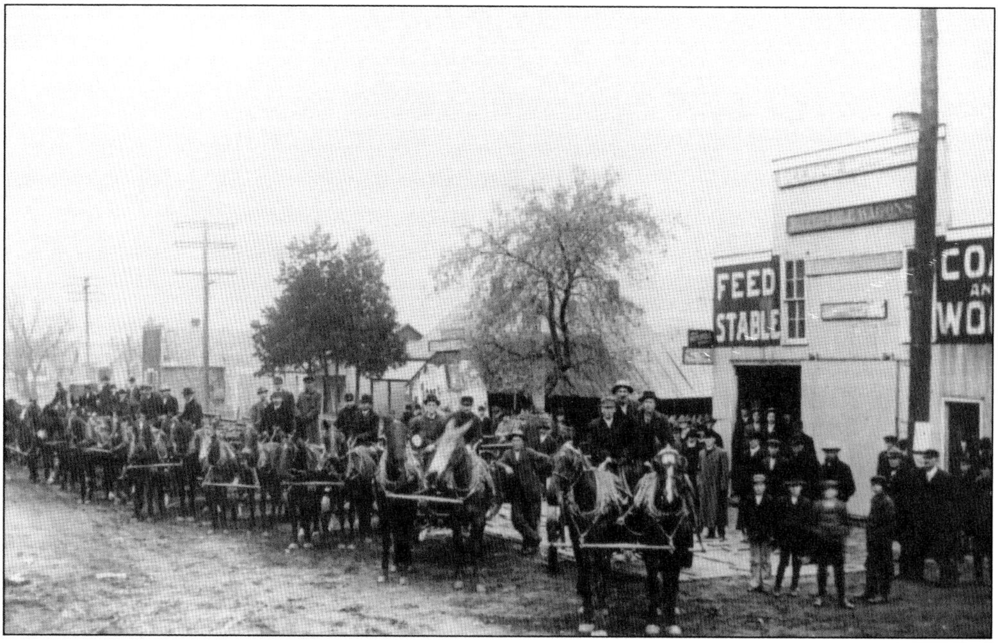


In this 1890s photograph, Barney Sextro, who operated a farm implement business west of the railroad tracks on Center Street in Marysville, is delivering new farm equipment to local farmers.

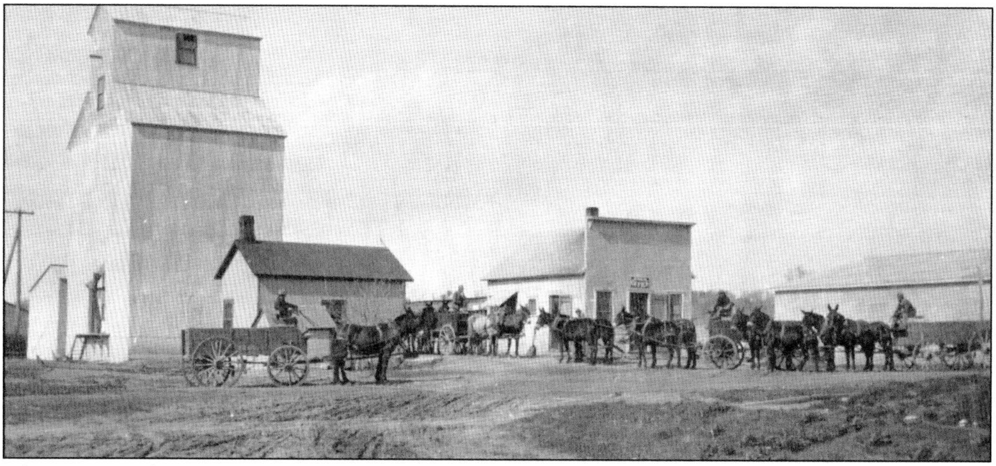

The cement elevator owned by Angus and William McLeod was built in 1889, and the small town of Marietta—with depot, stockyards, and a post office—grew around this. Competition in the 1890s by F.H. Peavey & Company was aimed at driving the McLeods out of business. On January 1, 1900, a new concept came to Kansas when the Marietta Farmers Elevator became the first farmers' cooperative elevator. A subsequent flood, wheat shortage, and fire, as well as continuing competition from Peavey, caused heavy debts and the cooperative reorganized and sold stock as the Marietta Stock and Grain Company. The cooperative venture was a success and Peavey sold out to them in 1910.

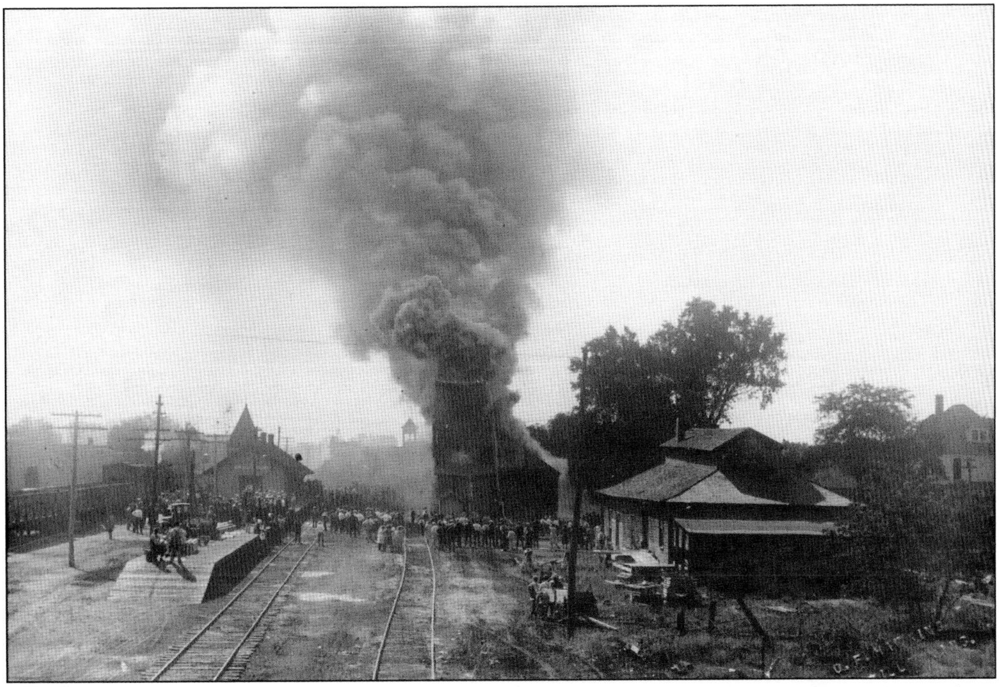

Elevator fires were not uncommon in early Marshall County. Midland Elevator, located on Seventh Street in Marysville, went up in flames on April 28, 1908. This view looks south along the railroad tracks; the third depot, built in 1880, is at left.

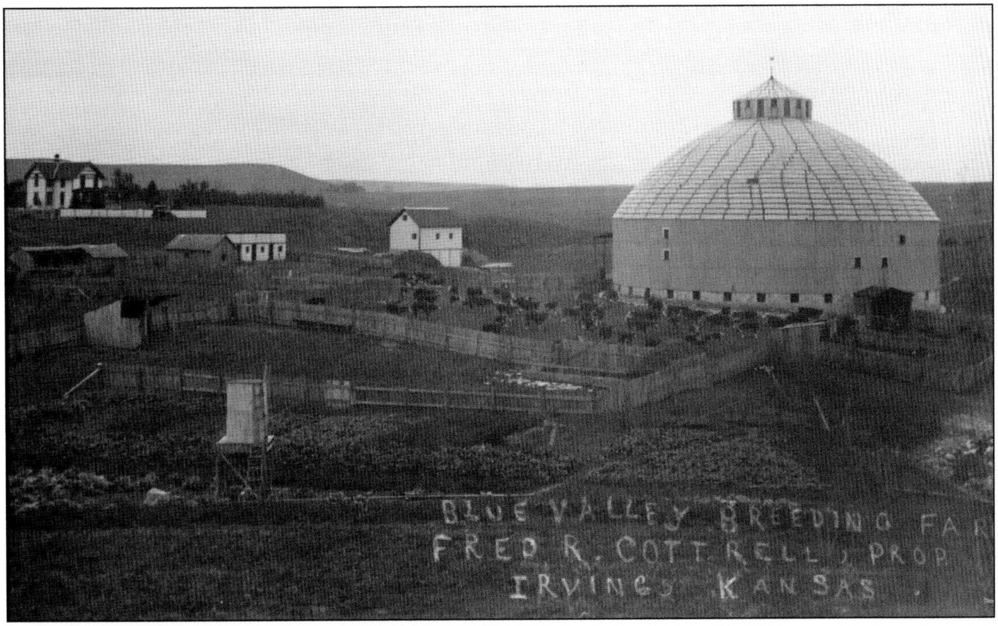


Featured in *Ripley's Believe It or Not!*, this round barn was built in 1909 by Fred Cottrell at his Blue Valley Hereford Ranch in Bigelow Township east of Irving. It was 100 feet in diameter and 80 feet high, and was built at a cost of $5,000. It had a capacity of 300 head of cattle, 500 tons of hay, and 10,000 bushels of grain. On July 27, 1946, a crowd of more than 10,000 people gathered at the ranch for a rodeo.

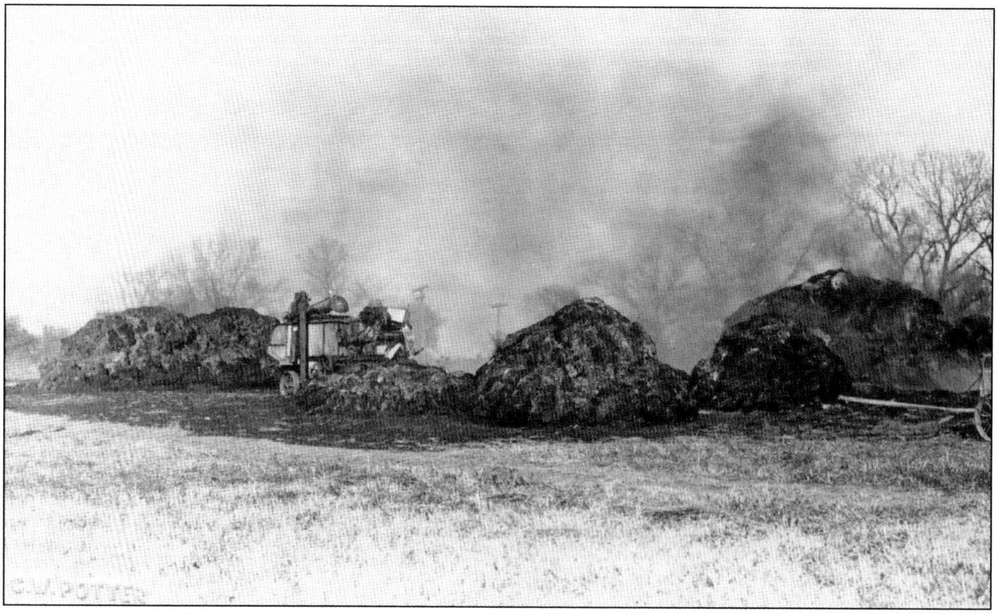

Wes Craven's thresher steam engine—a "Case outfit"—blew up in 1914 near the A.L. Breeding home. The thresher had run dry and exploded when cold water hit the hot metal. This photograph shows the smoke from the smoldering thresher and from some of the straw piles, which also burned.

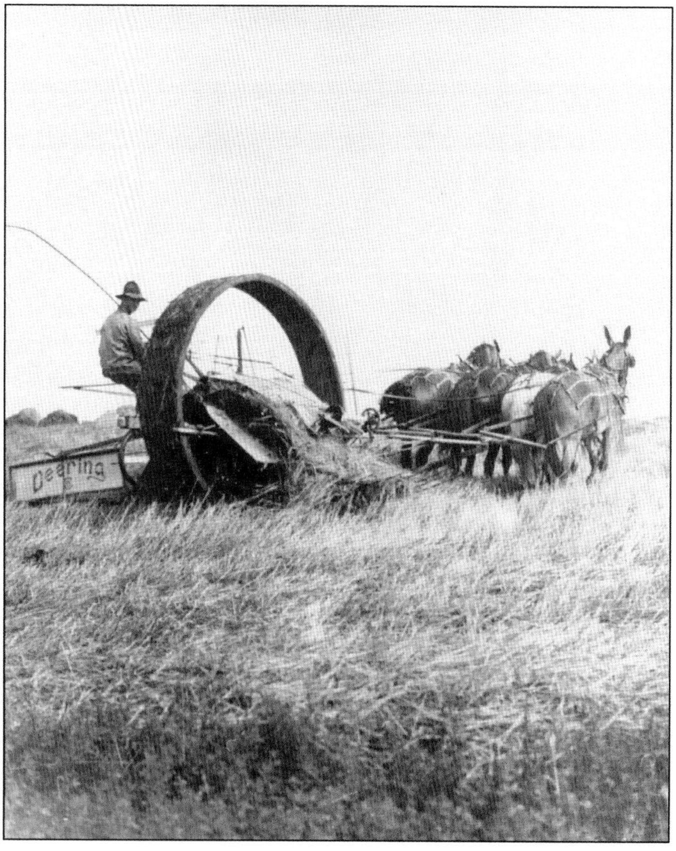


The summer of 1915 saw so much rainfall that crops were standing in water and some were rotting in the fields. Two towns, Oketo and Blue Rapids, recorded more than 43 inches of rain that summer—a record since weather stations were established in 1887. In his Marysville foundry, machinist Fritz Heinke invented a strap iron hoop two feet wide and 10 feet in diameter, wide enough not to get mired in the muddy fields. It was nicknamed the "Ferris wheel" by local farmers. The hoop was positioned under the binder's drive wheel. Once the drive wheel rested on a dry surface, the binder could not get stuck. This was the most efficient method for cutting wheat that season.

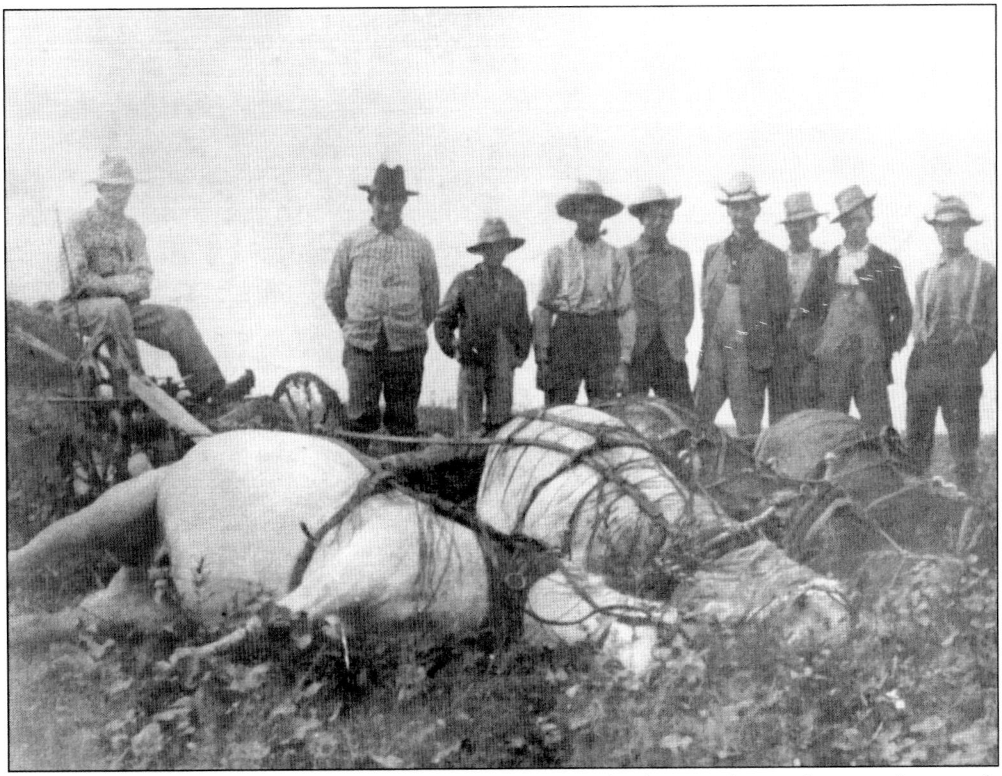

It was, unfortunately, not uncommon for lightning to strike farmers, livestock, or work animals like horses or mules when thunderstorms gathered suddenly over open farm fields. The ground current from a lightning strike outside Beattie on August 26, 1908, killed four horses belonging to Frank Naaf, who is on the plow at left. This would have been a costly loss, as horses were the engines of that period and often sold for $300 or more. In 1914, another Beattie farmer was hit directly and killed instantly, and several people standing near him were injured, some severely.

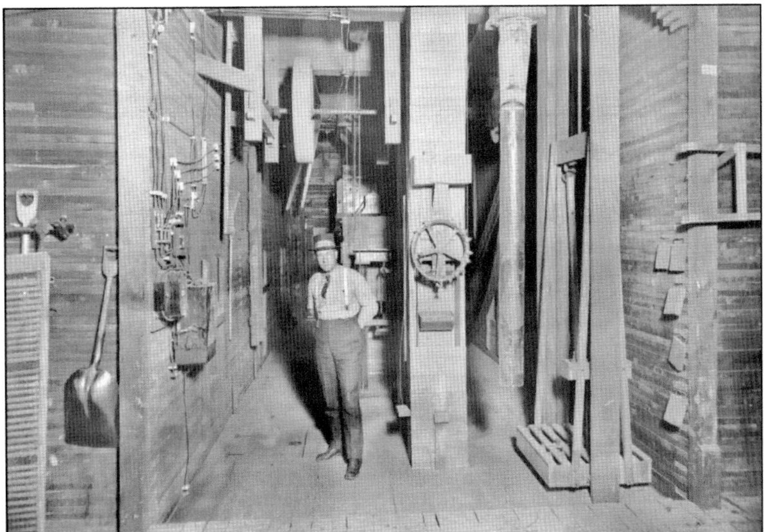

This is the interior of the W.T. Buck grain elevator at the Missouri Pacific Railroad line in Vliets, around 1910. At one time, the annual shipments through this elevator averaged 150,000 bushels of grain. By 1915, Buck owned and managed two elevators in this little village.

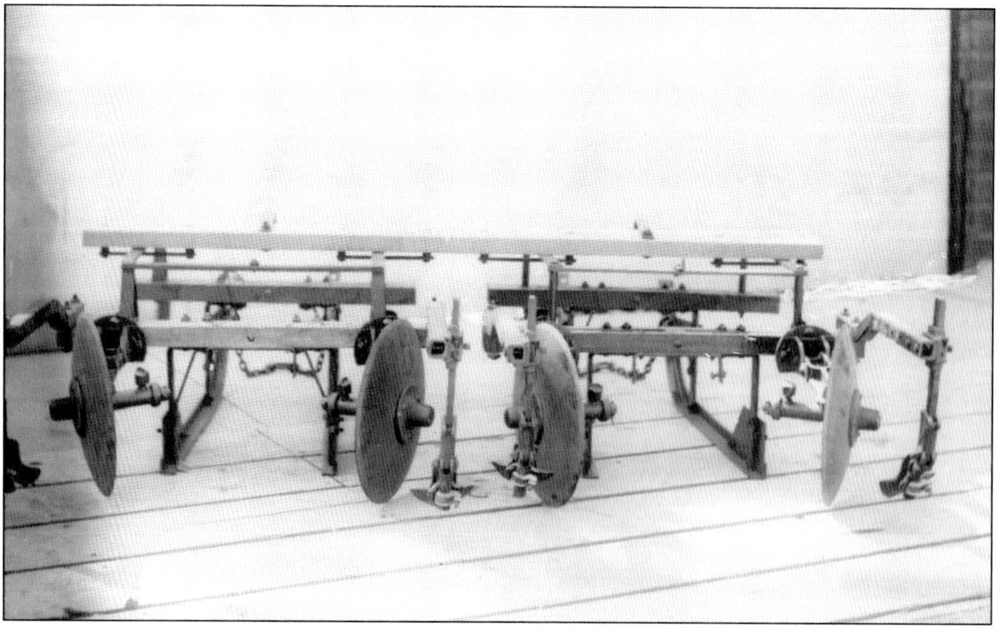

Beattie farmer and inventor Linden Kirlin gained international fame for his farming inventions. The two-row cultivator in this photograph revolutionized the cultivation of listed corn. In 1915, at age 67, Kirlin invented a shock absorber for Ford automobiles. Kirlin held at least eight patents, most for farming implements.

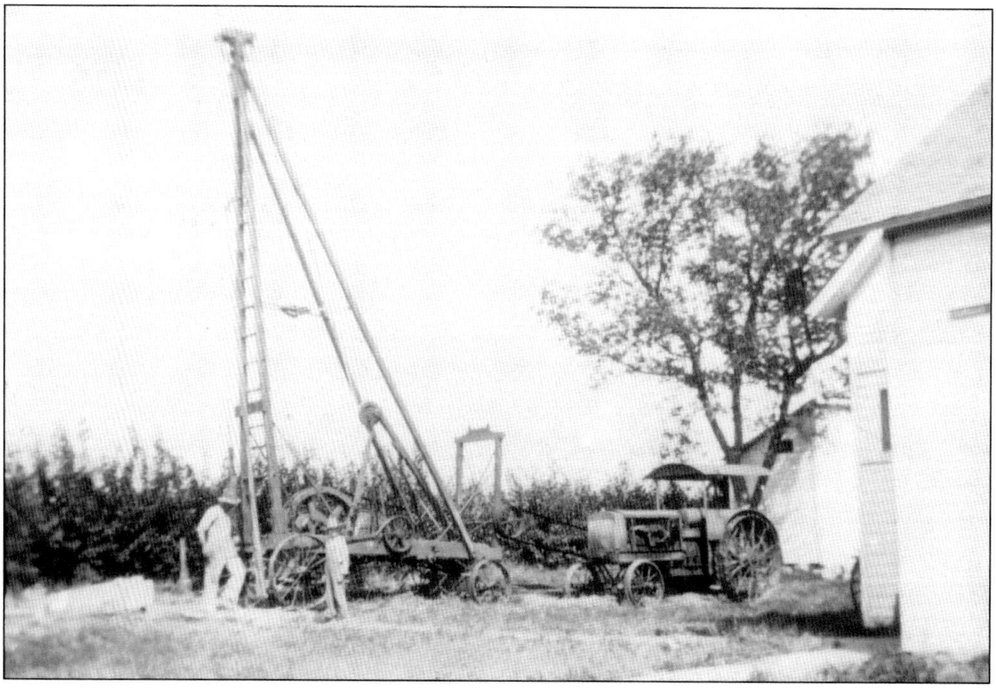

Water for house and farm was a necessity on the prairie. Rainwater or water carried from local creeks was used for everything from washing to cooking, but even the earliest settlers dug for groundwater as soon as they could. By the time this well was being drilled at an unidentified Marshall County farm, gasoline power had made the process easier and faster.

In addition to being a farmer, Otto Wullschleger was a well-known Marshall County historian and collector of Indian artifacts, especially arrowheads. He is seen here with his sons and a covered wagon hitched to a team of oxen. His farm was two miles northeast of Winifred.

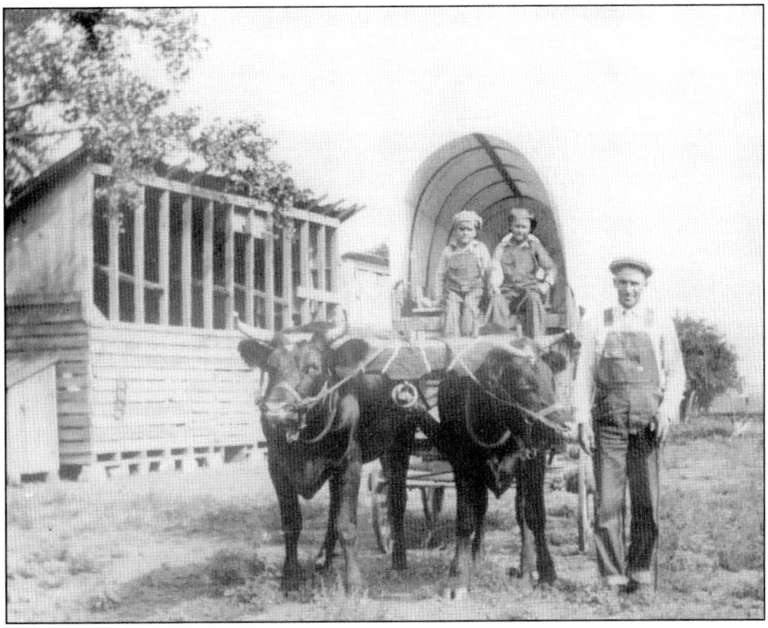

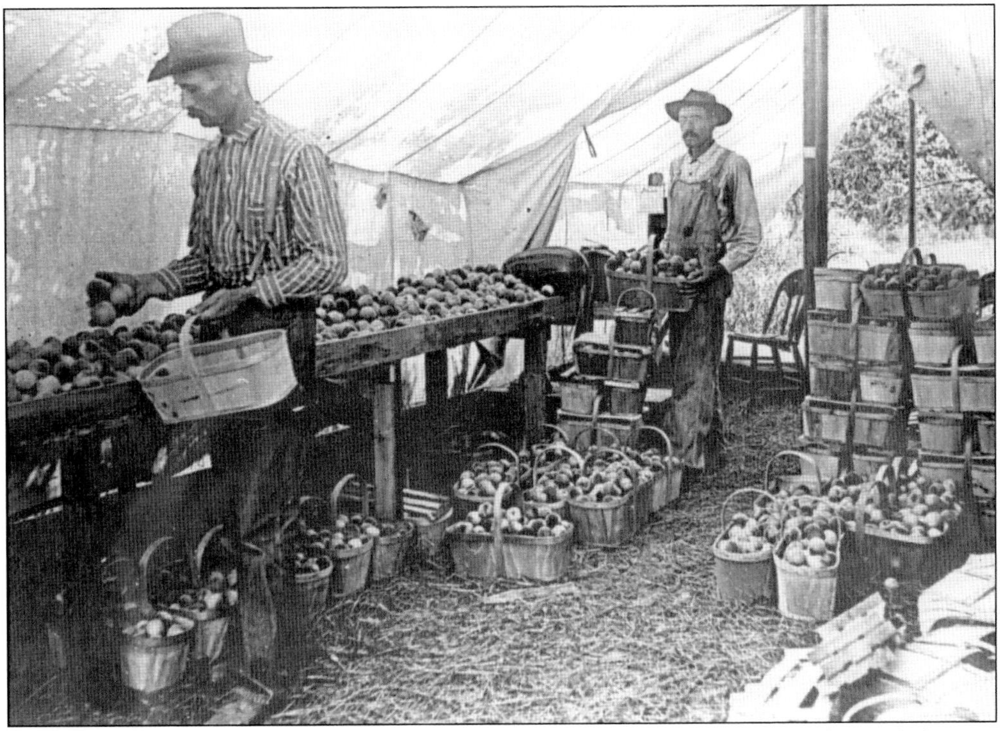

E.S. Nevins had an orchard southeast of Blue Rapids, where he grew both peaches and cherries. The Nevins family's sale shed, where peaches were sorted, weighed, graded, and packed, seen here in about 1930, was visited by hundreds of local families annually. At one time, there were at least two other peach orchards in the county.

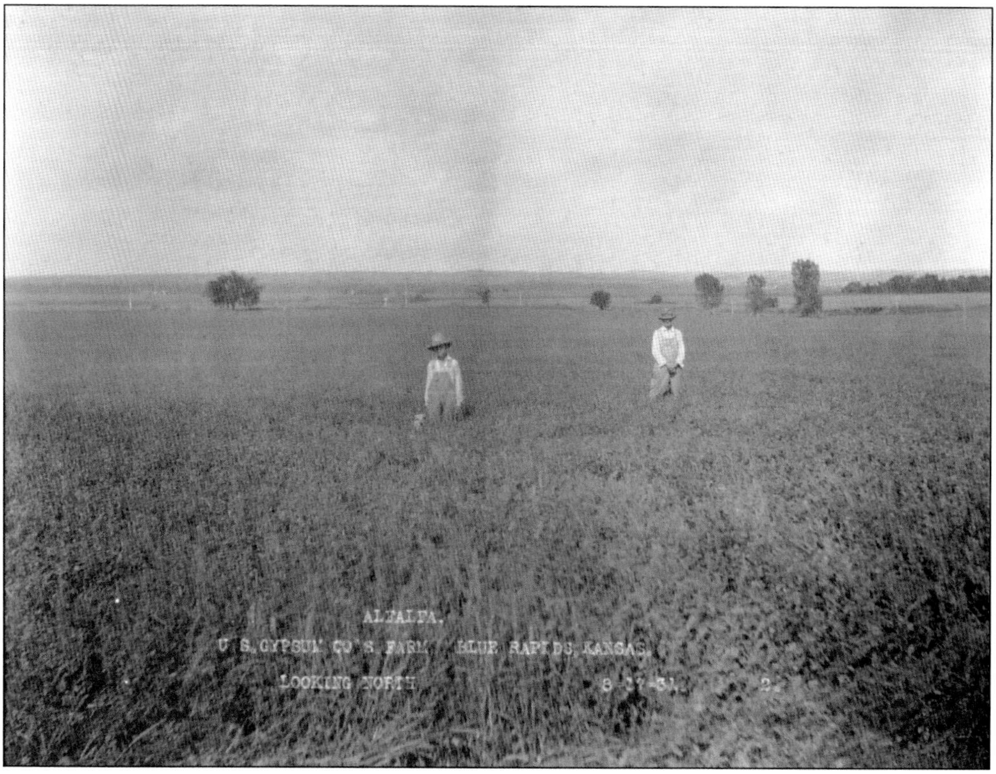


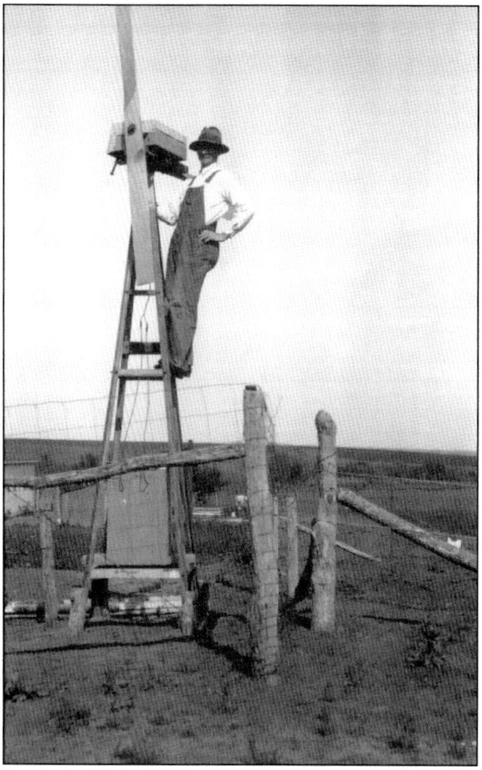

In the 1930s, the US Gypsum Company had a substantial farm near its plant just south of Blue Rapids. The farm had a manager's house, barns, pens for the mules that hauled the gypsum from the mines, and some housing for workers. In this 1931 photograph, farmhands are standing in the farm's alfalfa field.

Oketo farmer Ed Bach is tending to his homemade wind-powered generator in about 1935. The generator would have been used to charge batteries that provided direct current to power a radio or a couple of lights. At this time, kerosene lamps were still used in most farm homes. Most Marshall County residents living outside of town did not have electricity until the late 1940s.

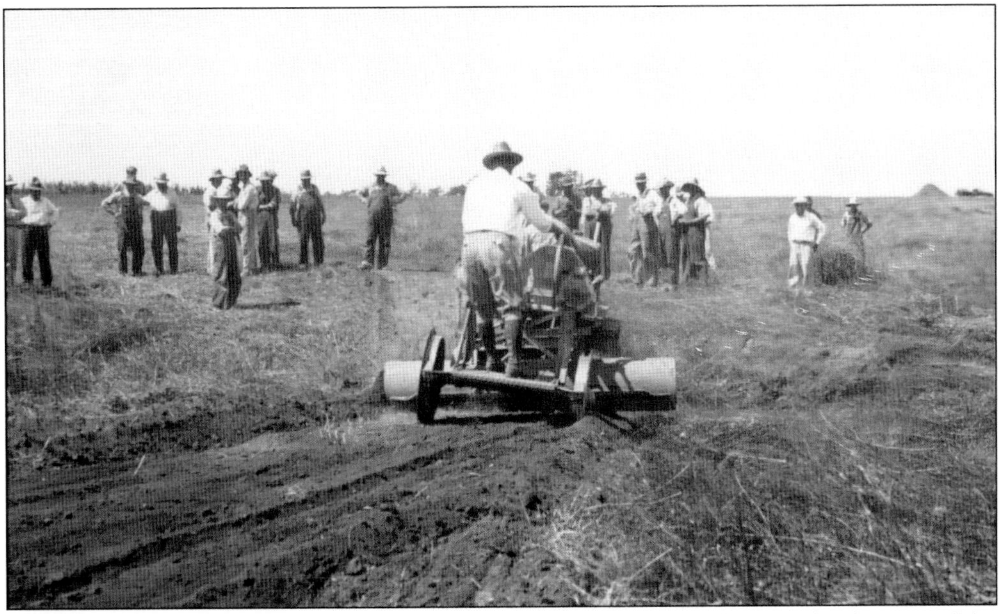

Farmers and townsfolk alike would have been hard-pressed to identify a beneficial aspect of the Dust Bowl. But these storms—created in part by poor farming practices—led to the creation of the Soil Conservation Service, which showed farmers modern, responsible farming practices. This is a product demonstration in 1931 showing how model broad-based terraces are started.

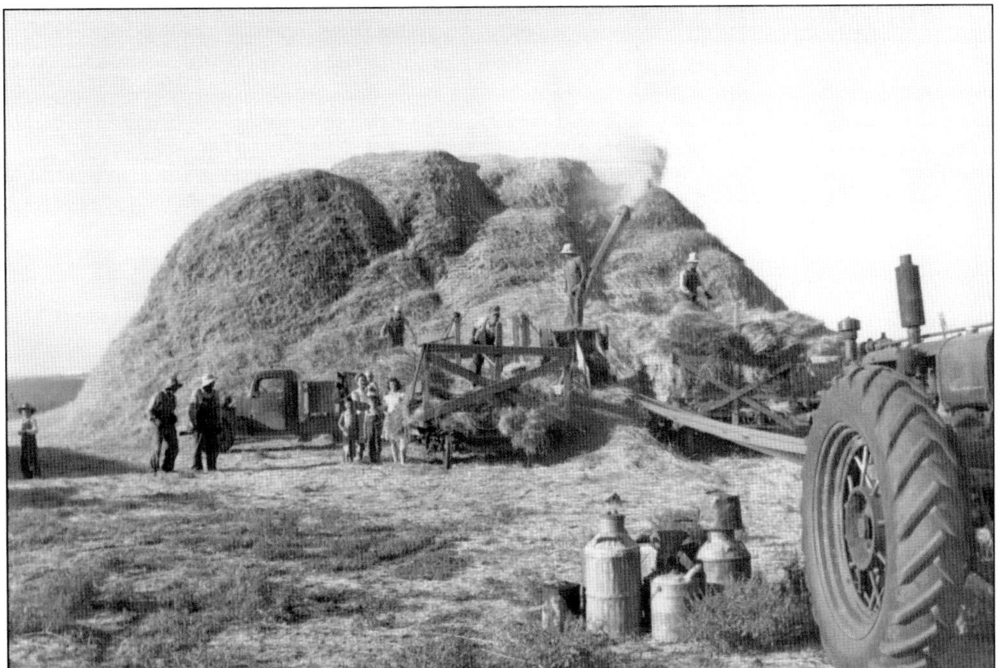

Farmers are threshing wheat or oats, making a small mountain of straw at a county farm. The pull-type thresher in this 1940s photograph is run by a gas-powered tractor.

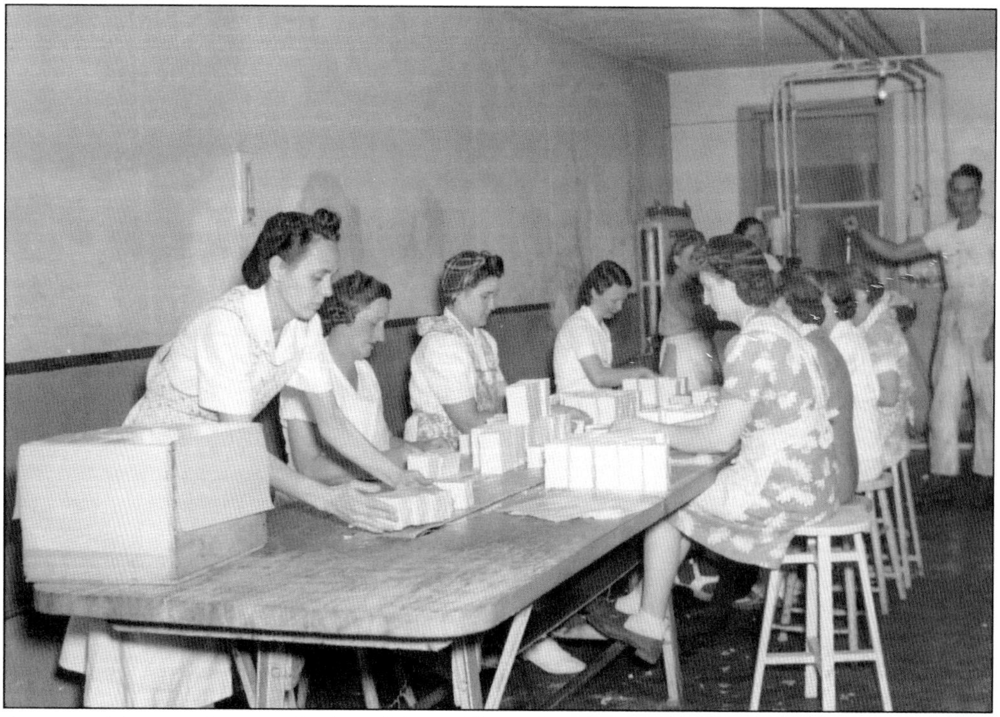

A state-of-the-art plant was built in Marysville in September 1925 by Armour & Company to replace its plant that had burned about six months earlier. As the company grew, this plant provided egg products, cheese, and butter. Workers in the print room at the plant are creating Cloverbloom Butter blocks in quarter-pound and one-pound blocks. After "printing," the blocks were wrapped and placed in cartons and boxes for shipment. The plant had government contracts during World War II, but sales slackened after the war. Armour sold the company to Perry Packing Company in 1947. Perry focused on eggs and merged with three others to become the largest egg packing company in the nation. Perry Packing closed in 1961.

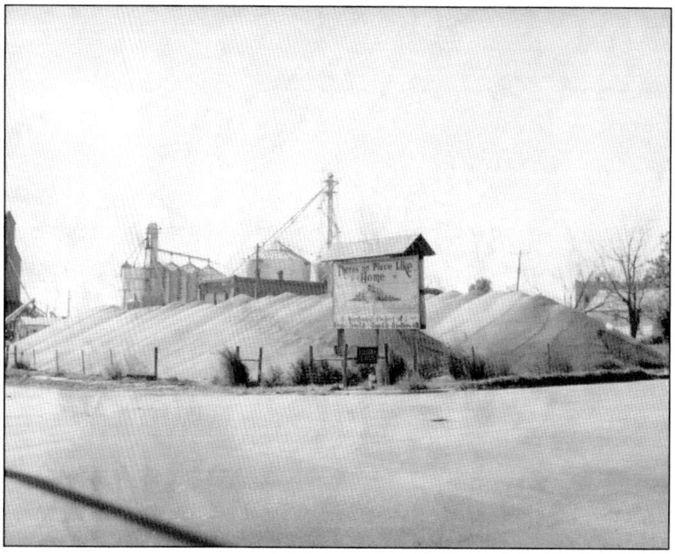


Milo was an important Marshall County feed crop for several decades, peaking between the 1950s and 1970s. As science found more uses for corn and corn prices rose, milo's popularity waned. Today, relatively little milo is grown in the county. Sorghum, known locally as kafir corn, was a type of milo grown much earlier in county history. In this photograph, milo from an abundant harvest is piled near the Home City elevator awaiting shipment.

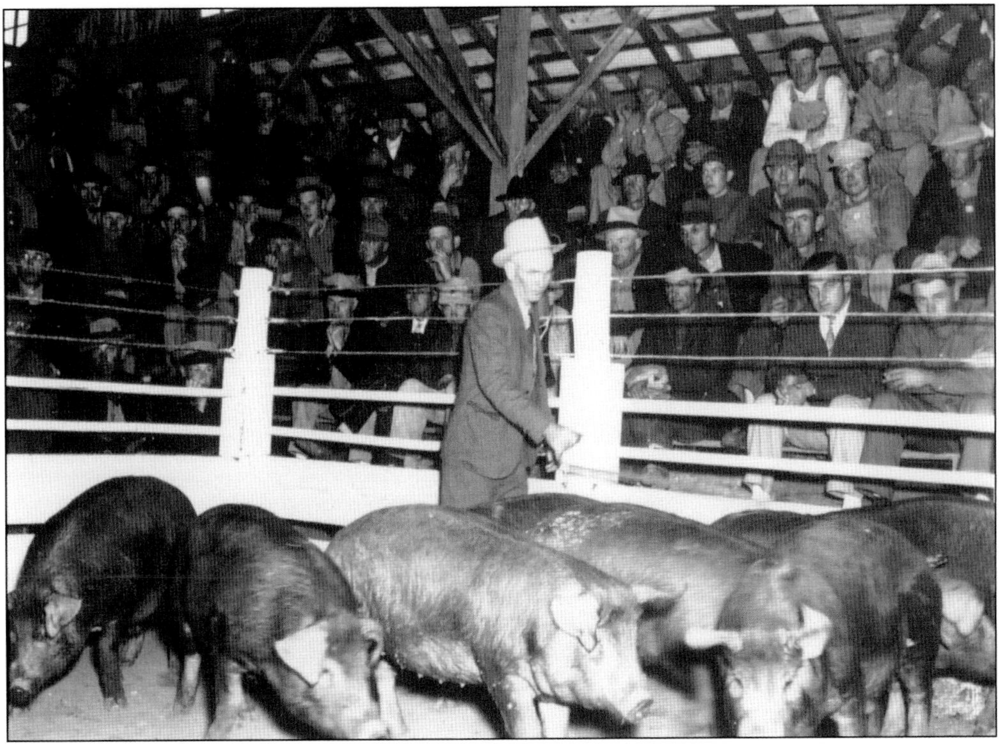

The A.L. Breeding Sale Barn was an important place for livestock auctions in the 1940s. The building was on the west bank of the river, close to the current junction of US 36 and US 77. It was razed in the late 1970s.

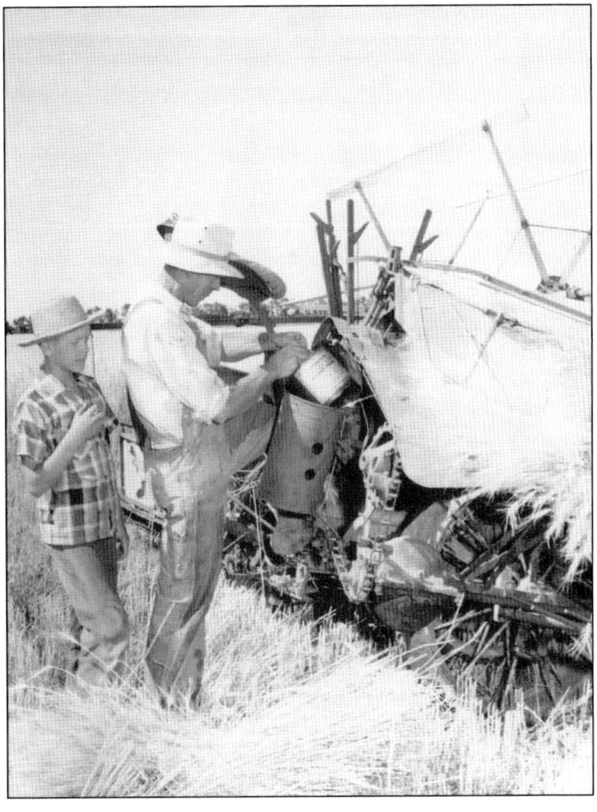

In this 1950s photograph, a county farmer and his son are changing twine on a binder. This would already have been a novelty as most farmers would have been using combines to cut and thresh their wheat.

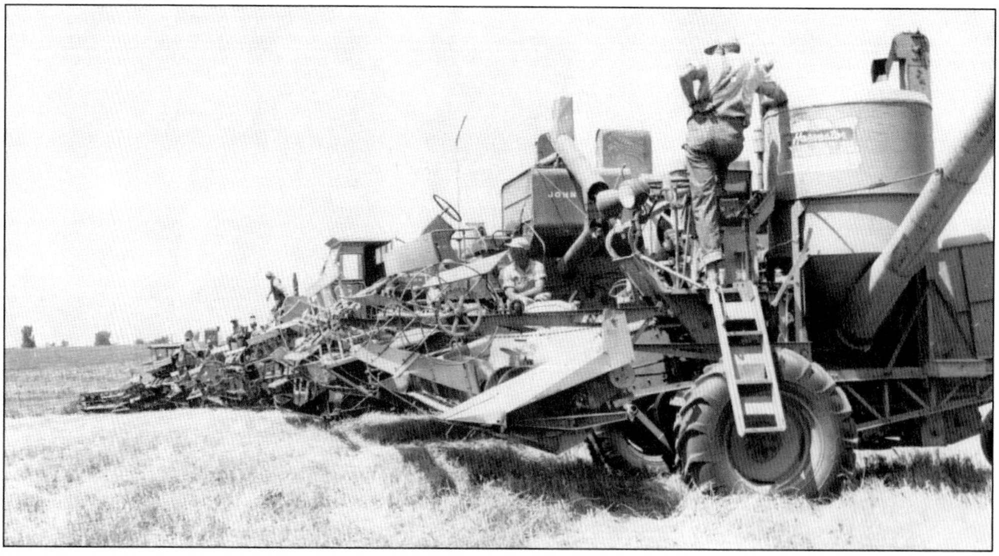

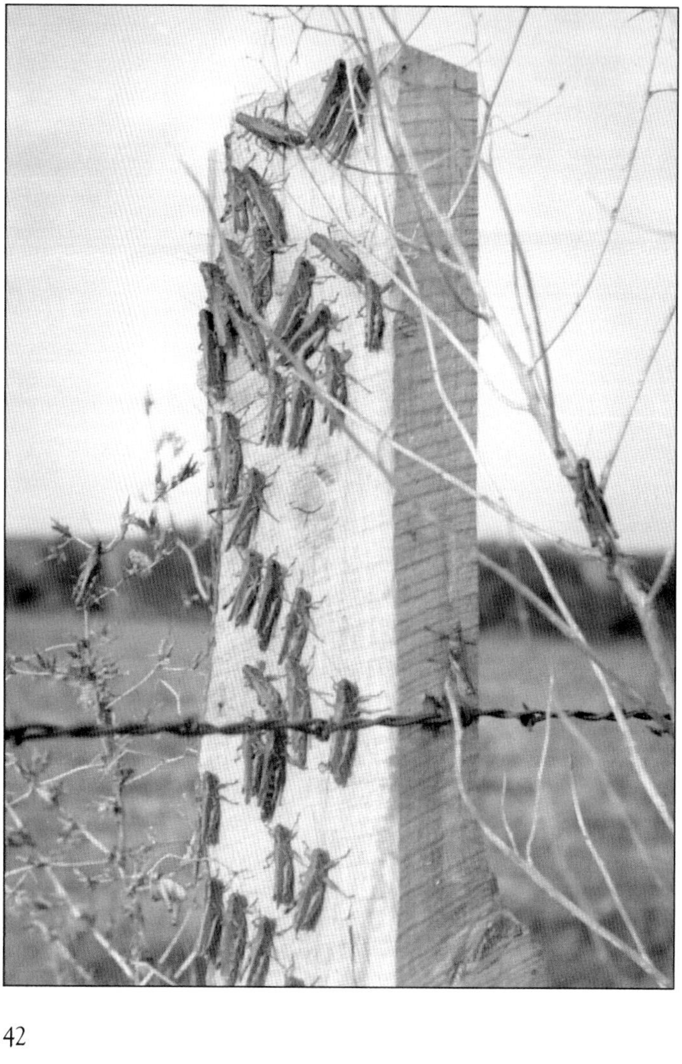

In July 1963, a fleet of 18 combines harvested 65 acres of wheat in just two hours on the Oketo farm of Henry Sedlacek Jr., who had died days before, at the beginning of harvest. More than 20 trucks hauled the grain to storage.

This photograph, taken September 8, 1949, shows a cloud of grasshoppers on the Joe Rundus Jr. farm, near Blue Rapids. Although, thankfully, not a common occurrence, several county histories mention summers where entire crops were lost to these pests. The first recorded grasshopper invasion in Marshall County was in 1866.

# *Four*

# Business and Industry

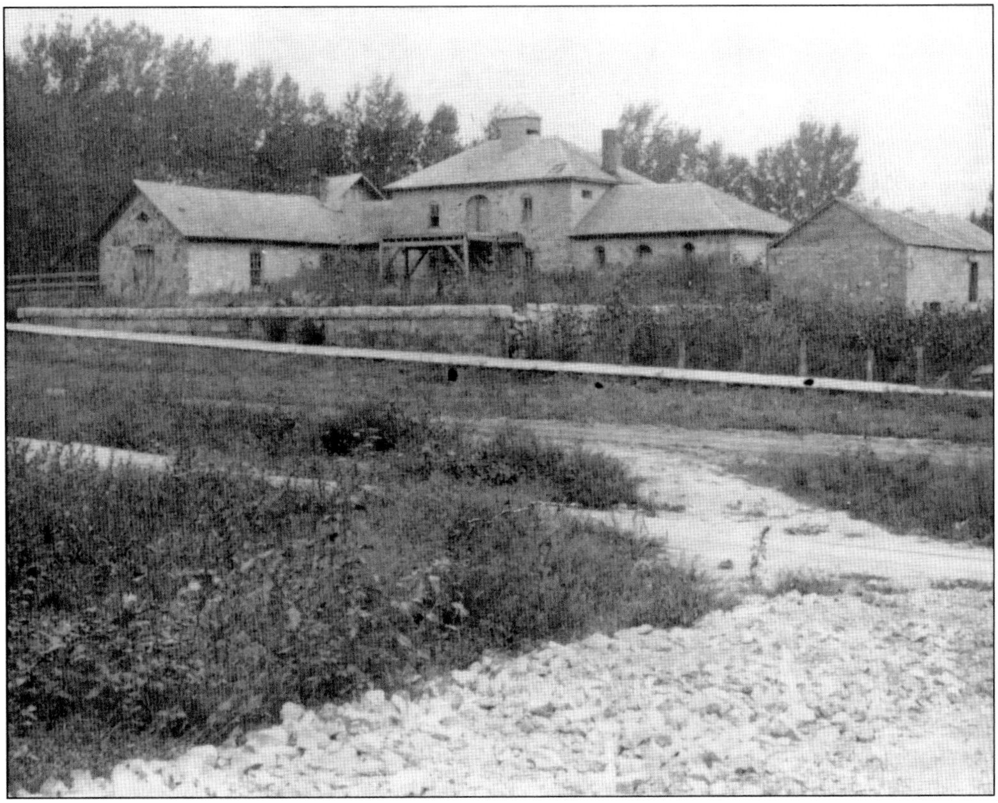

There was a large German population in Marshall County and good beer was part of their heritage. P.H. Kalenborn's Phoenix Brewery, seen here around 1884, was located in Marysville in the 1100 block of Broadway on the south side of the street. An 1873 newspaper advertisement states, "The Proprietor wishes to inform the Public that his facilities for manufacturing best Phoenix Beer is unsurpassed in the state. All orders filled promptly, and satisfaction guaranteed. Highest price paid for Barley at the Brewery."

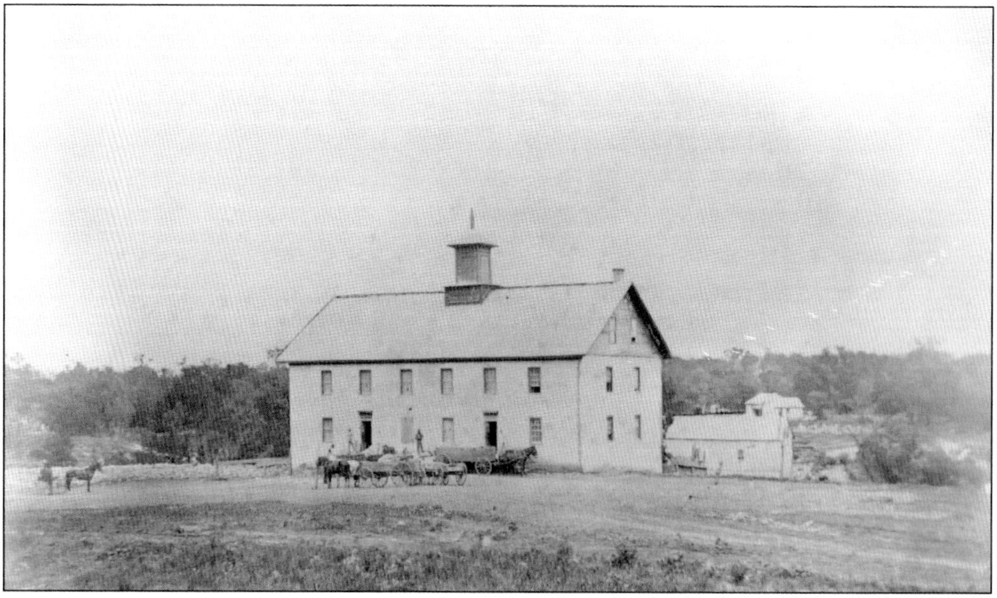

Perry and Jennette Hutchinson arrived in Marysville in 1859. When they had acquired enough money, Hutchinson purchased the water rights on the Big Blue River and started a dam. In 1863, he returned from service in the Union army, finished the dam, and built the only flour mill within 100 miles. In 1867, he built a larger mill, seen in this photograph taken August 15 of that year. When he began shipping by rail, his success was assured, and that success bolstered the economy of the entire area. The mill burned in 1905, but Hutchinson, undaunted, rebuilt. His house, directly across US 77 from the mill site, was built in 1872 and listed in the National Register of Historic Places in 1972.

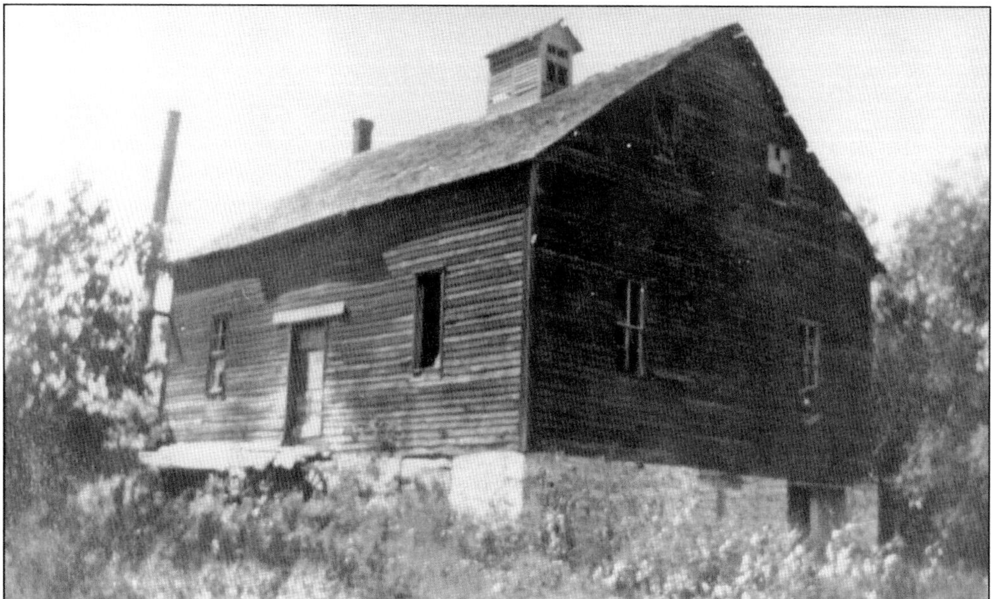

The first sawmill in Marshall County was built in 1855–1856 on the Black Vermillion at what would become the town of Barrett. Local black walnut logs were sawed for the A.G. Barrett home and for the Barrett Hotel in Marysville.

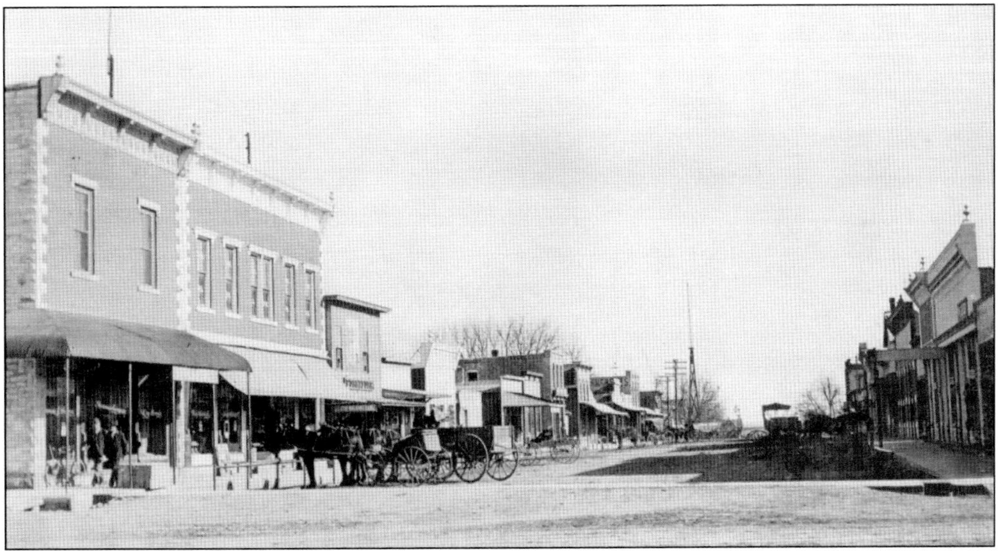

This is Commercial Street, the main street in Waterville, around 1907. The photographer is at the corner of Kansas Street, looking west. Waterville was platted in 1868, one hundred miles from Atchison, to be the westernmost railroad town on the Central Branch of the Missouri Pacific Railroad. The railroad contributed to the growth of the town, which peaked in population at 1,700 in 1910. The population in 2010 was about 690.

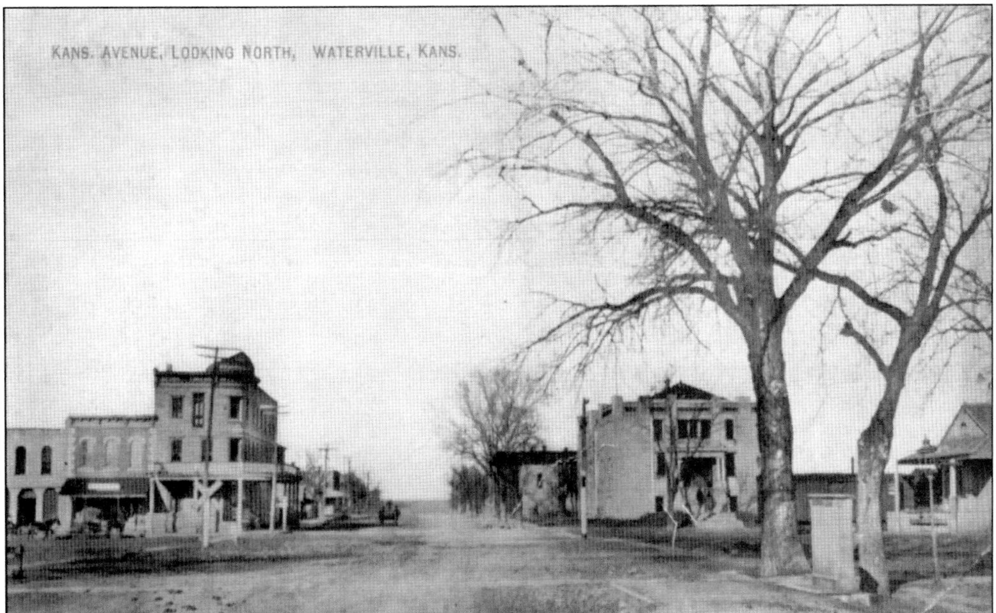


The Central Branch Railroad runs from right to left (east to west) in this 1907 postcard view, between the trees and the buildings about half a block away. The two-story limestone building on the right side of Kansas Street is Waterville City Hall and opera house. The building at left across the street is the Weaver Hotel, built in 1905. The Weaver was renovated and opened as an historic hotel in 2010; it was placed in the National Register of Historic Places in 1975. The city hall has been relocated and the opera house is currently undergoing renovation. Events and performances are held here periodically during the year. (Courtesy of LaVerna Arganbright.)

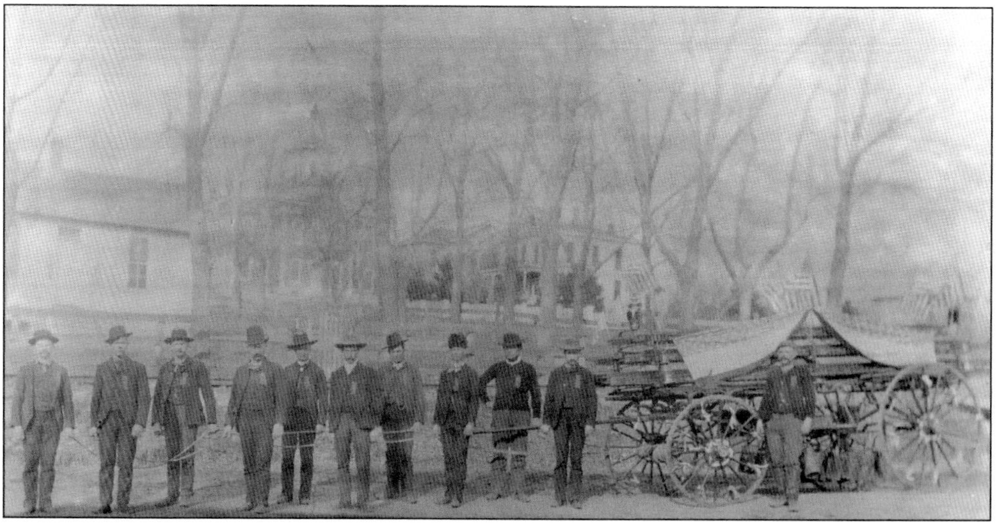

Members of the Marysville Fire Department are posed at the pull ropes of their fire wagon in 1885. It was slow and inefficient to hitch horses to fire wagons so early fire carts were "hitched" to the firemen.

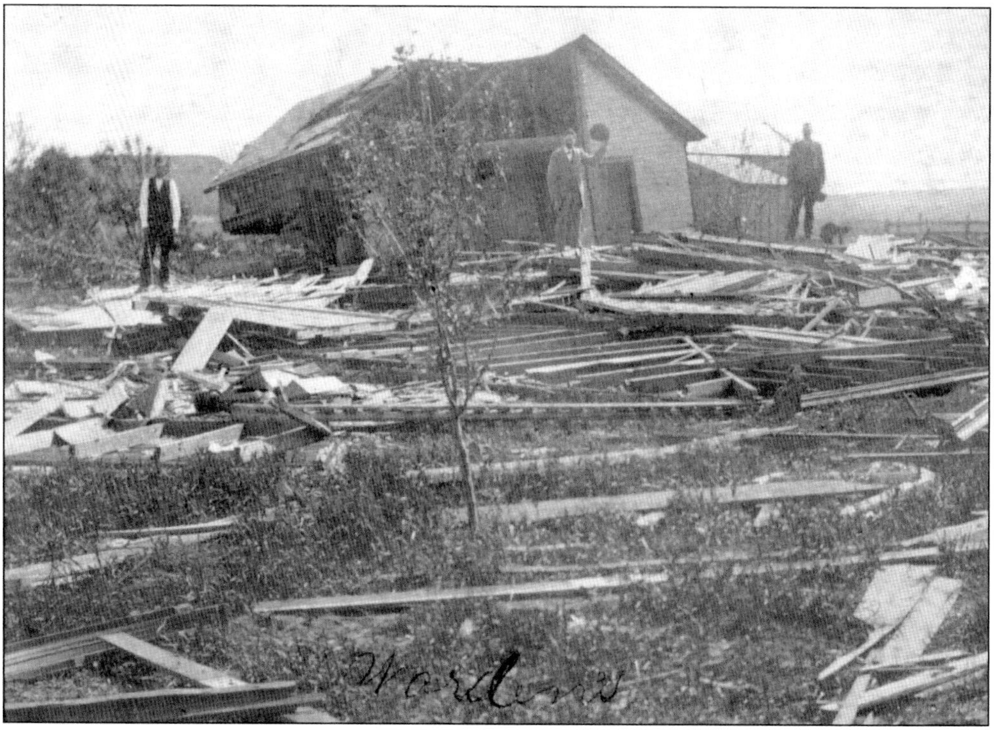

On May 30, 1879, the town of Irving was heavily damaged by two tornadoes about an hour apart. The damage path of the first tornado was 100 miles long. The second was described as a black cloud a mile wide. When the storms cleared, 14 people had been killed and about 50 injured. The school, most of the Presbyterian church, and 34 homes and businesses had been destroyed. The iron bridge east of the town was lifted off its piers and smashed into the river. It is estimated that these tornadoes would rank at F4 or higher on the modern Fujita scale. A persistent myth suggests these tornadoes were an inspiration for L. Frank Baum's classic, *The Wonderful Wizard of Oz*.

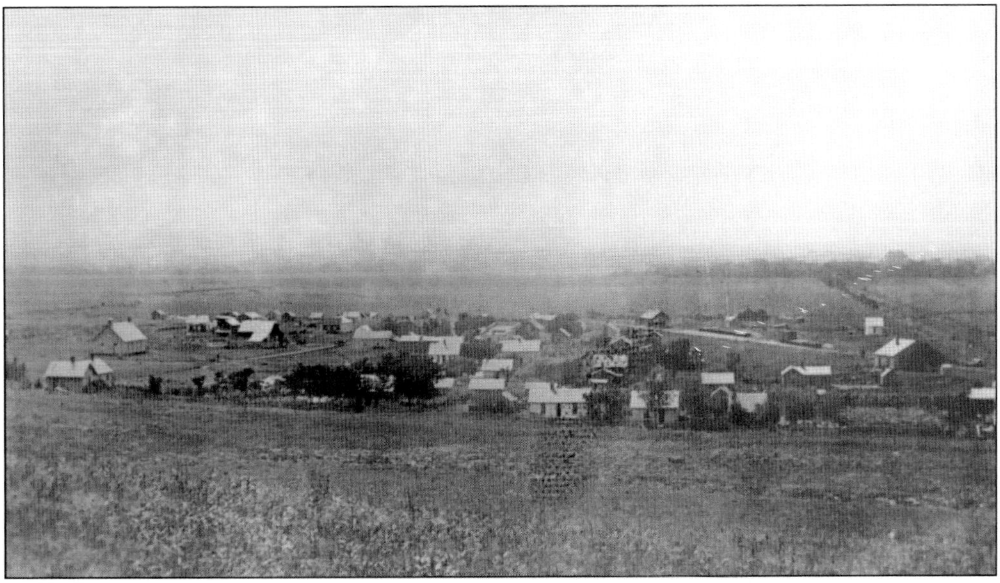

Bigelow was established in 1881 around the area's limestone quarries. This is a view of the small community surrounded by prairie in 1886. The population peaked in 1910 at 200. By then, the town had a popular dance hall, newspaper, church, and active community groups. Bigelow was one of three Marshall County towns demolished in the late 1950s to make way for the Tuttle Creek Dam project.

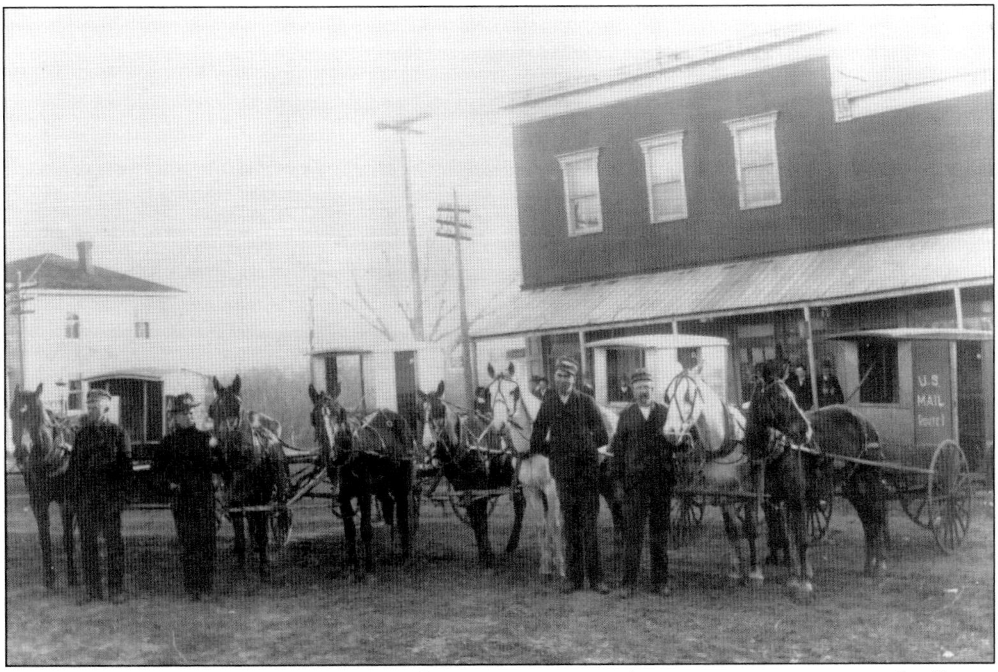


In the 1890s, Marshall County had 11 thriving towns, nearly as many unincorporated villages, and hundreds of rural homesites. The 1890 county census shows a population of 23,634. Residents went to town to pick up mail at the post office or had their mail delivered by mailmen who traveled by horse and mail-delivery carts over hundreds of county miles on unpaved streets and country roads. The Vermillion Post Office had four rural mail routes when this photograph was taken.

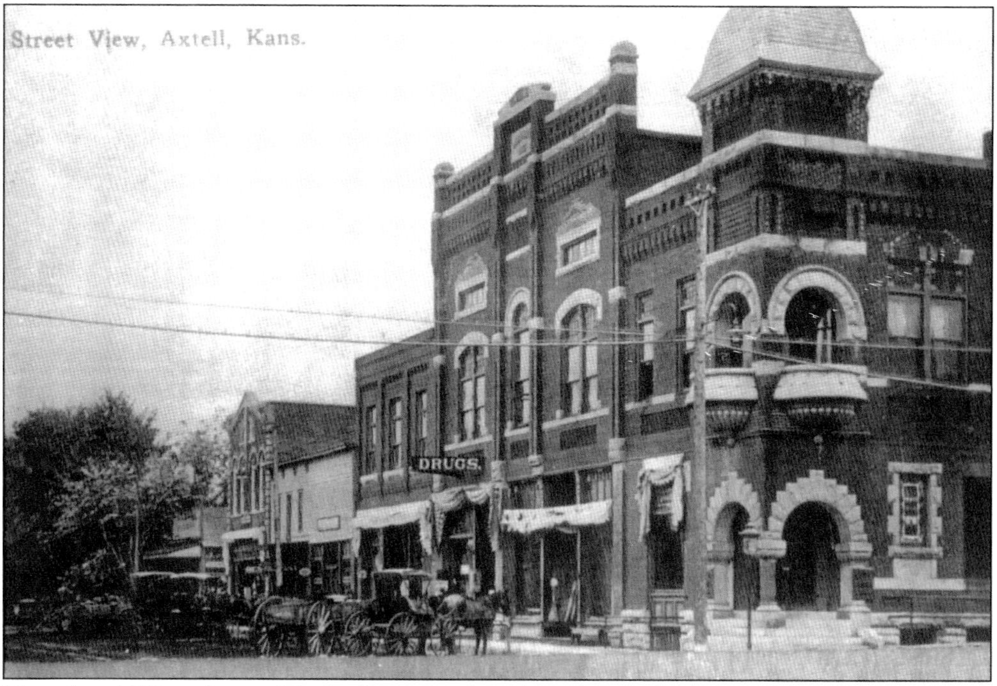


Platted in 1872 and served by both the St. Joseph and Grand Island and the Kansas City & Northwestern Railways, Axtell grew to be a thriving town with 42 businesses by 1917. In about 1908, the Citizens Bank, opera house, drugstore, and restaurant were among the businesses in this ornate brick and limestone building at the corner of Fifth and Maple Streets. In 1925, a bronze doughboy monument was erected here by American Legion R.R. Hendricks Post 214 to honor 150 men and 2 nurses from Axtell who had served in World War I.

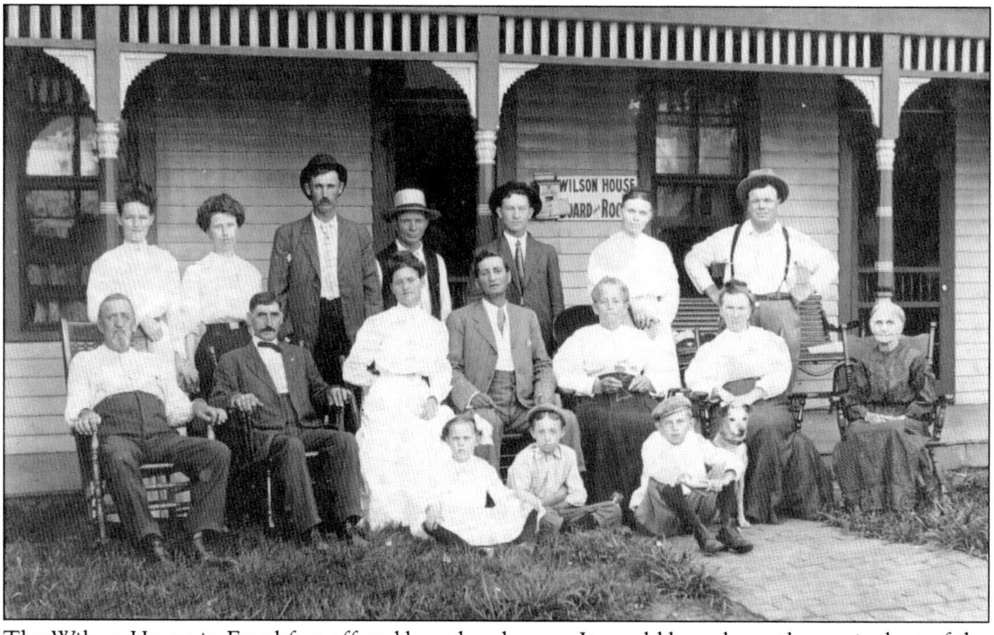


The Wilson House in Frankfort offered board and room. It would have been the equivalent of the modern long-stay motel, with some long-term residents and some people traveling for business.

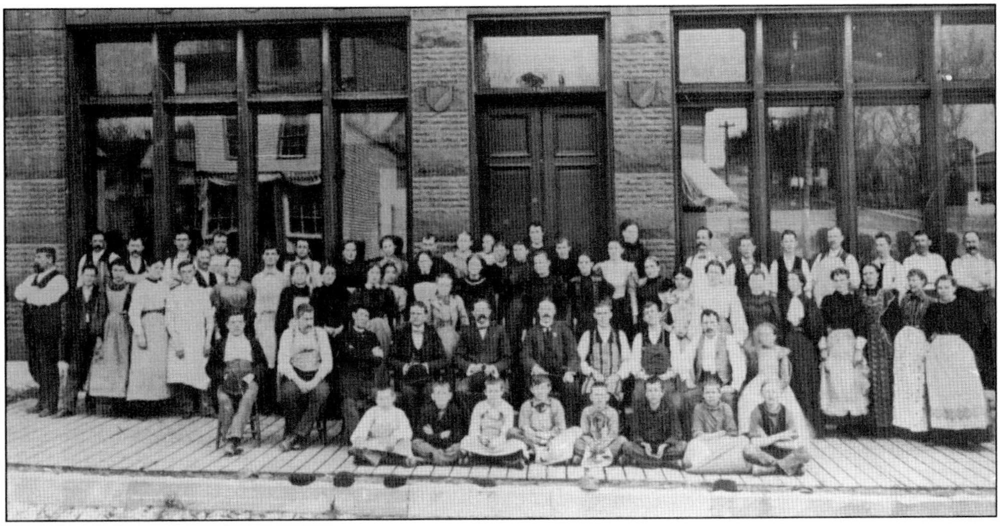

By the late 1800s, Marshall County had at least six cigar factories—one each in Blue Rapids and Frankfort, and four in Marysville. Of these, the Charles F. Pusch factory at the southeast corner of Broadway at Tenth Street in Marysville was the largest. In 1887, Pusch employed 32 and manufactured 1,500,125 cigars. When this photograph was taken in 1898, the factory employed at least 67 people. Notice the number of child workers in the photograph.

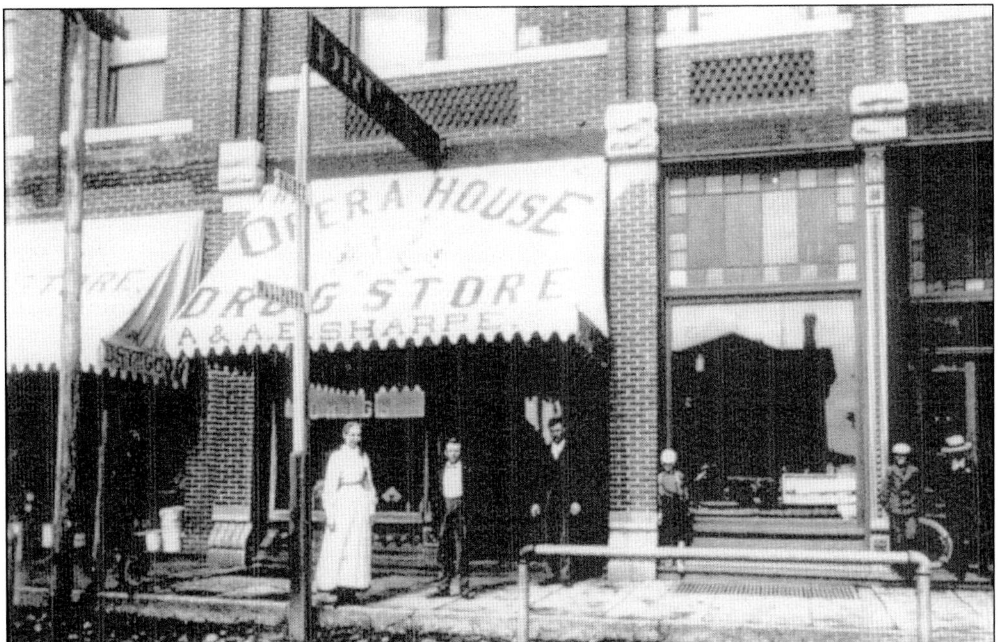


In 1898, the Axtell Opera House was located above the drugstore. Opera houses were small town auditoriums, used for meetings and dances, and for musical and theatrical performances by both local and traveling entertainers. In June 1912, the City of Axtell constructed an electrical line from Seneca to Axtell. With electricity in the opera house, moving pictures were shown there occasionally. Movies increased in popularity and required larger venues. In 1914, the local motion picture show proprietor took over the opera house and renamed it the New Electric Theatre. Admission was 10¢ and movies were shown three times a week.

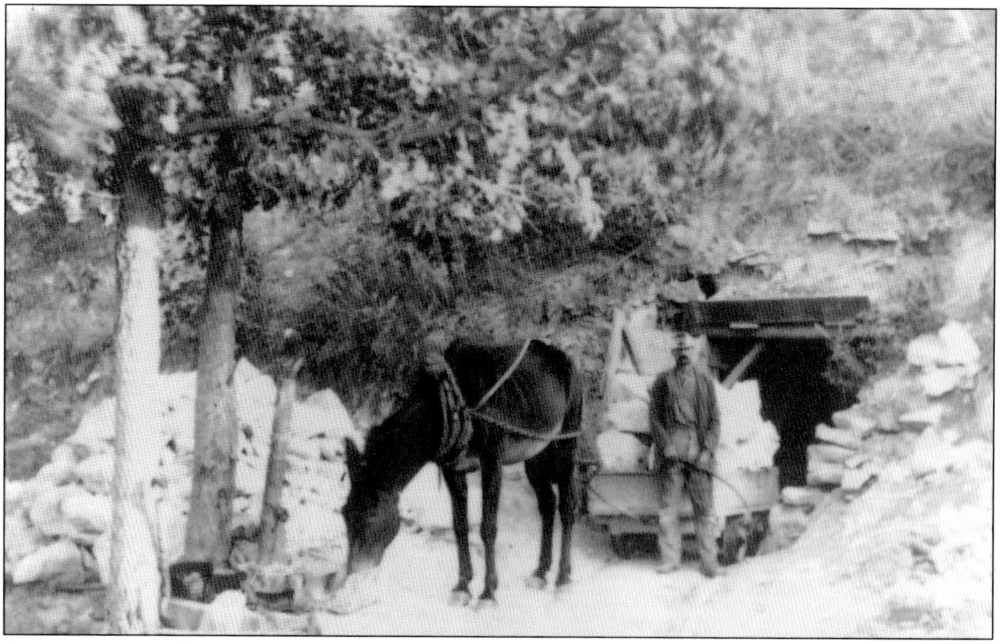

Gypsum mining has been the one constant industry in Marshall County since its founding. In 1857, an early settler discovered that the white rocks that turned to powder in his open fire made fine plaster for his cabin walls. The gypsum mining and plaster industry began in earnest in 1871. This photograph shows a mule feeding after hauling a load of gypsum from an early mine. The current mine, located between Marysville and Blue Rapids on US 77, operates at a depth of 100 feet. It is likely that the warren of tunnels mined in the Blue Rapids area since the 1870s would total more than 100 miles.

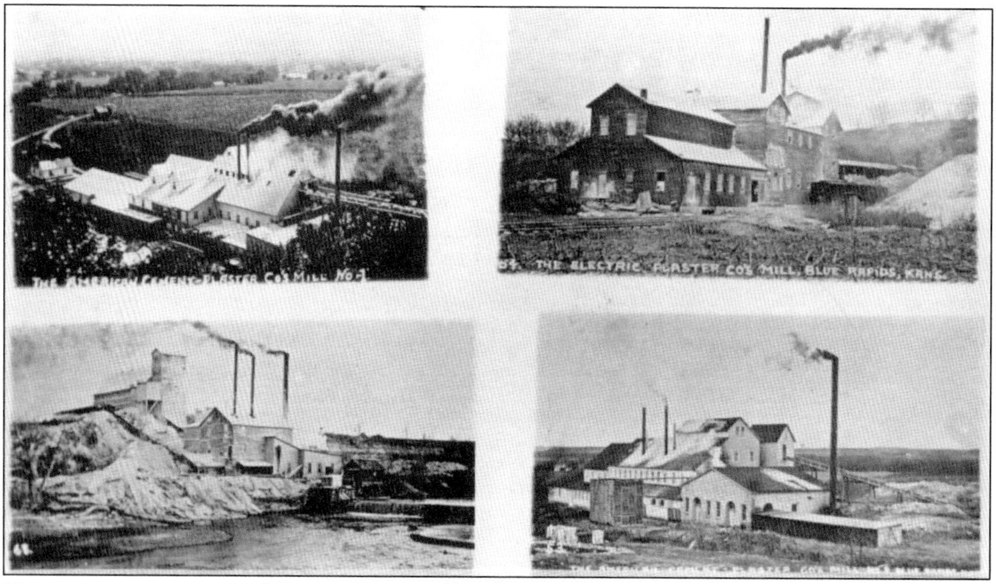


Once gypsum was mined, it went to a mill to become plaster. These mills were operating in 1907 around Blue Rapids near the gypsum mines. Today, walls are seldom plastered, and since the 1950s, most gypsum has been used in wallboard. Gypsum is also used in chinaware, marbles, chalk, plaster of Paris, fertilizer, toothpaste, and other common items.

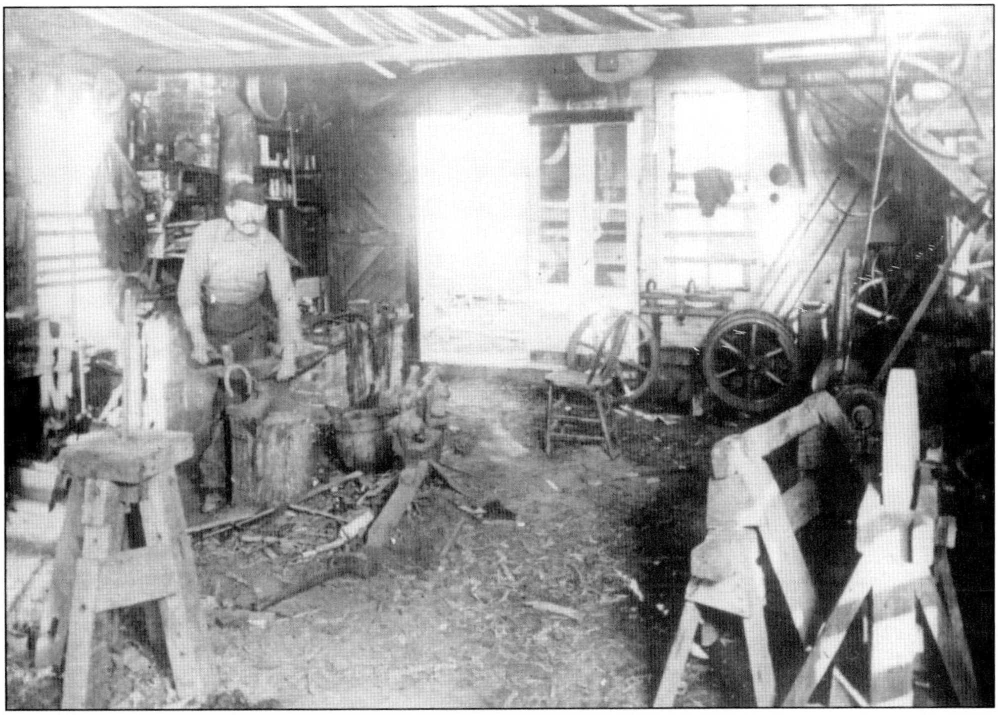

Jeff Smith is pictured at work in 1912 at Transue Brothers blacksmith shop in Summerfield. Blacksmithing was Summerfield's oldest continuous business. James and George Transue bought out the town's first blacksmith, Thomas Hutton, in 1893 and built themselves a new shop on the same site in 1898. In 1946, after 55 years of blacksmithing, George Transue sold the shop to Dale "Tinker" Robeson, who kept many of the Transues' tools and equipment and was in business even longer, 1946 to 2008. Current owners David and Elizabeth Zahm have restored the shop and reopened it as Transue Brothers Blacksmithing Museum. The building was entered in the National Register of Historic Places in 2009.

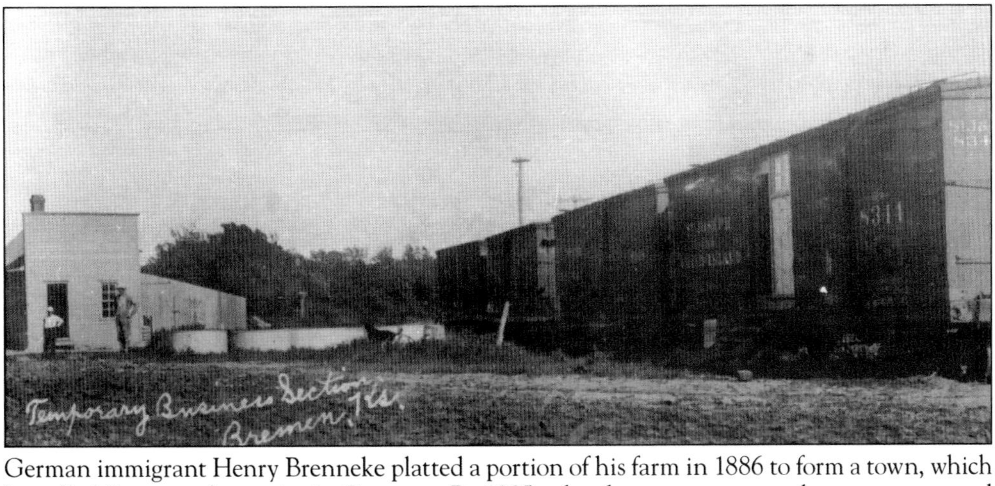


German immigrant Henry Brenneke platted a portion of his farm in 1886 to form a town, which he called Bremen after a city in Germany. By 1905, a hardware store, general store, tavern, and other stores were in Bremen. On March 18, 1908, the entire town burned down. The Union Pacific Railroad provided boxcars to house Bremen businesses while the town was rebuilt. (Courtesy of Dennis Richardson.)

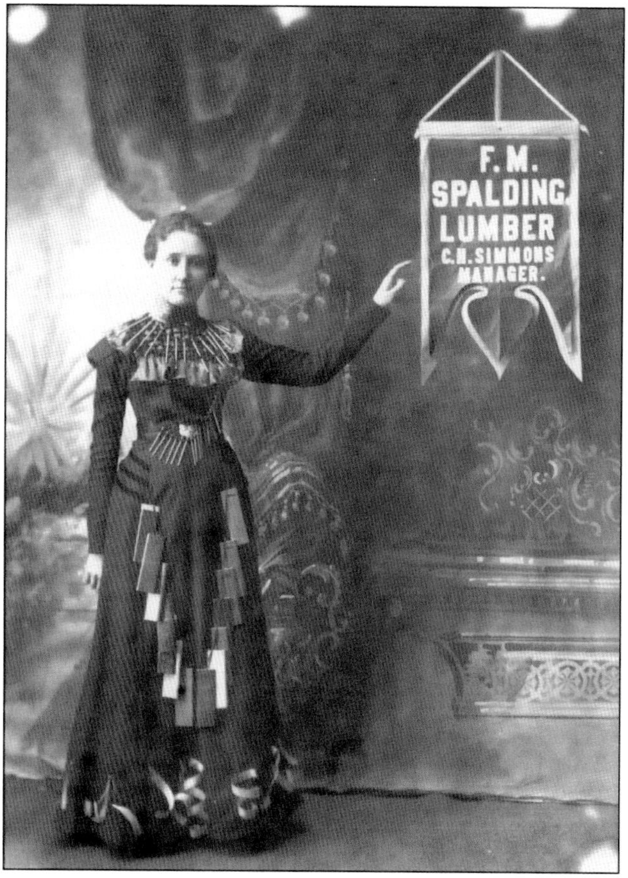


Kate Moser, representing F.M. Spaulding Lumber, is posed in an outfit decorated with nails, wooden molding, and wood shavings. Moser was one of nine models advertising Marysville businesses in a merchandising contest around 1900.

Marietta was founded in 1881 and, like many other towns, grew around a railroad line. The businesses along Main Street in this view from about 1910 are, from left to right, Marietta State Bank, a café, Bull Brothers General Store, Victor Bull's hardware store, Sam Rockwell's blacksmith shop, and the Marietta dance hall over the produce station. By 2014, all the businesses were gone, and only the elevator remained.

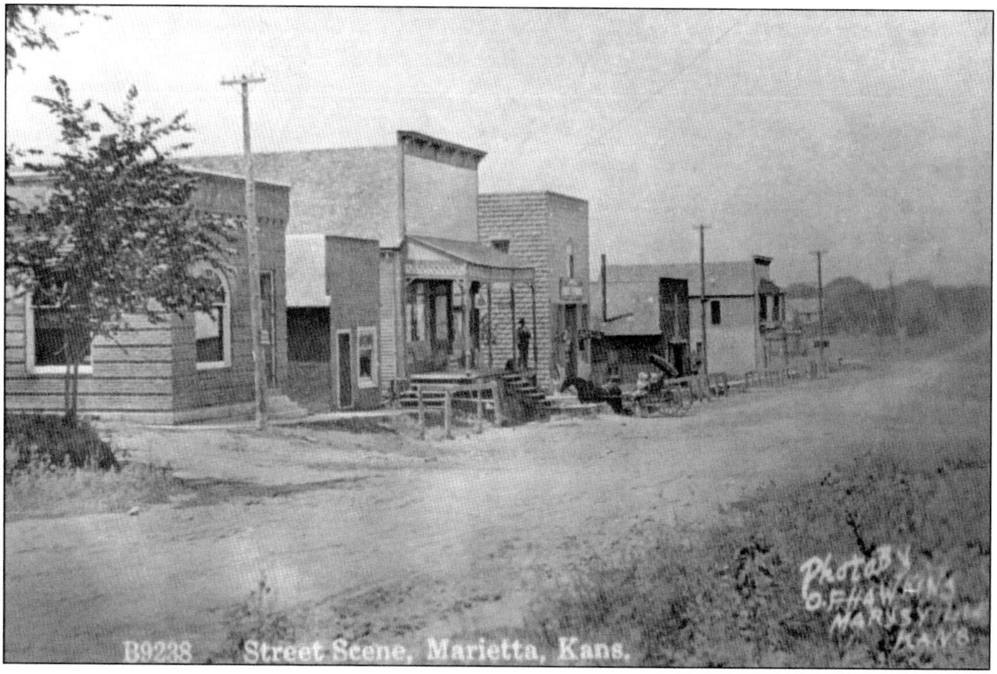

The Marysville flagpole stood in the middle of the intersection at Broadway and Tenth Street in 1917. The spot is now on US 77 (Tenth Street), one block south of US 36 (Center Street).

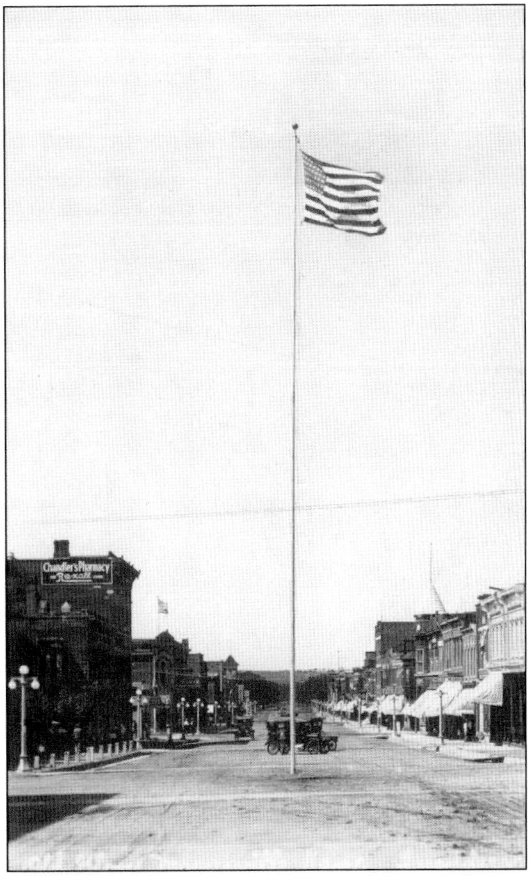

Plant engineers maintain the 21,000-pound, six-foot flywheel in the Beattie Electric Light Plant around 1915. The town's population at this time was about 450.

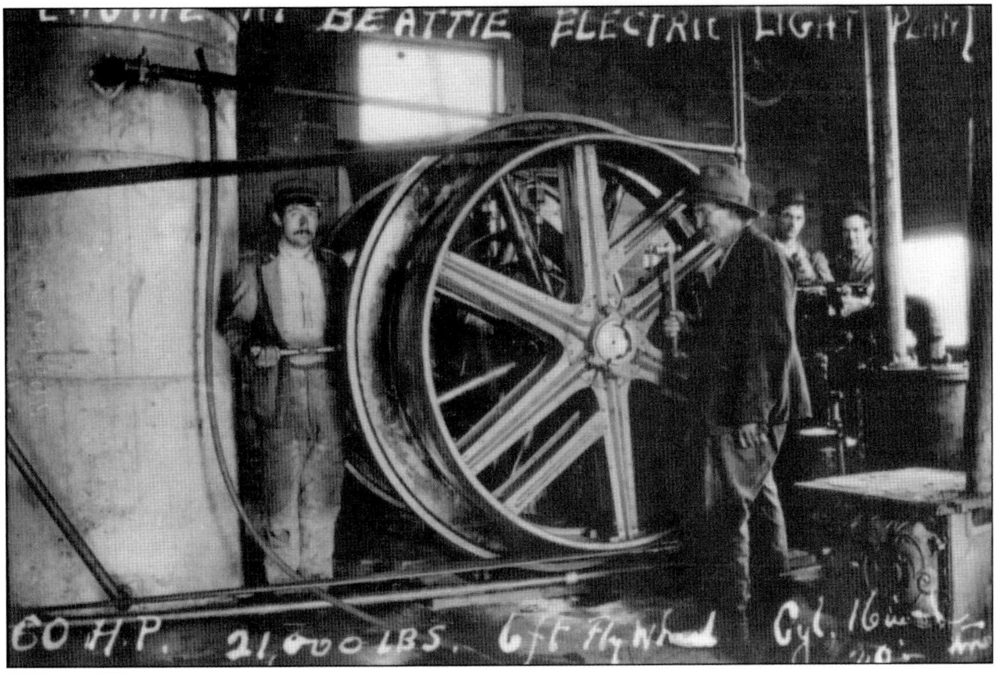

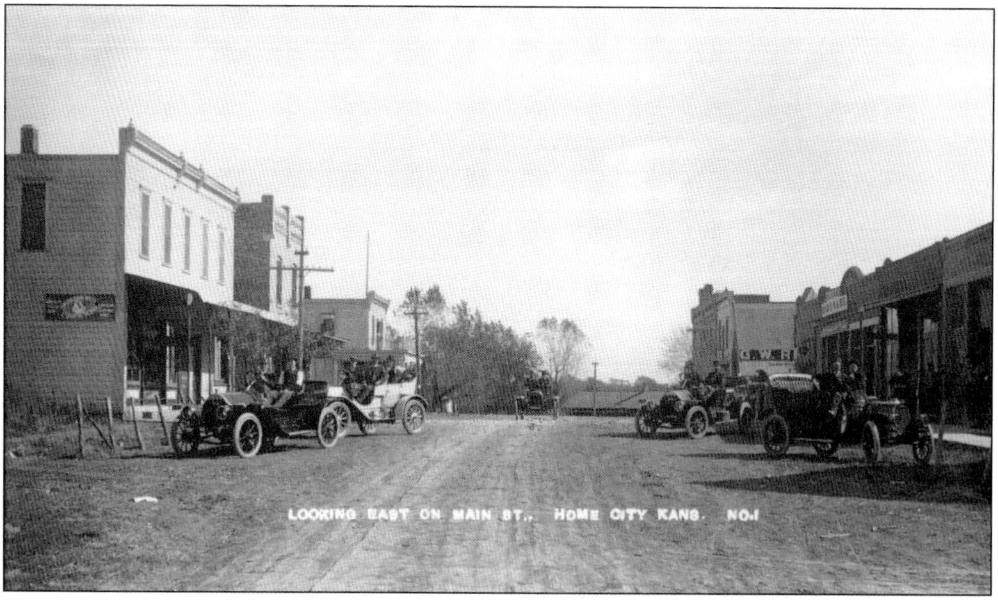


The town of Home got its name from its first post office, which was established in someone's home in 1878. It is still known simply as Home by the US Postal Service, but anyone familiar with the town refers to it as Home City. This eliminates potentially confusing answers to questions like, "Where did you take this year's wheat?" "Home." By the time this photograph was taken, the town had been rebuilt following a devastating fire in 1905.

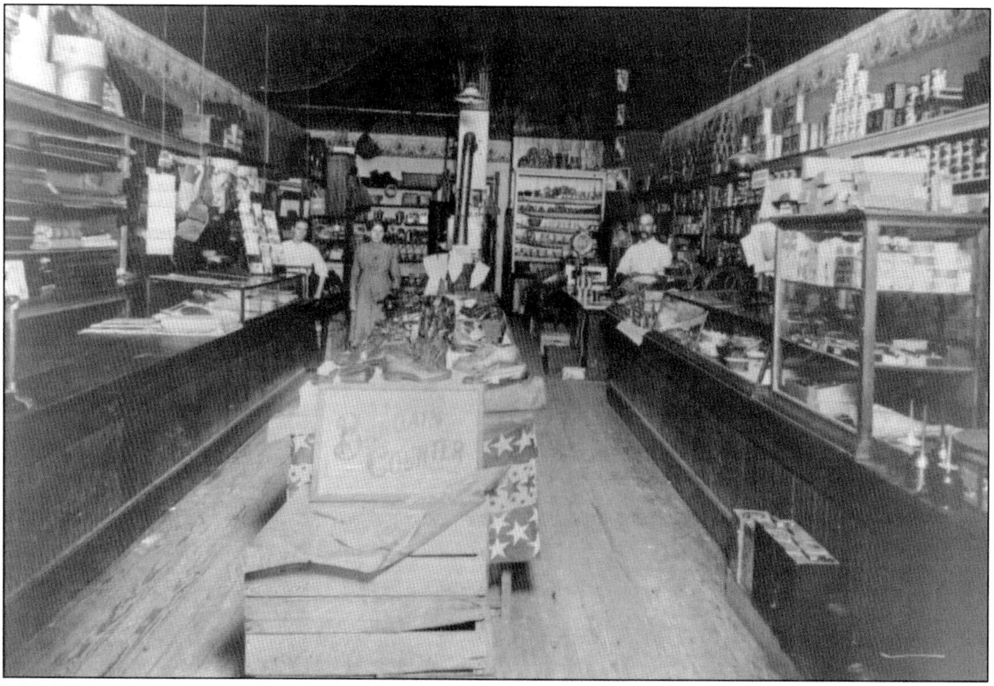

The Vliets store offered anything local residents could need in 1913. In the store are, from left to right, Blanche Owen, Adela Anderson and I.M. Owen. The "Bargain Counter" sign in front of the shoes and boots suggests the owners knew that the way to a customer's heart was through the pocketbook.

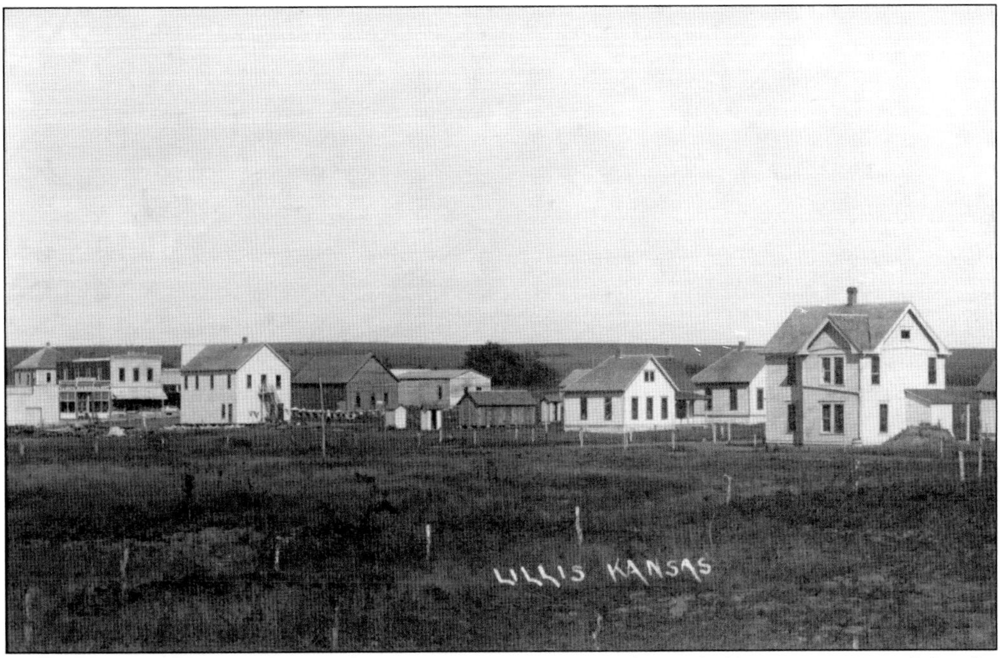


Lillis was chartered in 1906 in the southeastern portion of Marshall County. Named for the Right Reverend Bishop T.F. Lillis of Kansas City, the town was located on the Marysville and Topeka railroad "cutoff." This is a view of Lillis as it appeared about 1910. Today, two businesses, occasional weddings and funerals at St. Joseph's Catholic Church, and an annual St. Patrick's Day parade keep the little town alive.

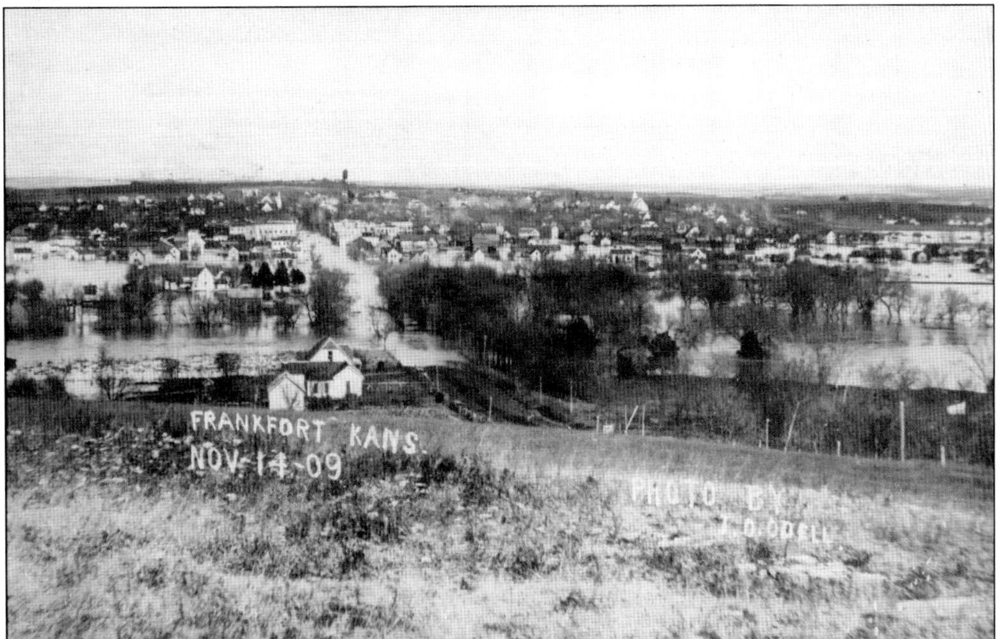


The population of Frankfort was a little more than 1,400 when the town was flooded in November 1909. Frankfort floods were recorded with photographs in 1903, 1906, 1908, 1909, 1917, 1941, 1943, and 1958. In 1963, a dike was built along the Black Vermillion River.

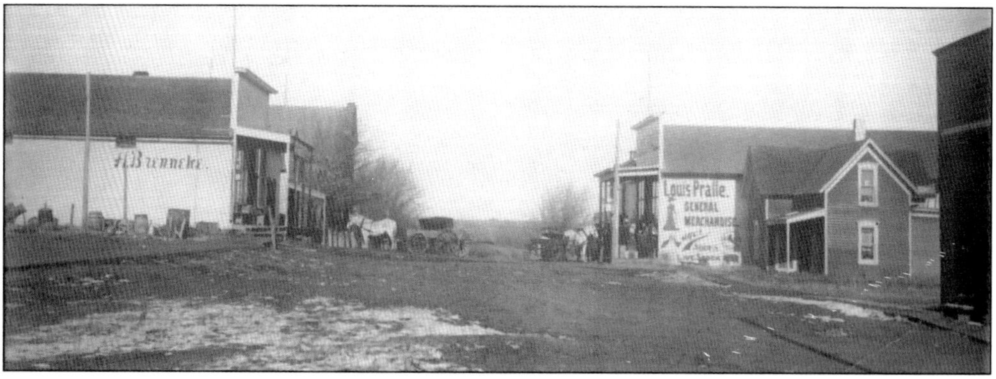


In 1905, when this photograph was taken, Bremen was a small but flourishing town, one in which people not only knew one another but recognized all the horses. At left is the first store owned by Henry Brenneke. Otto Holle's team of white horses is hitched in front of the Fischer tavern, and the tall building is the hardware store. The home at the right belonged to Louis Pralle, and in front of his store is Fred Bartel's white horse. A fire in 1908 destroyed the business district.

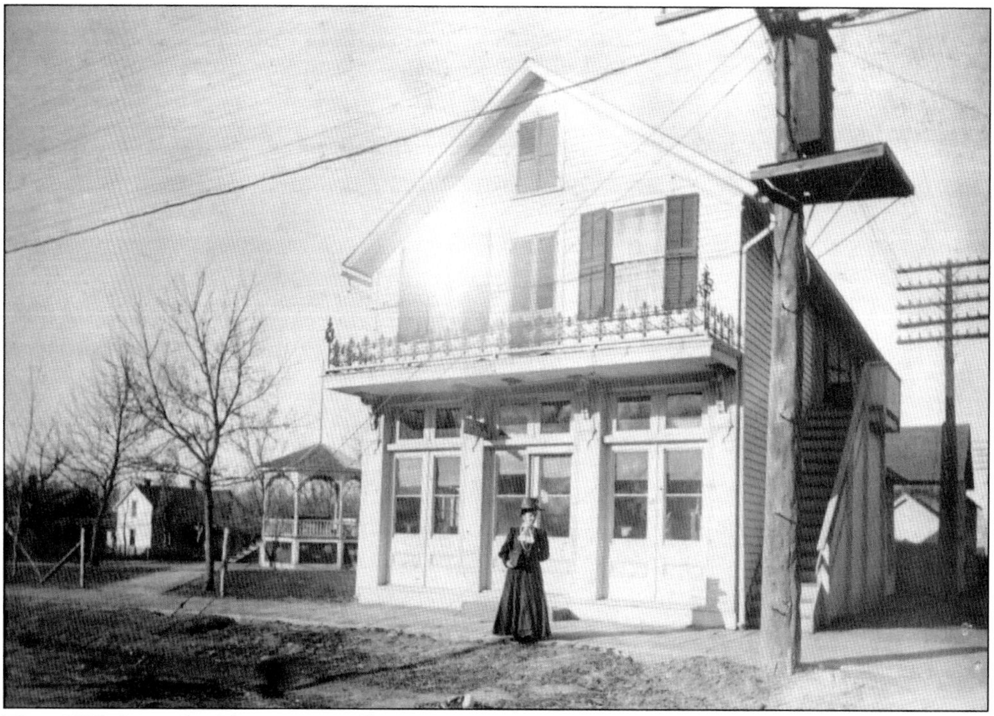

This 1870 frame building, originally on Broadway, was the second location of the Exchange Bank of Schmidt & Koester. In 1882, the bank put up an elegant two-story brick building as its third location, and this structure was moved around the corner to a new site (pictured here), 107 South Ninth Street. It was used as a dressmaking and millinery shop and then for the first independent phone company in Marysville. Standing in front is Ora Lamb, operator for the telephone exchange.

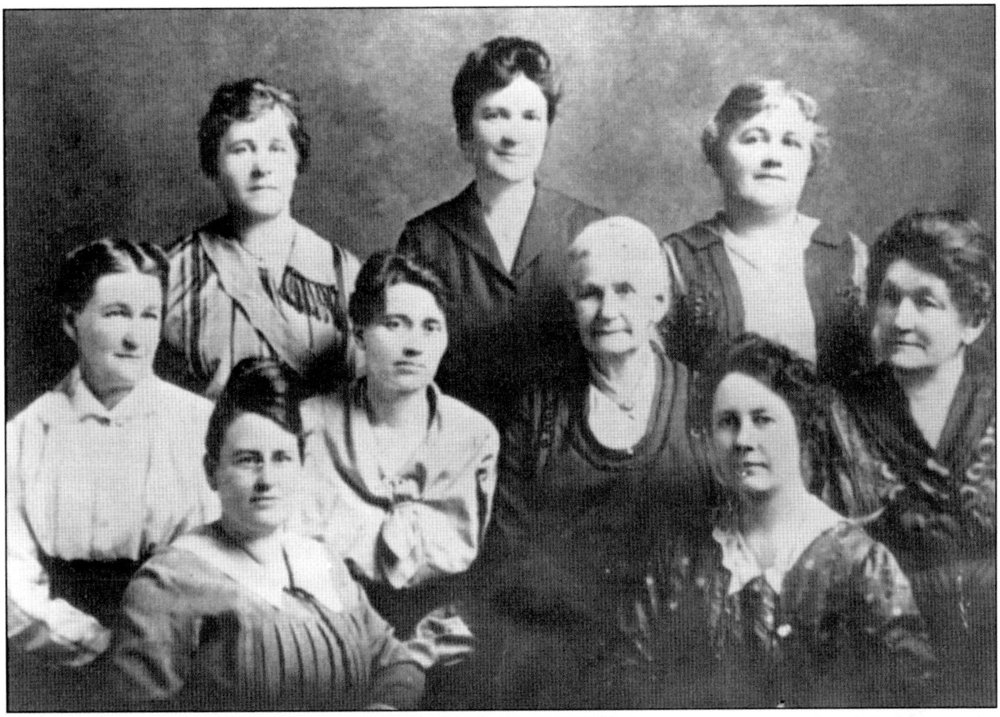

Though still unable to vote in state and federal elections, Kansas women won the right to vote in city elections in 1887. In 1917, Oketo had an all-woman city council. Mayor Lavinia (Mrs. Z.H.) Moore (second row, third from left) was a former teacher at the Otoe Indian school and wife of the town banker. The city treasurer and a member of the council were her daughters-in-law. This was the second all-woman city government in the county, after Beattie in 1899.

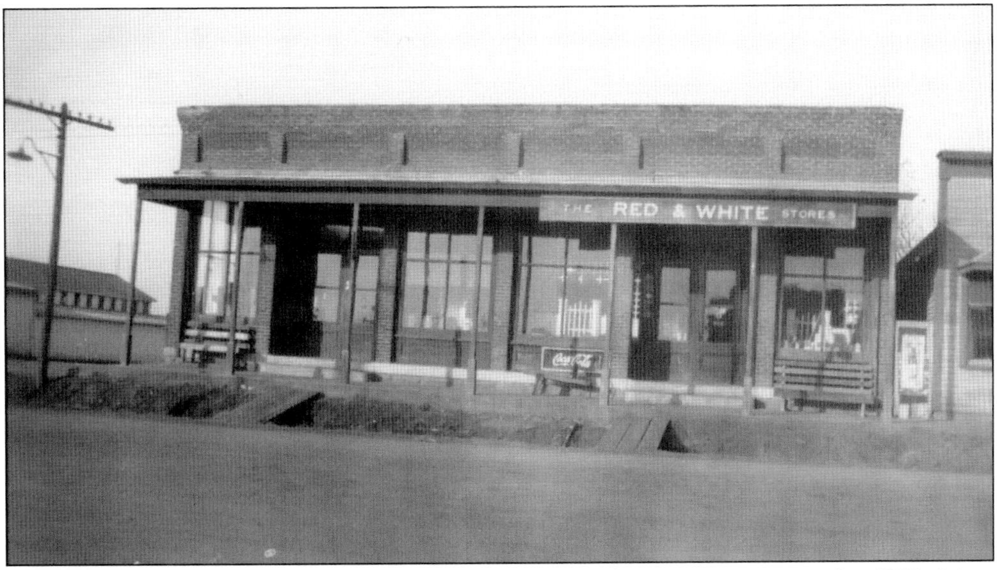


The first settlers arrived in Herkimer in the late 1850s, but the town was organized in 1878. Adam Keller, who owned land adjoining railroad property, platted a town and planned to name it Bryan in honor of a passenger conductor on the local railroad. The Post Office Department refused to accept the name, so Keller chose Herkimer, after his hometown in New York.

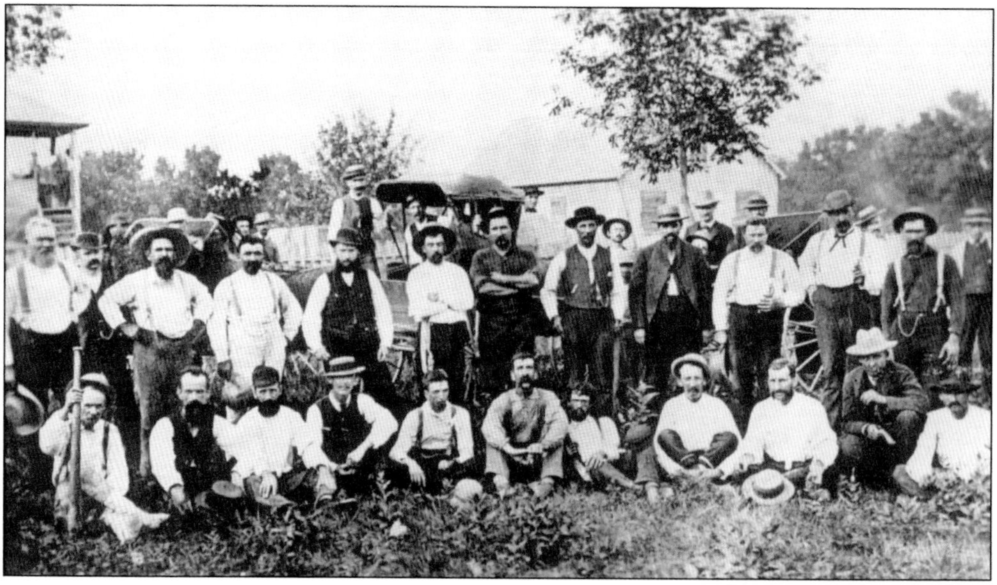

In the summer of 1884, Marysville businessmen joined sides on baseball teams called the Fats and the Leans, then met at the county fairgrounds to battle for bragging rights. Players included a barber, blacksmith, merchant, druggist, miller, lawyer, farmer, grocer, bandleader, two cigar makers, and others. Although the final score was not recorded, a newspaper account notes there were several kegs of ice water for refreshment.

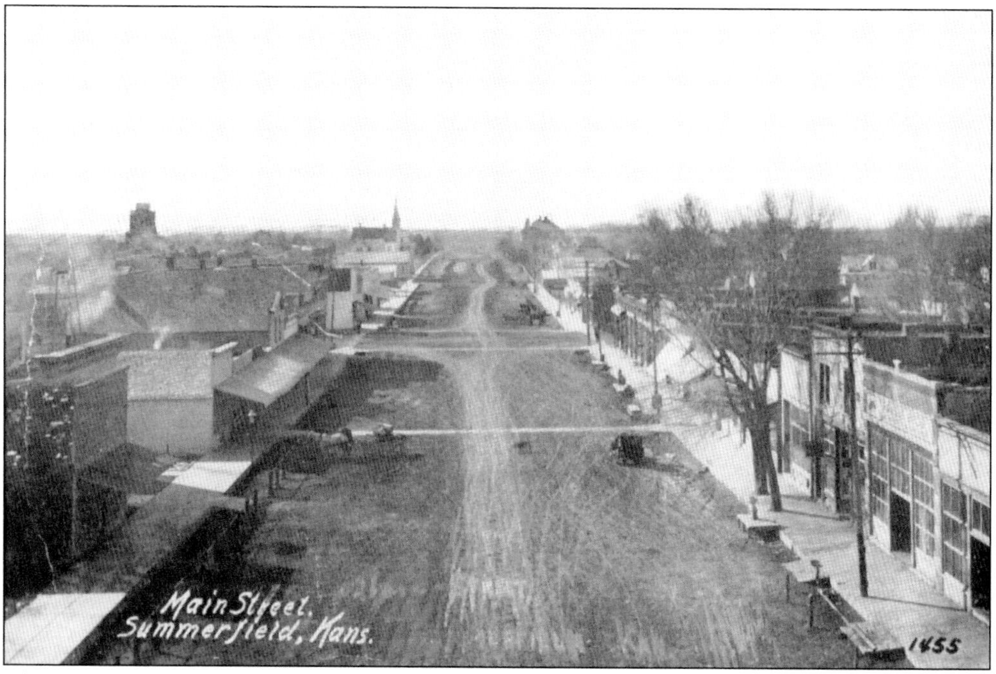


This postcard view of Summerfield, taken from atop the windmill in about 1909, shows the blacksmith shop at the lower right corner. At that time, the population of the town was 554, its peak. Today, the town is home to about 150 residents.

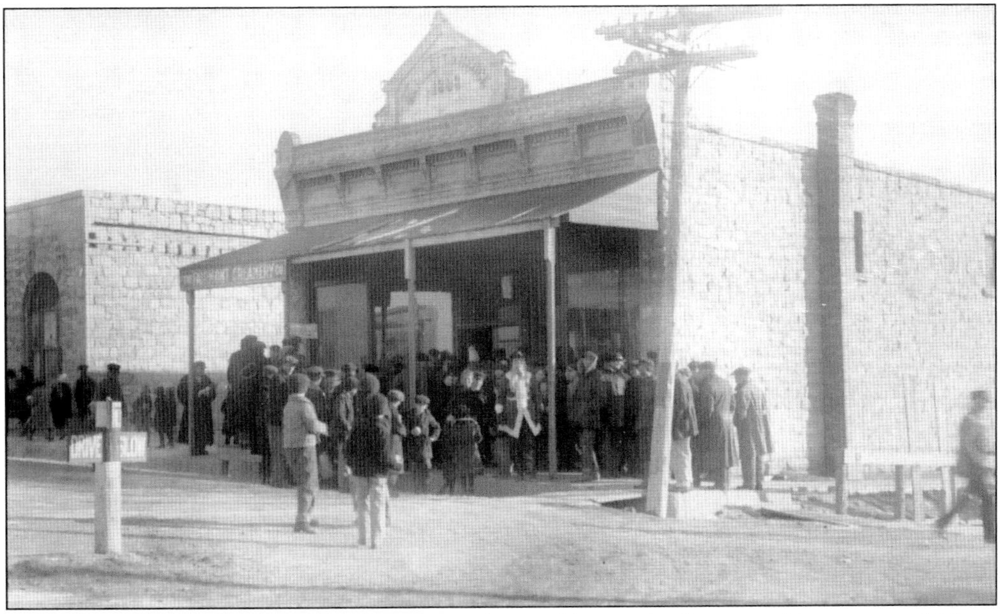

Children and adults have come to town to see Santa Claus at the Fairmont Creamery and Oketo Farmers' Store in 1923. This store was located at the southeast corner of Center and State Streets, west of the Oketo Opera House and directly across the street from the Z.H. Moore store. The Moore store was built in 1884 from locally quarried limestone. It was entered in the National Register of Historic Places in 1976 and is now the Oketo Museum.

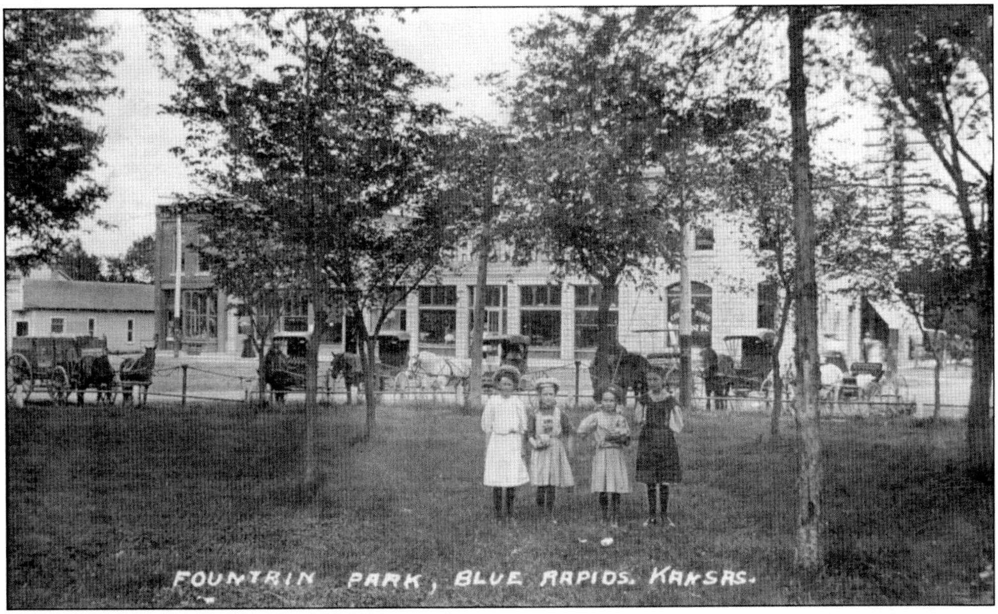


Sometimes fondly referred to as the "squircle," the tiny parkland in the center of the Blue Rapids business district is both the town square and circular roundabout. Hundreds of parades have circled this square since the city was platted in 1870. It is located one block south of US 77. The Blue Rapids Museum and the Holm log cabin are on the south side of the square. In 2012, a *Monument to the Ice Age* was constructed in the park to celebrate the glaciers that formed the rivers and landscape in the area.

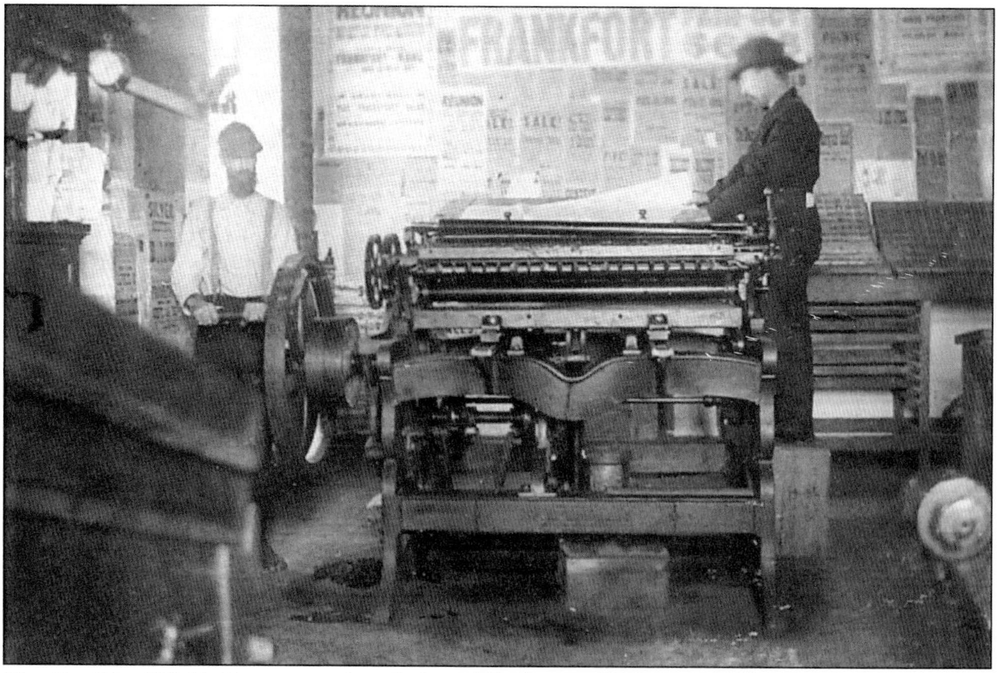


The *Frankfort Weekly Review* was founded in 1893. George William Shedden, owner and editor, is standing on the right in this view of his print shop in the early 1900s. The *Review* folded in 1909. Marshall County's first newspaper, the *Palmetto Kansan*, was established in December 1857 and lasted only seven months. The *Waterville Telegraph*, established January 1, 1870, is the longest-running newspaper in the county, having been in publication for 145 years.

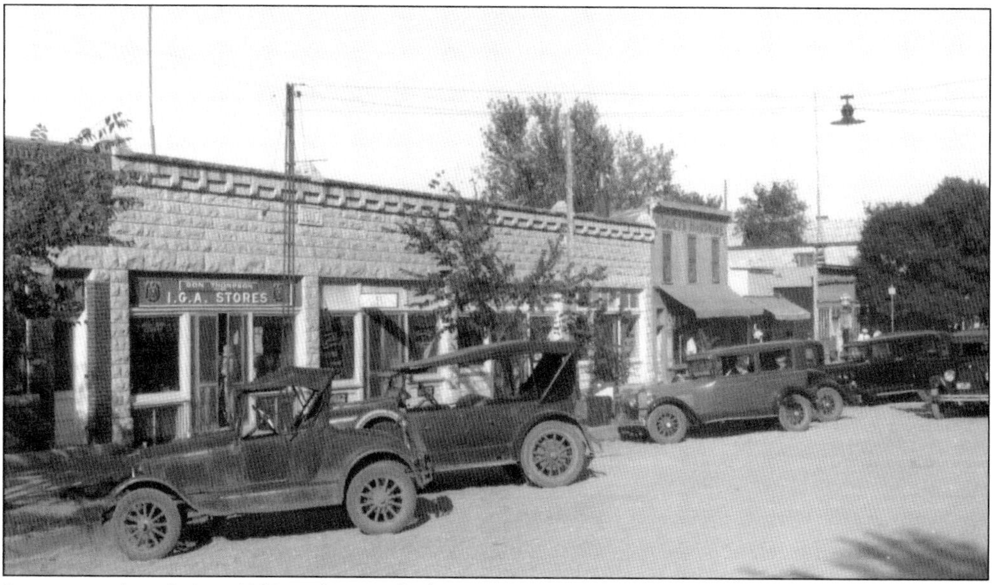


Irving was founded in 1859 and named after author Washington Irving. This view of the north side of Main Street in Irving was taken September 24, 1930. Over its history, the town suffered floods, fires, tornadoes, dust storms, and swarms of grasshoppers in the farm fields—just like other county towns. Despite being a year into the Depression, the fall of 1930 was a time of calm weather and relative prosperity in Irving.

Between the 1860s and about 1920, ice blocks were cut from local rivers and streams in the winter, stored in icehouses, and covered in layers of wood shavings or wood planks. The Marysville ice plant at 602 Spring Street was built in the late 1910s. The plant's huge steam engine, shown here in January 1929, ran compressors that compressed ammonia to freeze water. Compressed ammonia was notoriously unreliable and ice plants occasionally exploded, one of the reasons plants were often built not adjoining other buildings. Plant ice also ran the risk of contamination if ammonia leached into the water during compression. The plant closed in the 1960s.

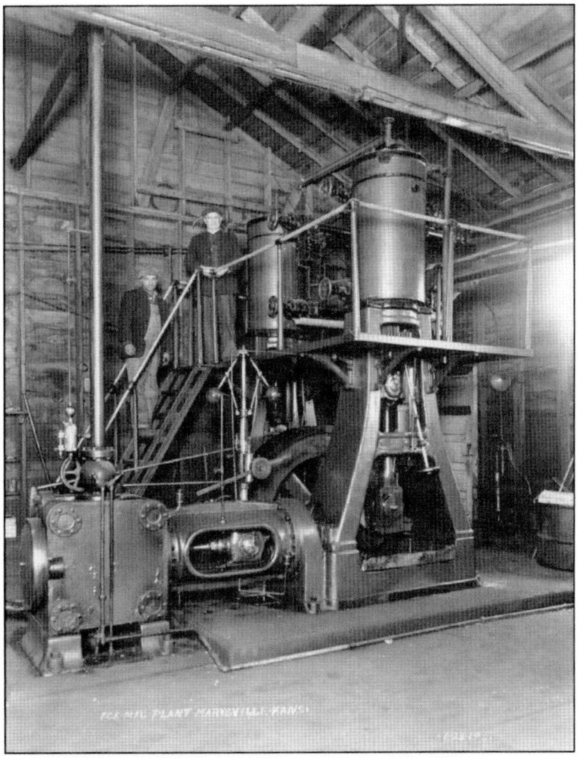

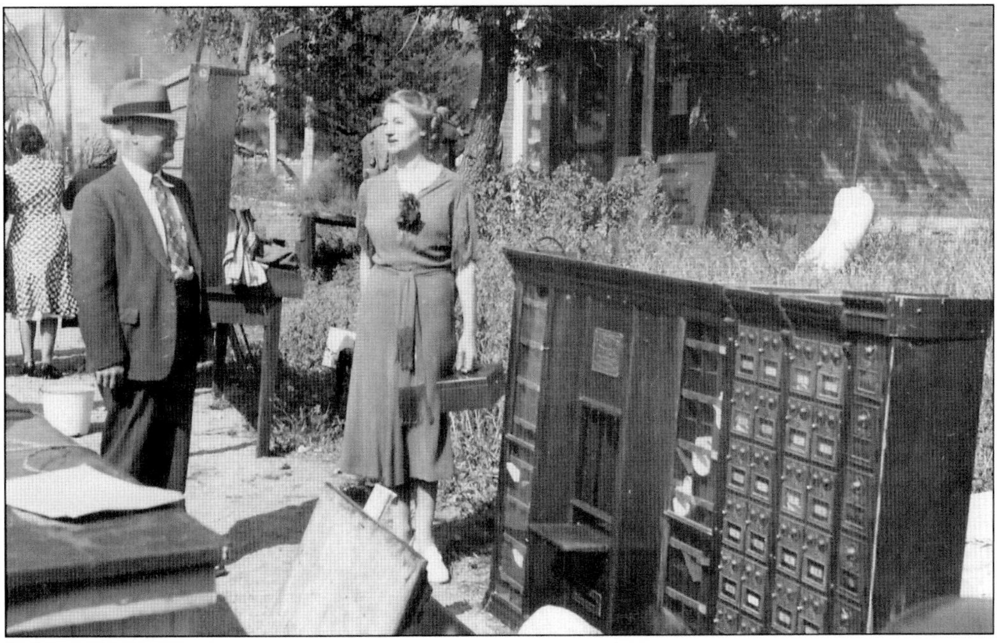

On September 26, 1939, a fire started in a Home City creamery a block away from the Tangeman Store and the post office, which was next door. The wind carried an ember and started a fire first at the Tangeman Store and then the post office. The firefighters were able to remove the mail and post office boxes. At left is Home City resident R.O. Crouse, and at right is postmistress Marie Oehm, protecting the postal property. The cashbox is in her hand.

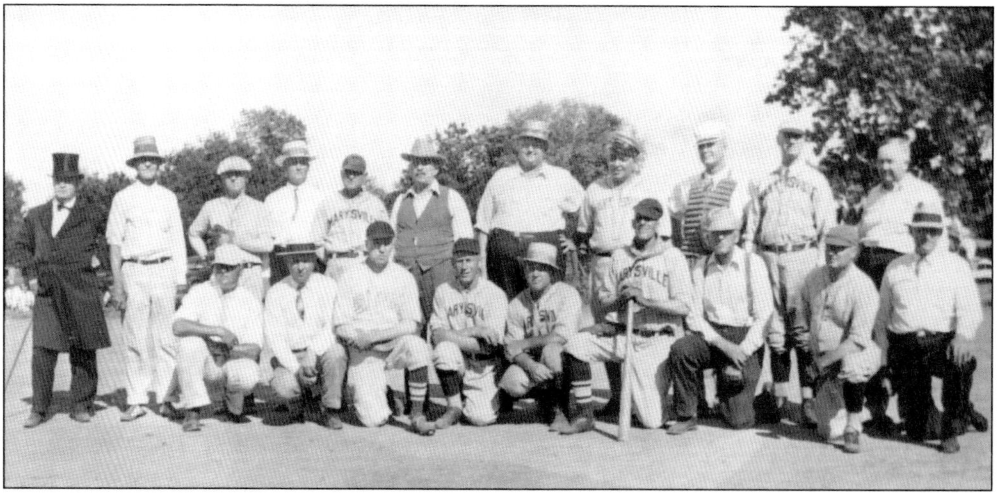

Nine Republicans and ten Democrats ran for Marshall County sheriff in 1932. Someone suggested that was enough for a baseball game. On July 1, a game was played at the athletic ground in northwest Marysville, with Mayor G.M. Ware (at left in beaver hat and frock coat) as umpire. A beer keg was set up at third base, for those who made it that far. After an hour and ten minutes—three innings—the game was called with the score tied at 11. "Too hot," said the umpire, who had been blindfolded for the last inning to demonstrate his ability to call 'em as he saw 'em. In November, the Democrats' catcher, Martin Flanagan, was elected sheriff.

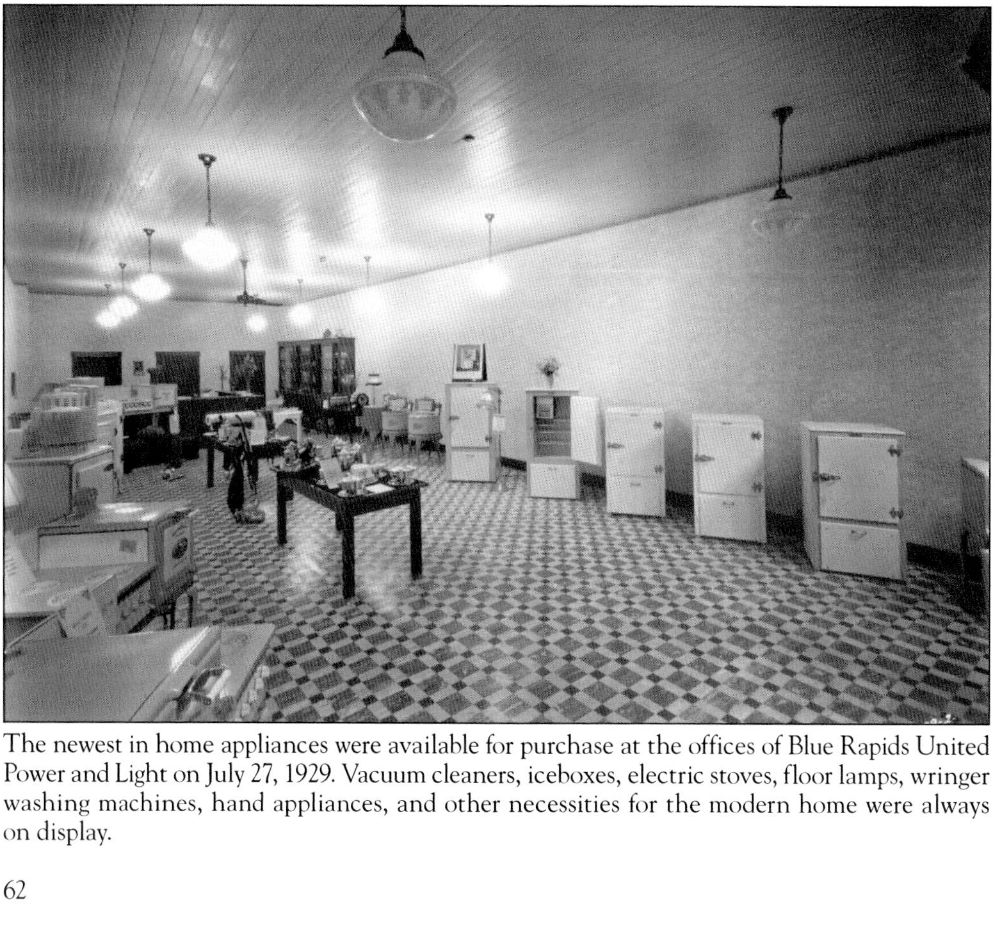

The newest in home appliances were available for purchase at the offices of Blue Rapids United Power and Light on July 27, 1929. Vacuum cleaners, iceboxes, electric stoves, floor lamps, wringer washing machines, hand appliances, and other necessities for the modern home were always on display.

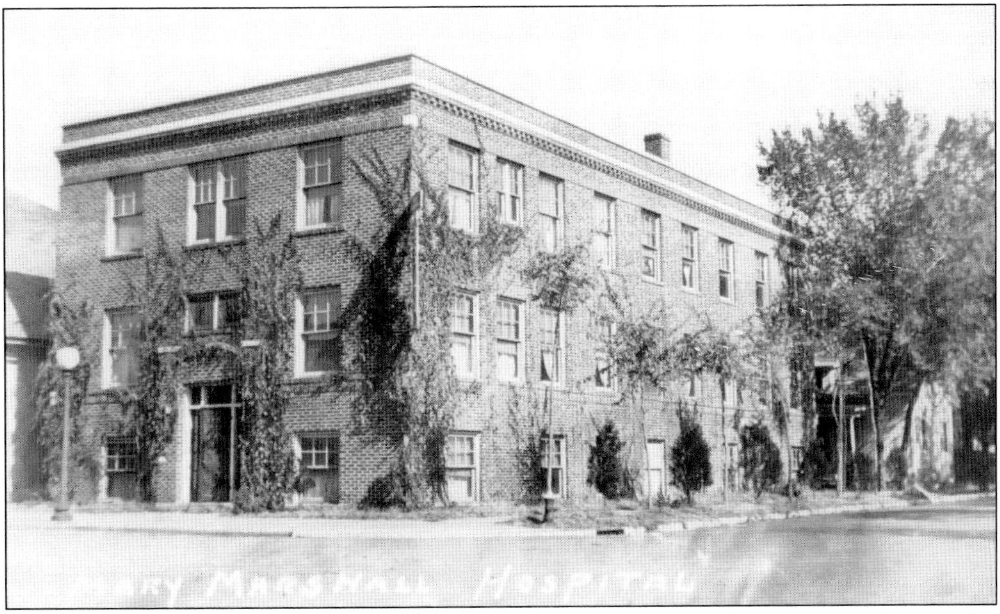


Mary Marshall Hospital was located at the corner of South Eighth and Elm Streets in Marysville. Built by Dr. W.S. Roney in 1920, the hospital was later converted into the Elms Hotel, and later to the Carriage House Apartments.

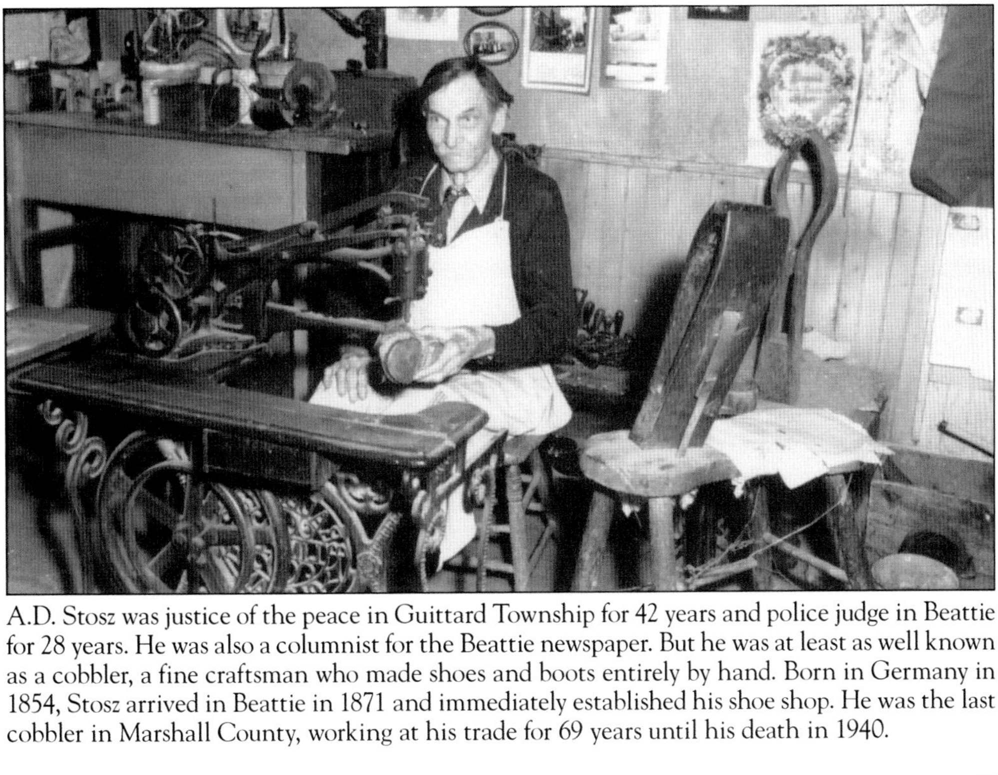

A.D. Stosz was justice of the peace in Guittard Township for 42 years and police judge in Beattie for 28 years. He was also a columnist for the Beattie newspaper. But he was at least as well known as a cobbler, a fine craftsman who made shoes and boots entirely by hand. Born in Germany in 1854, Stosz arrived in Beattie in 1871 and immediately established his shoe shop. He was the last cobbler in Marshall County, working at his trade for 69 years until his death in 1940.

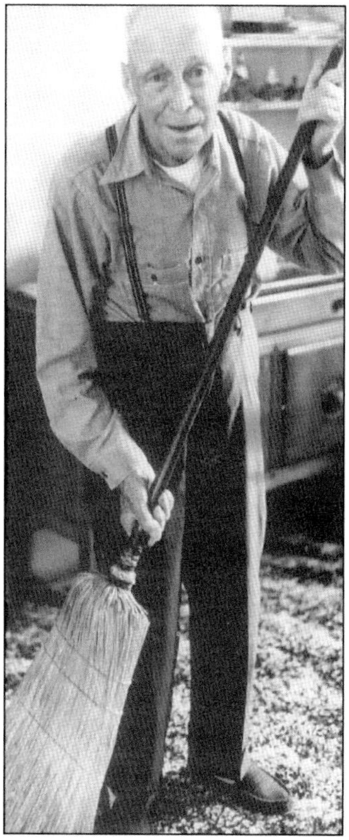

In the late 1800s, Marshall County was the broomcorn region of Kansas and Willard Sabin was its "Broomcorn King." By the 1880s, he was planting more than 500 acres of broomcorn near Frankfort. The entire broom was made by hand in a factory near the farm. The straw was wired to the broomstick, then hand sewn with heavy twine. The Sabin men managed the farm and factory; the women cooked for the crews. Sabin's son Alex is holding the oversize factory display broom during an interview in 1977.

The Ford Model A was first produced on October 20, 1927, but was not sold until December 2. Whether potential customers or just curious, these men have gathered at Arbuthnot's Ford Service at 713 Broadway in Marysville on December 13 to take a look at Ford's replacement for the Model T, the first new Ford in 18 years.

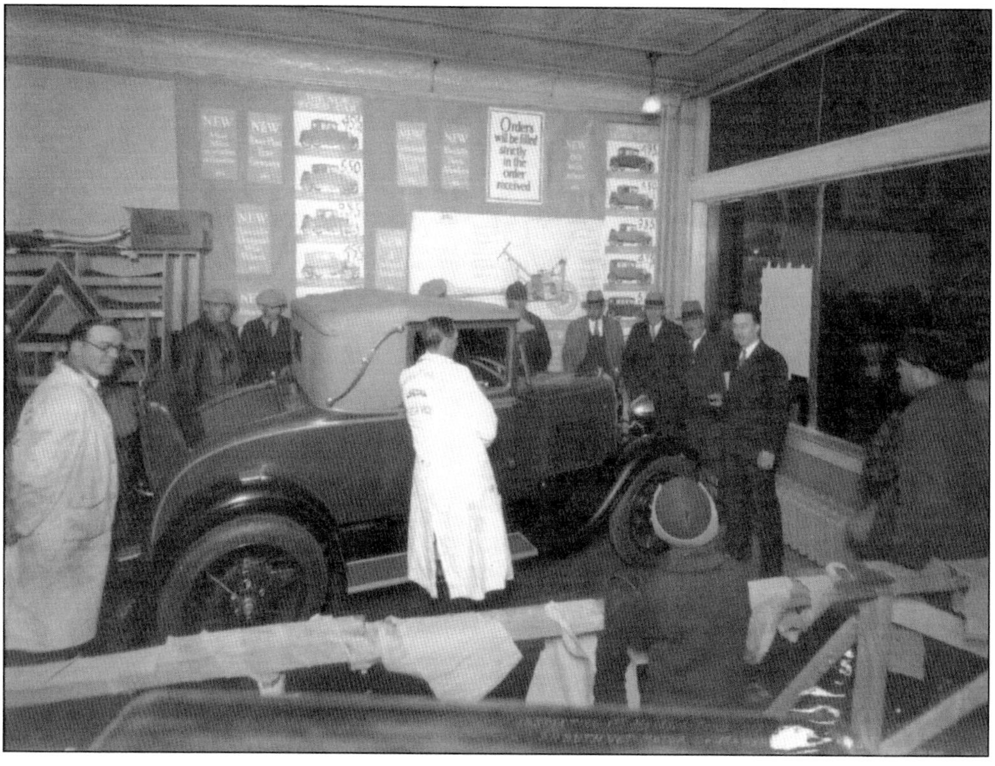

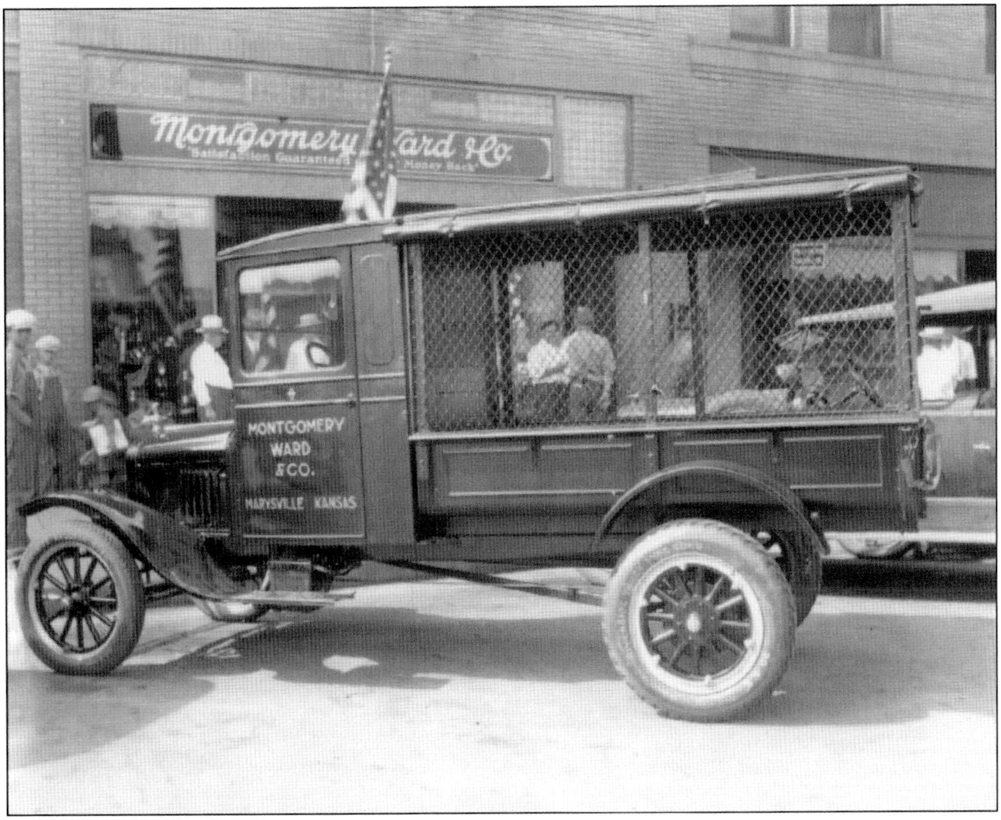


The nation's first Montgomery Ward "merchandise exhibit" opened in Marysville on August 14, 1926. More than 6,000 people—some of whom had traveled more than 100 miles—signed the guest register that day. Although Ward's entire inventory of 33,000 items could not be displayed, products from fashionable clothing to bicycles and radios to radiators were showcased and could be ordered from the catalog. In February 1928, eighteen months later, this catalog store became a retail store. This van delivered merchandise throughout the county. In 1930, a new retail store opened at Ninth Street and Broadway. It closed on Christmas Eve 1968.

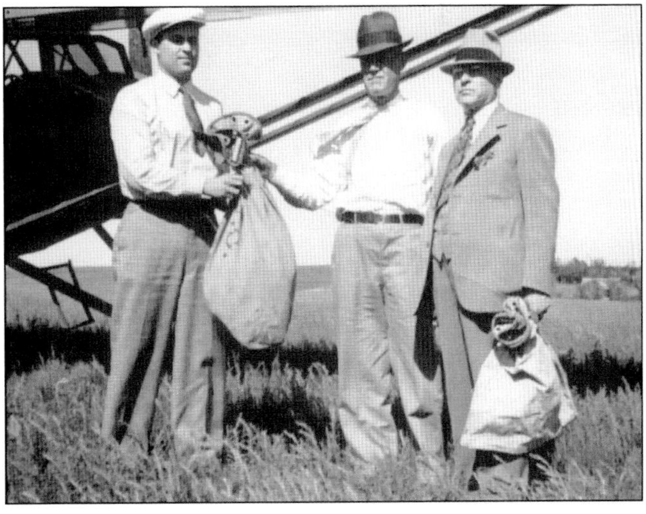

There was a time when mail went by truck or train. On May 19, 1938, airmail came to Marshall County. The first (and only) airmail to and from Marysville traveled via small plane, arriving and leaving from a farm field landing strip on the Charles Kloxin farm. On the left, pilot Elza Stone is receiving the outgoing mail—1,364 letters—from Oscar Joseph, mail messenger. At right, postmaster H.M. Brodrick holds the incoming mailbag.

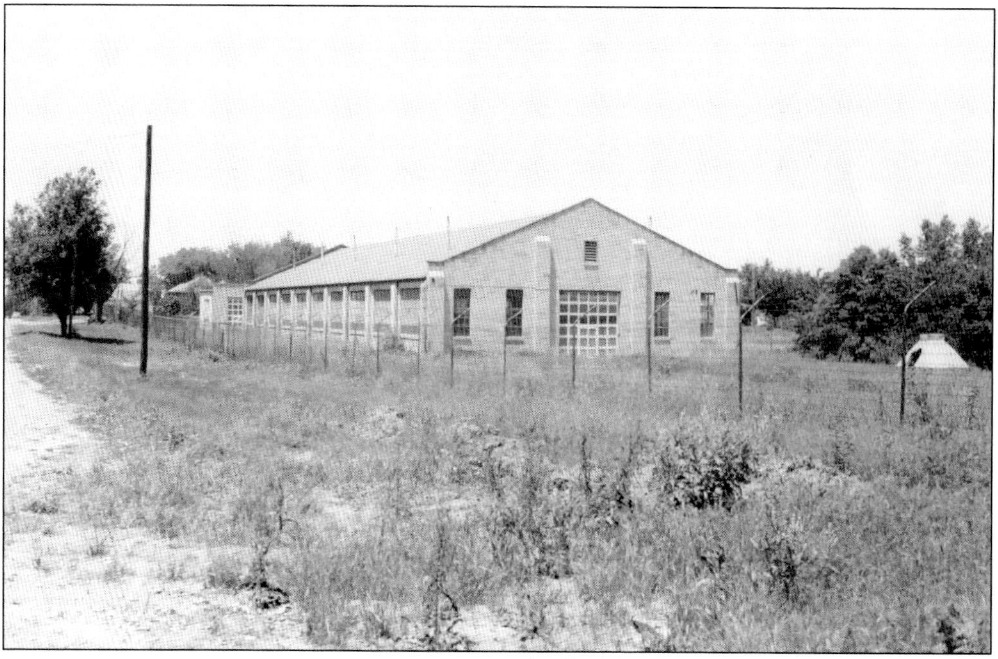

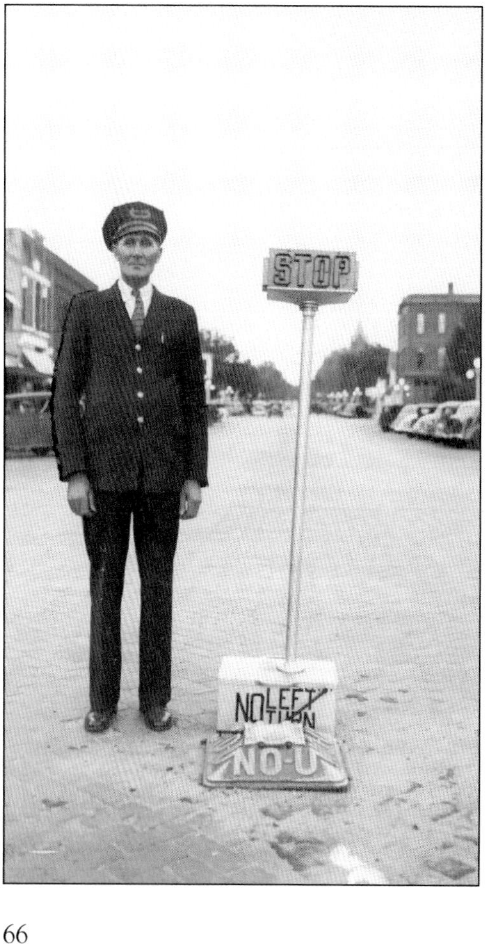


This building played an important—and secret—part in World War II. Firing panels for the Manhattan Project Trinity test site were assembled at this factory. Air-to-ground rocket launching circuitry was also assembled here. Waterproof walkie-talkie units for Navy life rafts and the 98A transmitter were also made here. Although employees knew they were fulfilling secret military contracts, they did not know the intended use of the products. Generally known as the "Radio Factory," the building was a manufacturing plant after the war for tractor radios, intercoms, and speakers. It closed in the mid-1950s. The building was constructed by the CCC in 1941 and originally was used as the camp's machine shop.

This traffic sign was used on Broadway, Marysville's main street, at "busy times." Tom Blodgett, three-term county sheriff and Marysville police chief from 1934 to 1947, is standing at Eighth Street and Broadway in the late 1930s. Blodgett owned a farm near Irving and was a renowned pitcher on county town teams.

# *Five*

# IN TIMES OF TROUBLE

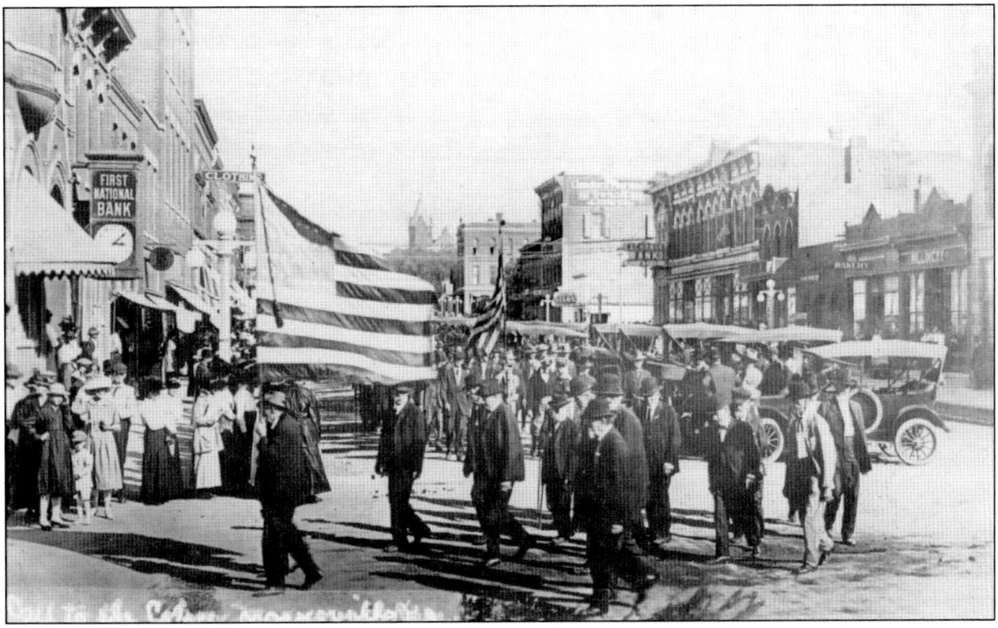


The Selective Service Act, enacted in May 1917, authorized the federal government to raise an army for America's entry into World War I. In this photograph, taken October 3, 1917, and entitled by the photographer *Call to the Colors*, veterans of the Civil War and the Spanish-American War—some of Marshall County's earliest residents—lead the county's third contingent of draftees to the Marysville depot, where they boarded a Union Pacific special train. The 50 men following the second flag joined several hundred other men from Kansas and Nebraska for training at Camp Funston, about 75 miles south of Marysville, before sailing for Europe. Although 28 Marshall County men died in this "War to End All Wars," all those in this photograph returned home safely.

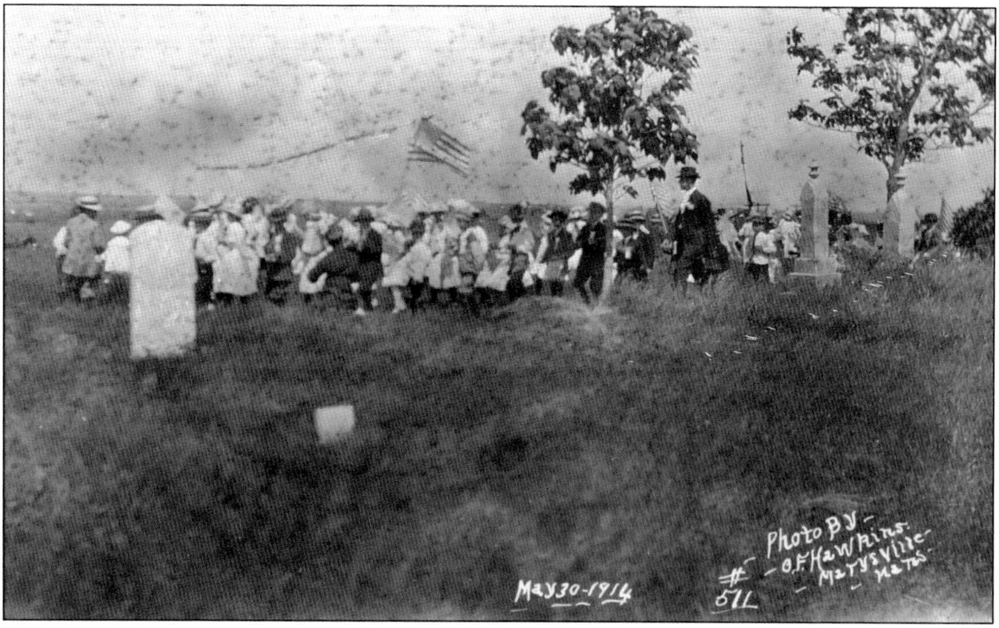


The Marysville Cemetery was incorporated in 1879. Early Decoration Day ceremonies, like this one on May 30, 1914, consisted of a parade of students, city residents, and veterans. Tributes were made and flowers left on the graves of soldiers. By the 1880s, many towns across the country referred to this solemn occasion as Memorial Day, but a name change was not formalized by federal law until 1967. Like Marysville, many Marshall County towns continue to hold services at local cemeteries each Memorial Day.

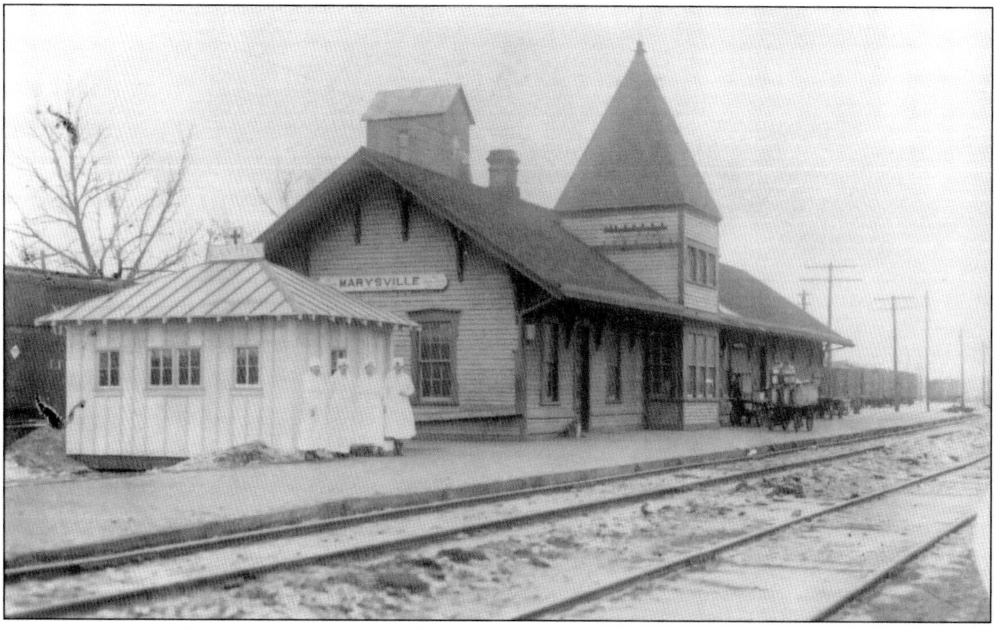


Local women staffed a canteen service located at the south end of the 1880 Marysville depot on Seventh Street during World War I. This photograph, taken in 1919, shows four Red Cross volunteers awaiting the arrival of a train. Soldiers could get sandwiches, cookies, pie, cake, and coffee. They might also get letter-writing assistance or a friendly chat.

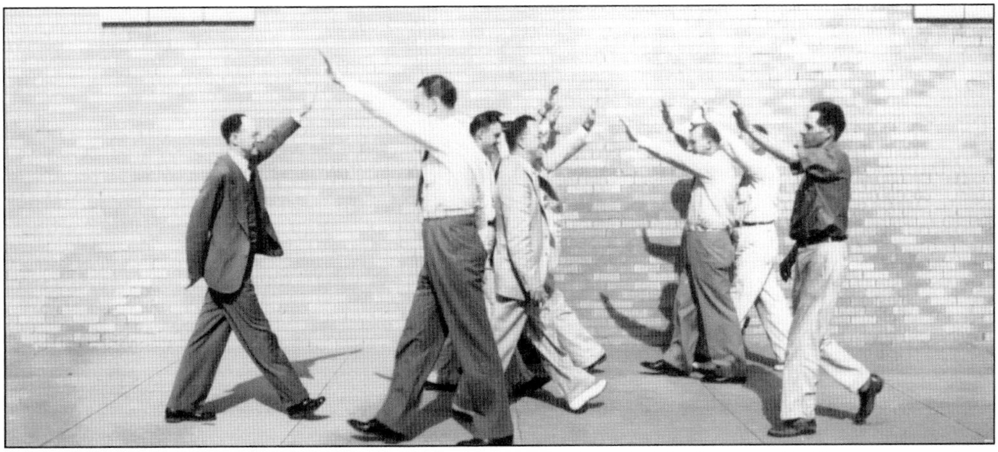

The National Anti-Bund Association of America was founded by Marysville Kiwanis members in February 1938. Adolf Hitler's philosophies had gained some attention in parts of the United States and the German American Bund (federation) was looking to attract American members. Local Kiwanis members published a prospectus citing the Bund as a plot to overthrow American democracy and inviting Americans to join the Anti-Bund, "a non-profit organization, organized . . . to bring [to the] attention [of] the American people the dangers of these Un-American organizations, in particular, the German-American bund; and to bring to the attention of the American public that we want this to continue to be a free democracy!" Its officers included Red Rerhuf, Tnediserp, Tsidnagaporp, Citelhta Rotcerid, and others (to understand the titles, read them backwards). The slogan on its letterhead was "Americanism is our only 'ism.'" When members met on the street, they saluted with their left hand and exclaimed, "Lieh!" An article about the Anti-Bunds appears in the November 8, 1938, *Look* magazine.

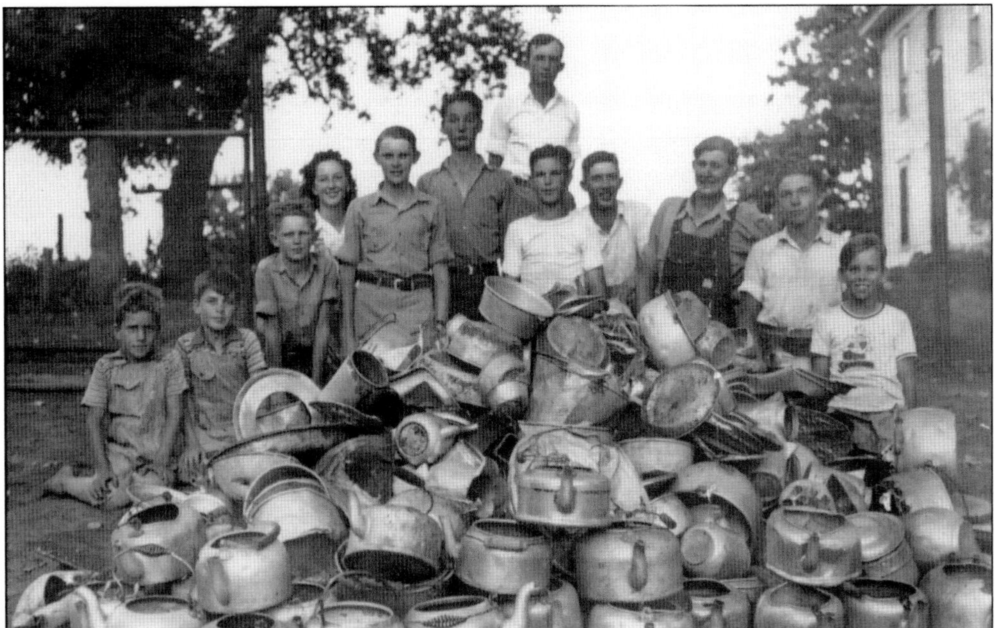

In July 1941, all Marshall County 4-H clubs gathered scrap aluminum for the war effort. Members of the Sunflower 4-H Club of Marietta visited 329 farm homes in Herkimer, Oketo, Balderson, and Marysville Townships and collected the greatest amount in this drive—245 pounds.

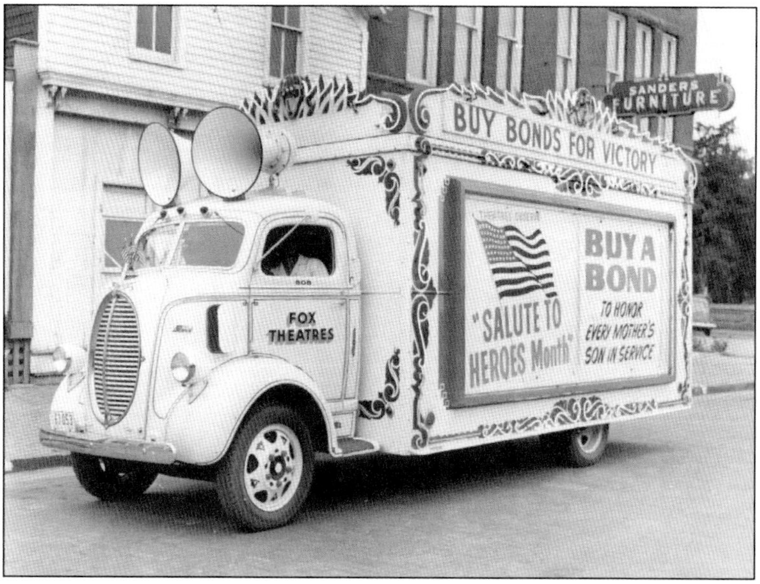


A Ballyhoo truck was in Marysville in September 1942 to advertise a war bonds sales drive being sponsored by the Liberty and Isis Theatres in Marysville and thousands of other theaters throughout the nation.

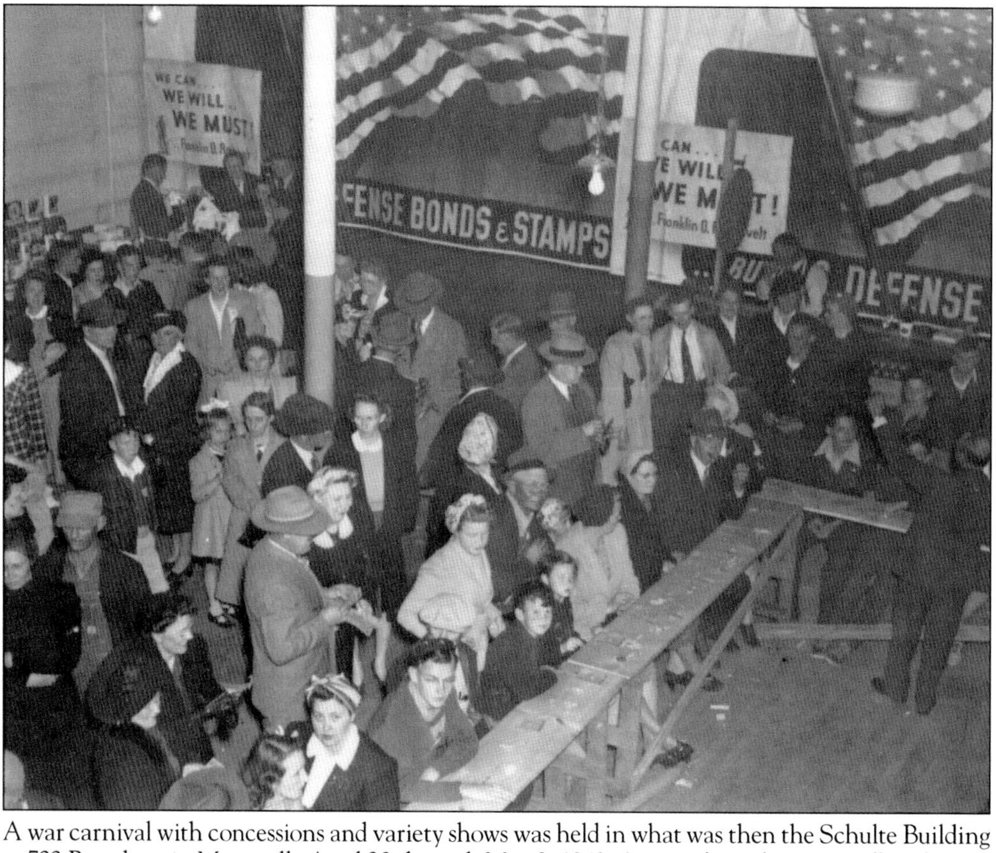


A war carnival with concessions and variety shows was held in what was then the Schulte Building at 722 Broadway in Marysville April 30 through May 2, 1942. An article in the *Marysville Advocate* on May 7, 1942, reports that the net profit of $478.19 from the three nights of the event would be used to give farewell parties for Marshall County men leaving for the armed services and for canteen work for troop trains coming through Marysville.

Hundreds of local women were involved in activities in support of the war effort. They baked treats for soldiers coming through town, attended bond sales events, and sent thousands of cookies, lap robes, pajamas, tray favors, and other items to veterans' hospitals. Here they are folding bandages for the Red Cross.

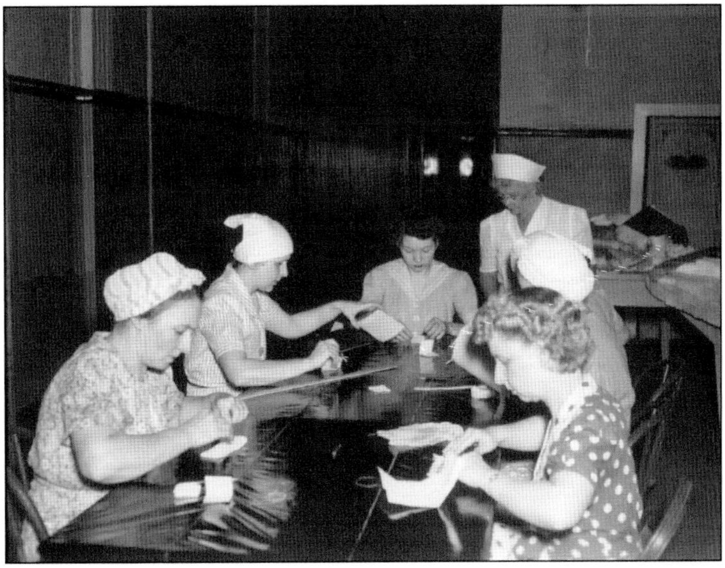

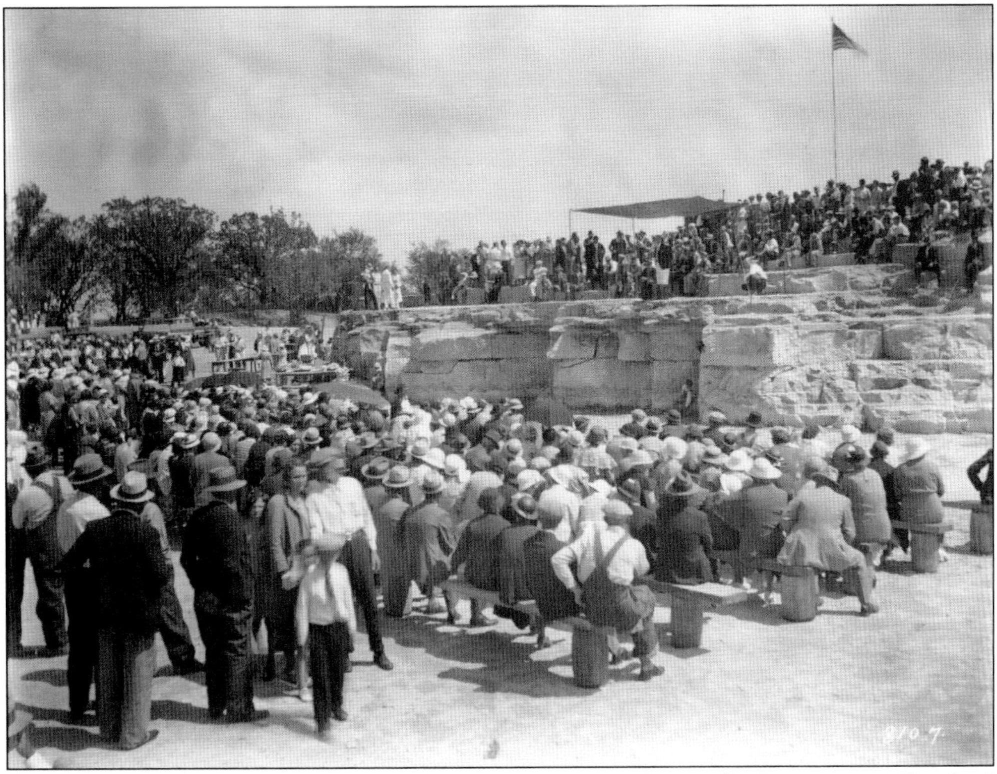

Relief agencies provided thousands of jobs for Americans during the Depression. The Civil Works Administration (CWA) lasted only five months, but nearly 7,000 Kansans worked on CWA road projects between November 1933 and the end of March 1934. On May 15, 1934, Gov. Alf Landon addressed more than 1,500 local residents at the limestone quarry in Beattie, reporting that Kansas was second in the nation in the number of people working through the CWA program and complimenting Marshall County on the use it had made of locally quarried crushed limestone in road building.

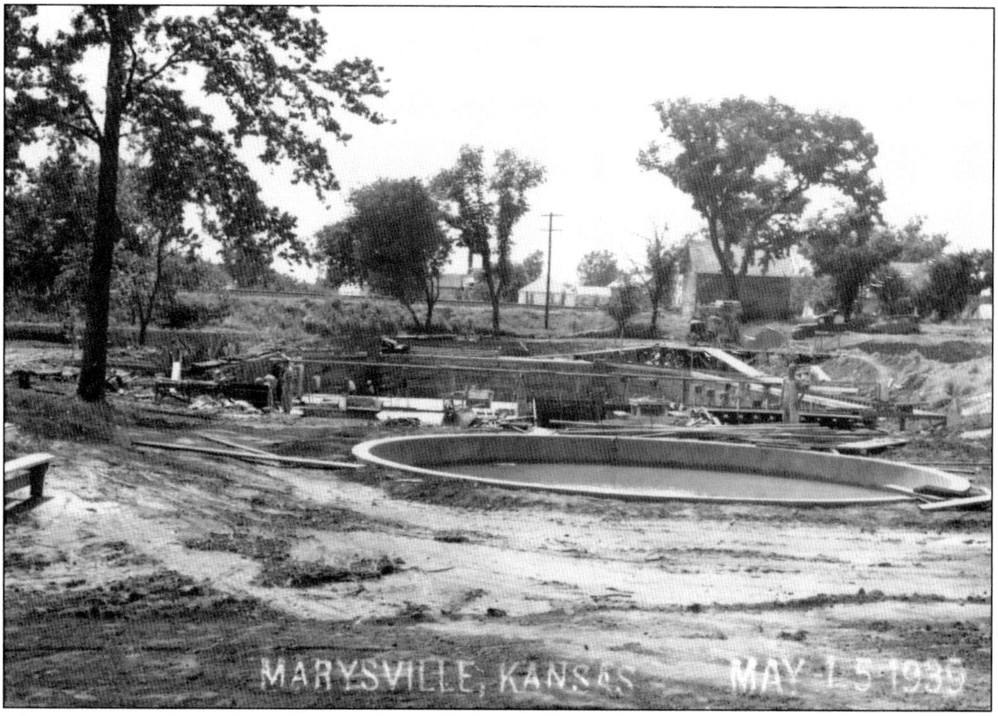


The swimming pool in Marysville City Park was built by Works Progress Administration (WPA) workers in 1939. This view shows a nearly completed wading pool in the foreground and work in progress on the large pool. This pool and the park around it were submerged by the flood of 1941. It was replaced by a pool on higher ground in 1953. That pool, in turn, was replaced by a new pool that opened in summer 2014.

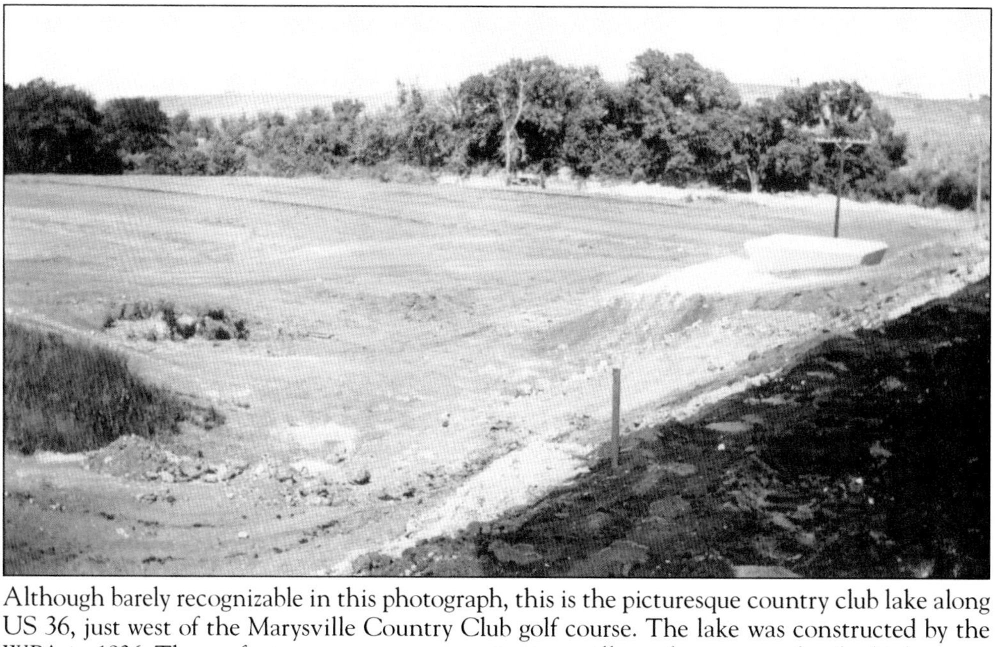

Although barely recognizable in this photograph, this is the picturesque country club lake along US 36, just west of the Marysville Country Club golf course. The lake was constructed by the WPA in 1936. The six-foot-square cement opening is a spillway that goes under the highway.

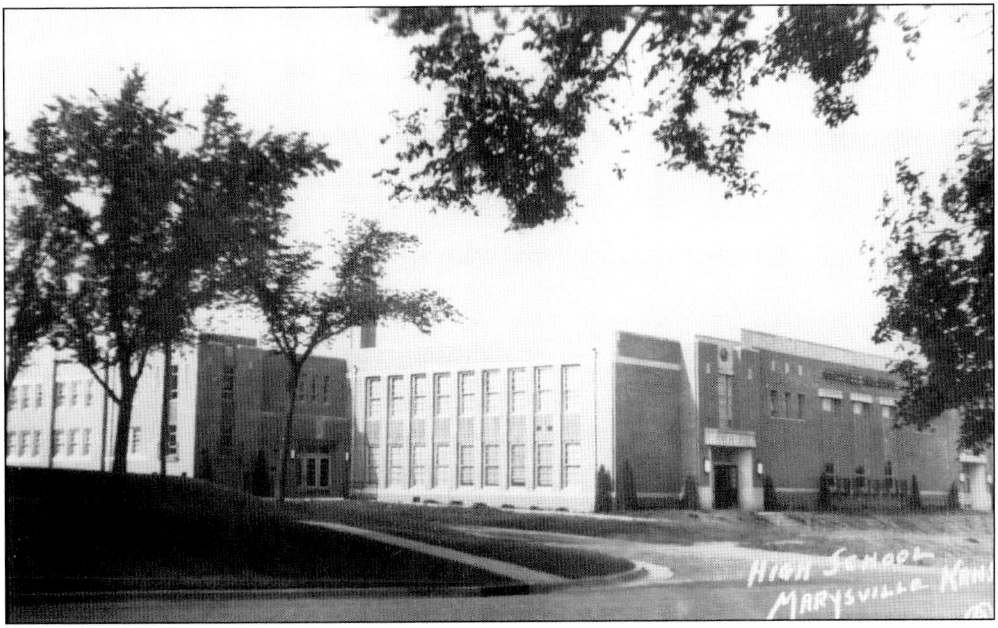


Marysville High School was constructed at Walnut and Eleventh Streets by the Public Works Administration (PWA), another of the Depression-era federal government work programs. Students began school in the new building on February 20, 1939. This photograph was taken during summer of that year.

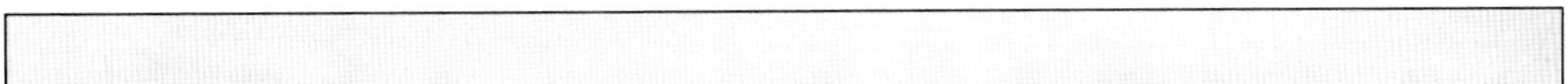

A new stadium and locker building (far end of the stadium) were built during 1936 by WPA workers. The locally quarried stones used to build the locker were from the 1877 jail that had been located at the top of the hill seen here. This 1939 photograph shows the entire high school stadium complex. Between 1936, when the high school was still at Tenth and Carolina Streets, and 1939, when the new high school was built, the locker was used by sports teams at the stadium.

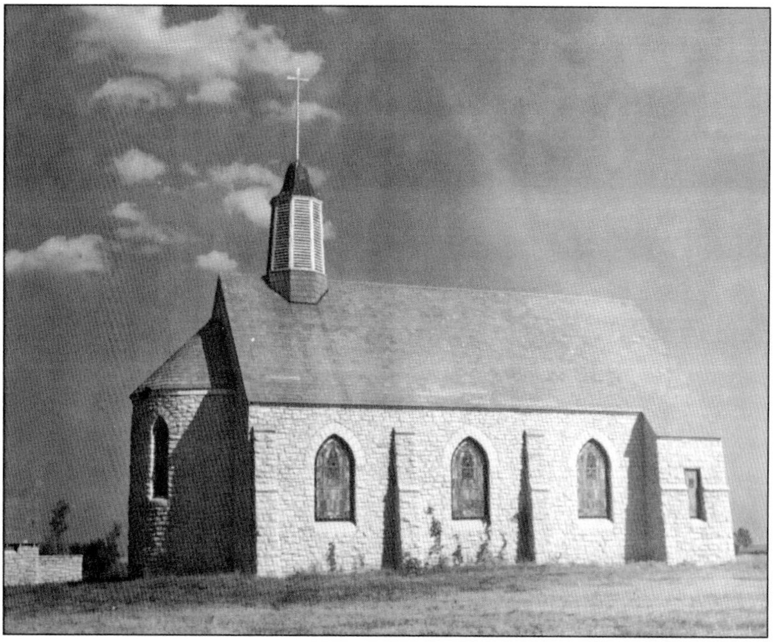

This beautiful chapel in the Marysville City Cemetery, built in 1939, was another WPA project. The chapel dedication was held on Sunday, October 18, 1942, but it has never been used. This photograph showing the original spire and stained glass windows was taken October 5, 1942. The chapel has since fallen into disrepair.

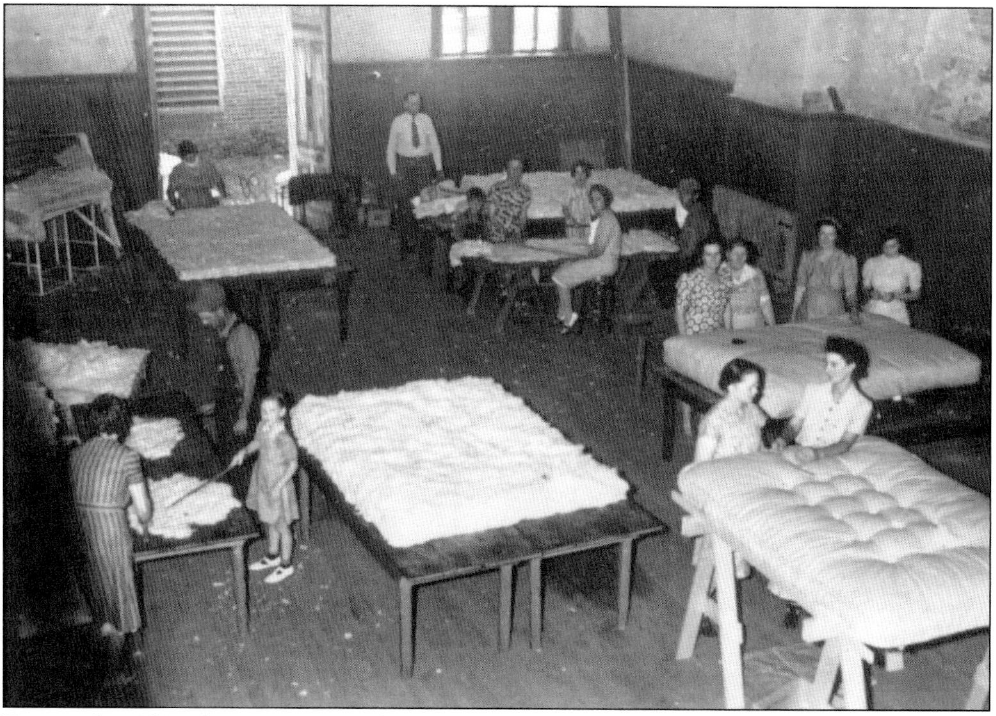

During the 1930s, the WPA operated a mattress program at Turner Hall in Marysville. Families who could not afford a new mattress could make one for free through this program. Cotton sufficient for the size of the mattress was cut from a cotton bale, shaped, and covered with striped ticking. The cover was stitched closed; then the mattress was tufted and buttoned down. Women, often with children in tow and friends or family along to help, could construct a mattress in a couple of days.

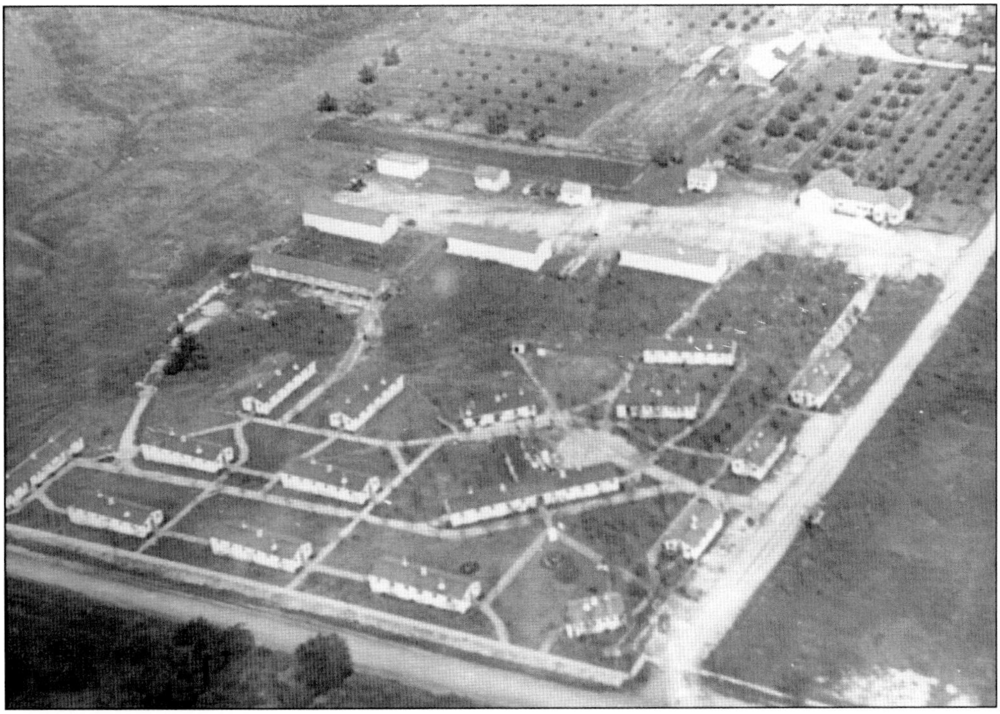

Franklin Delano Roosevelt was elected in 1932 on the campaign pledge of a "New Deal" to help put Americans to work during the Depression. He was inaugurated on March 4, 1933, and on March 21, Congress created the Civilian Conservation Corps. Marysville had one of 21 CCC camps in Kansas. CCC workers throughout Marshall County constructed buildings, built roads, created small stone or brush dams on local farms, and planted hundreds of trees. This aerial view of the camp, located at Sixteenth and North Streets in Marysville, shows the barracks. The farm in the background was on the grounds of the County Home. Lions Park now occupies this CCC location.

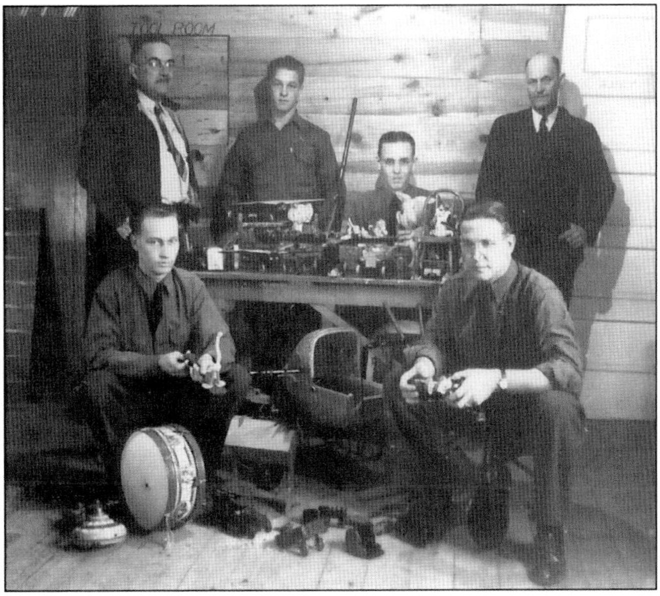

Toys were real luxuries for many families during the Depression. These CCC workers are repairing toys for distribution at Christmas, around 1935. Toys were also repaired or made by National Youth Administration (NYA) workers.

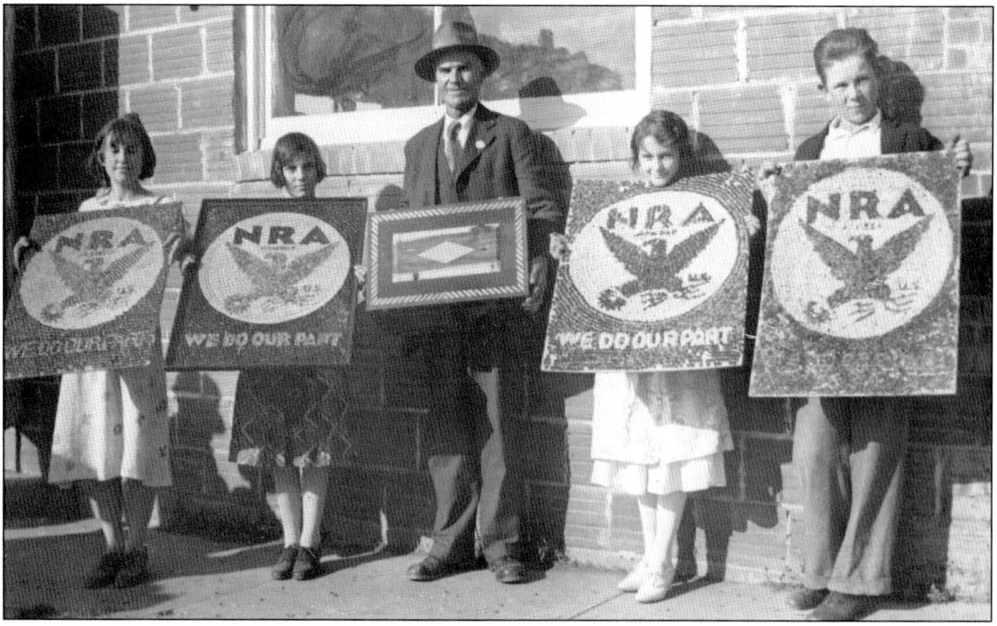


The National Recovery Administration (NRA) was created in 1933 by Pres. Franklin D. Roosevelt, who intended the program to help curb destructive competition and set fair prices. The program was declared unconstitutional by the US Supreme Court in 1935, but out of this program came the National Labor Relations Act. This Corn Emblem Contest in Marietta, probably in 1933, features the NRA emblem. Pictured, from left to right, are Monica Raymond, Mabel McBrien, J.A. Howell, Mary Schroller, and Dale Mayhew.

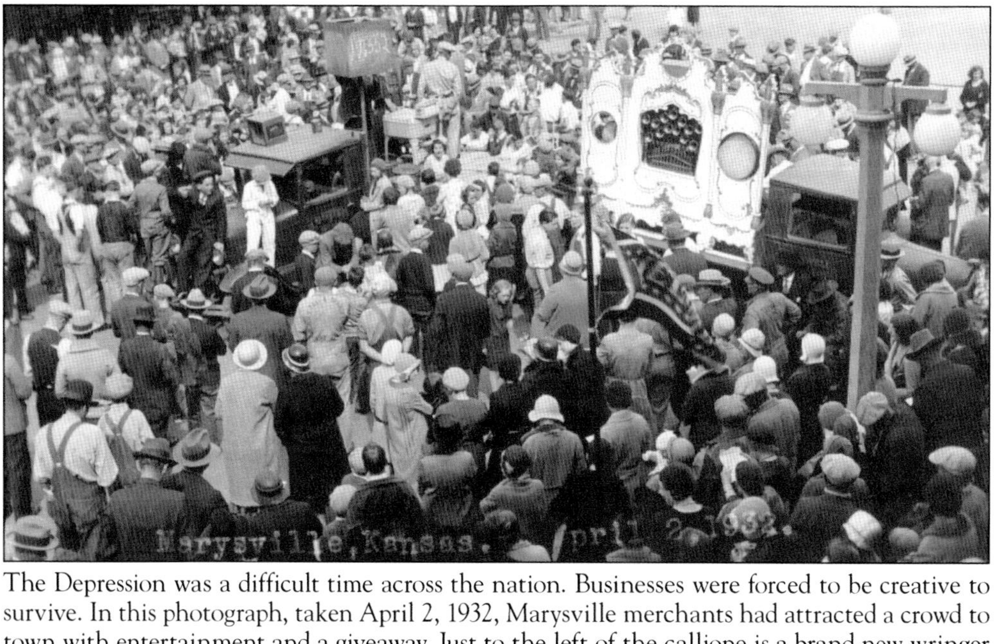


The Depression was a difficult time across the nation. Businesses were forced to be creative to survive. In this photograph, taken April 2, 1932, Marysville merchants had attracted a crowd to town with entertainment and a giveaway. Just to the left of the calliope is a brand-new wringer washing machine on a flatbed truck. The man leaning on the washer is probably the donor. Although there would have been smaller items given away, this was likely the major lure on this Saturday. Similar events were held periodically throughout the Depression.

## *Six*

# A Sense of Community

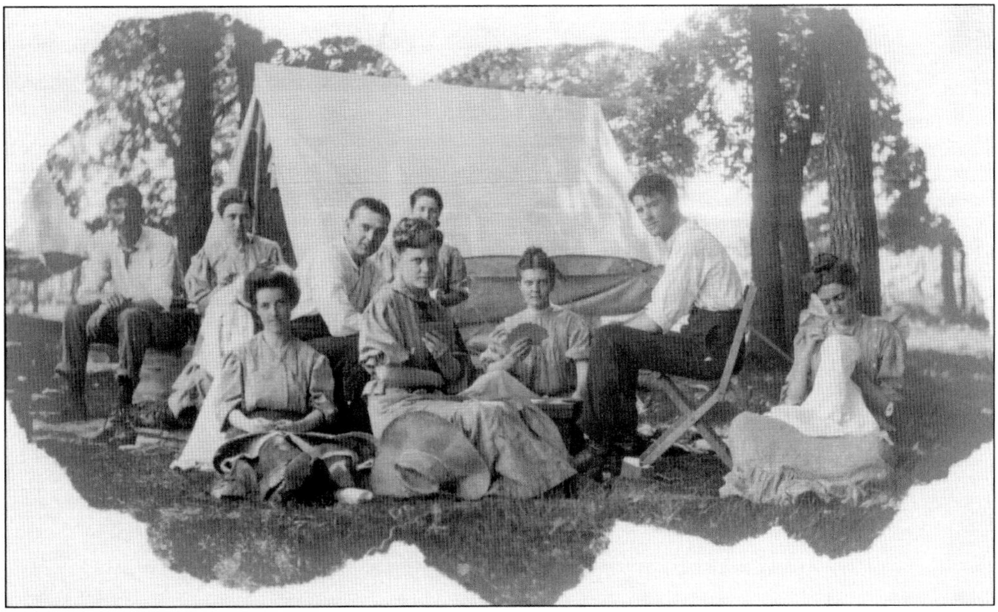

By all accounts, the summer of 1907 was a scorcher. Picnic groves, city parks, local ponds, and rivers provided a few hours of recreational relief for most families. More affluent young men and women (and their chaperones) left home for several weeks and constructed tent cities in shady groves at local farmsteads. There, they lounged with books and cards, cooked in comfortable tent kitchens, dined in gauze-sided "dining rooms," and slept on comfortable mattresses in naturally air-conditioned canvas tents.

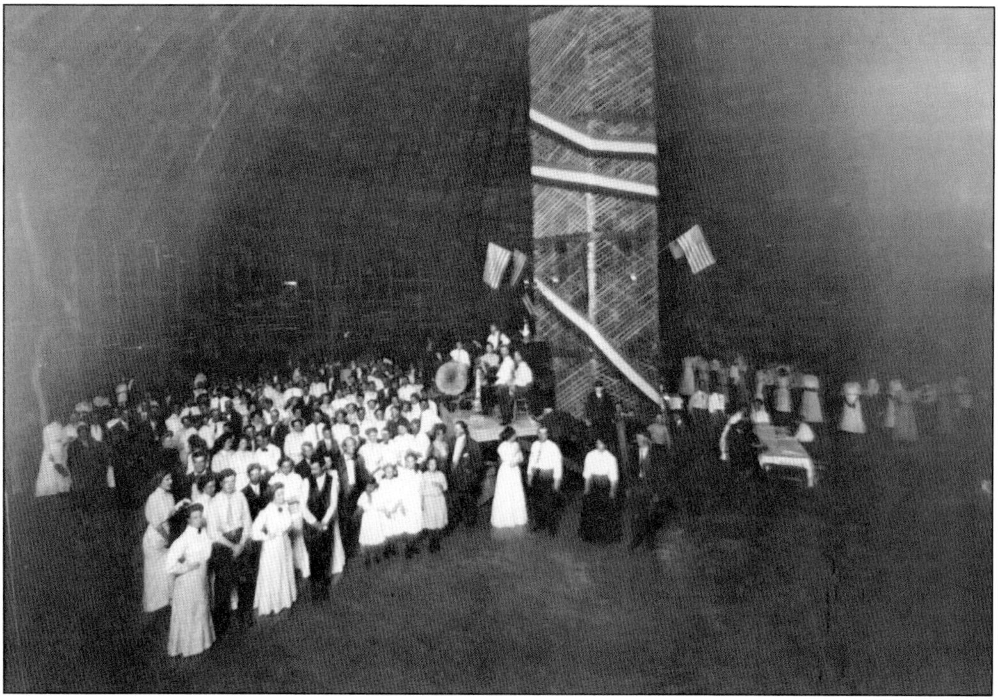

Nearly 500 people attended this Dedication Dance in Fred Cottrell's big round barn near Irving on August 17, 1909. The 17 automobiles parked outside along the basement wall were said to be the most seen at one time in Marshall County. The grand march was led by Cottrell's wife, Kate, and August Johnson, the master mason who had laid the basement walls.

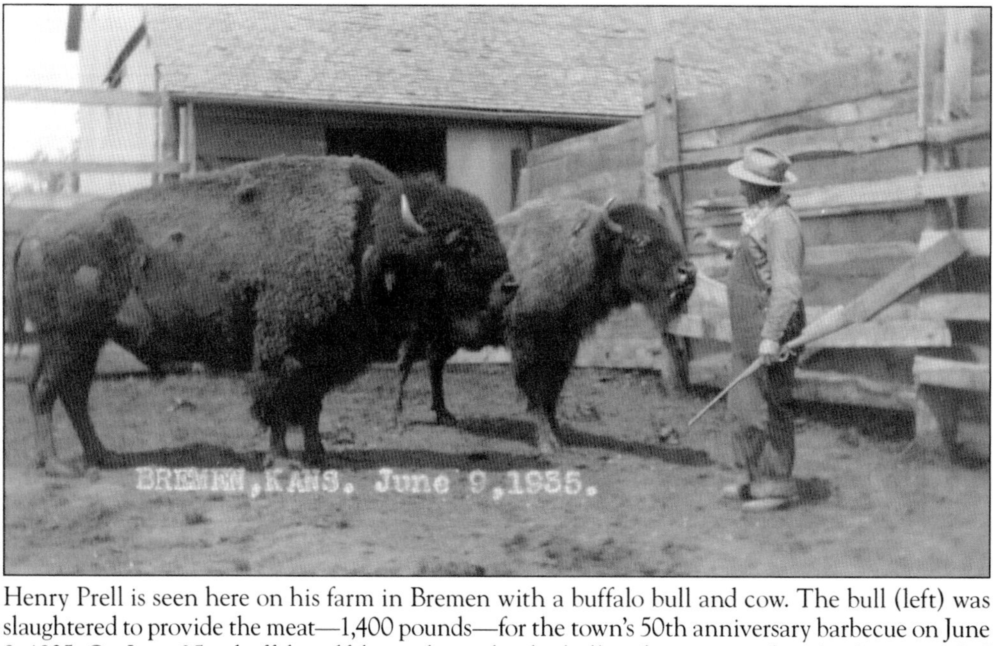


Henry Prell is seen here on his farm in Bremen with a buffalo bull and cow. The bull (left) was slaughtered to provide the meat—1,400 pounds—for the town's 50th anniversary barbecue on June 9, 1935. On June 25, a buffalo calf, born the night the bull and cow arrived at the farm, startled Prell's team of horses. The team trampled and killed the 46-year-old farmer. The bull's head was mounted and is on display in the Marshall County Courthouse museum.

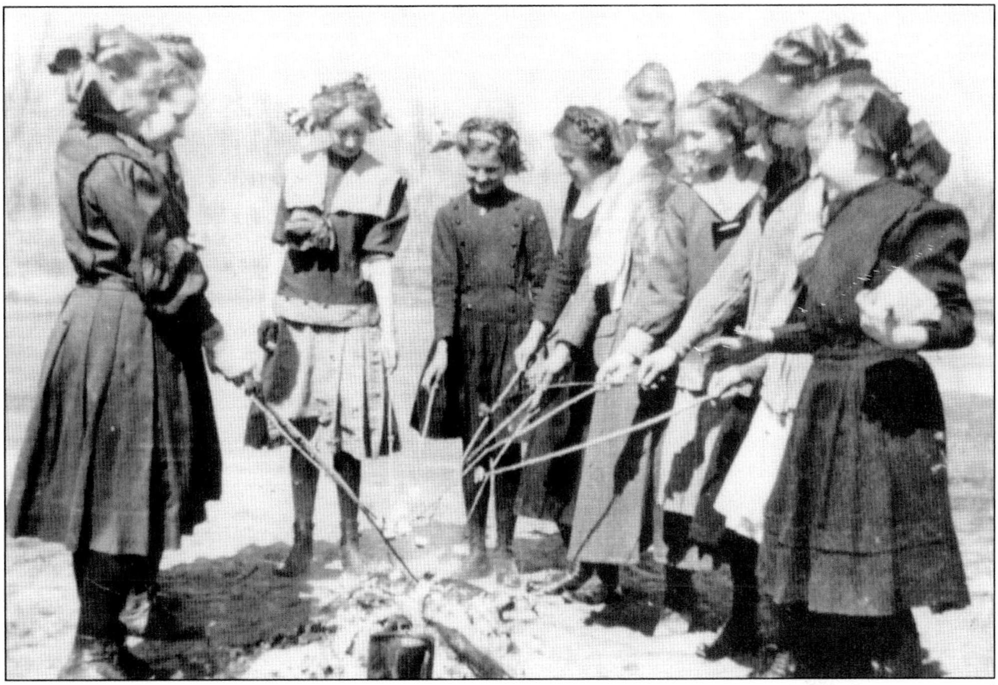

Juliette Gordon Low organized the Girl Scouts in March 1912. The first Marshall County Girl Scout troop was formed just two years later in Blue Rapids. In this 1914 photograph, the Scouts are roasting marshmallows over a campfire.

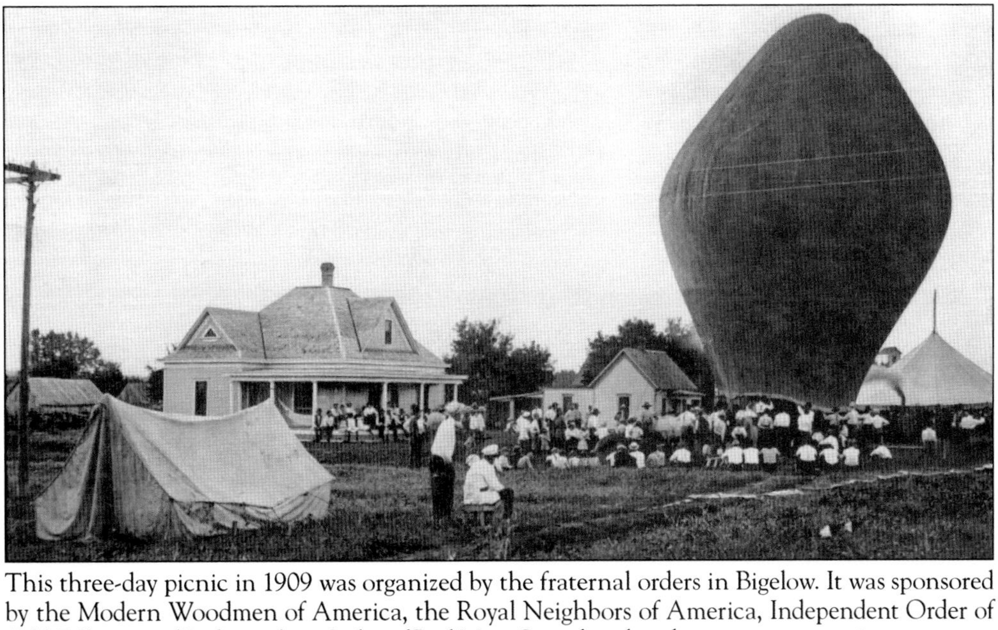

This three-day picnic in 1909 was organized by the fraternal orders in Bigelow. It was sponsored by the Modern Woodmen of America, the Royal Neighbors of America, Independent Order of Odd Fellows, and Independent Order of Red Men. Speeches, band concerts, concessions, a merry-go-round, high dive, and balloon ascension were among the scheduled activities. A baseball game between the Bigelow town team and the Black Diamonds, a well-respected Marshall County black baseball team, was held the second day. Teams from the Negro League, most notably the Kansas City Monarchs, played frequently in Marshall County.

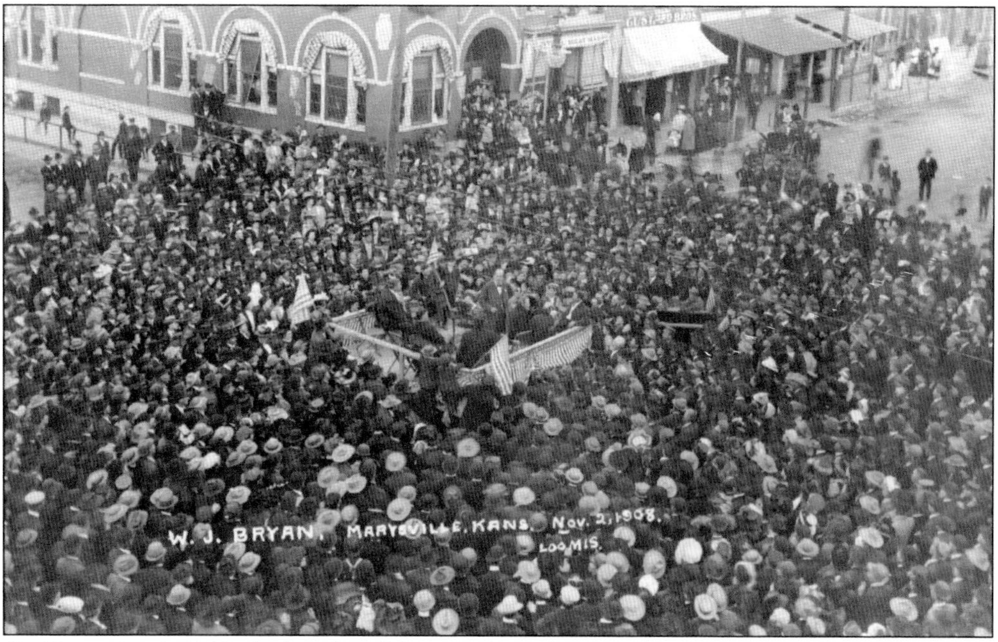


On November 2, 1908, the last day of the presidential campaign, Democratic candidate William Jennings Bryan appeared in Marysville. According to the *Marysville Advocate-Democrat*, Bryan spoke for nearly an hour to a crowd estimated at 6,000–7,000. The following day, the nation's voters elected Republican William Howard Taft to be the 27th president of the United States. Bryan lost in Marshall County by 768 votes of 5,806 cast. This was his third and last run for the presidency, having been defeated in 1896, 1900, and finally in 1908.

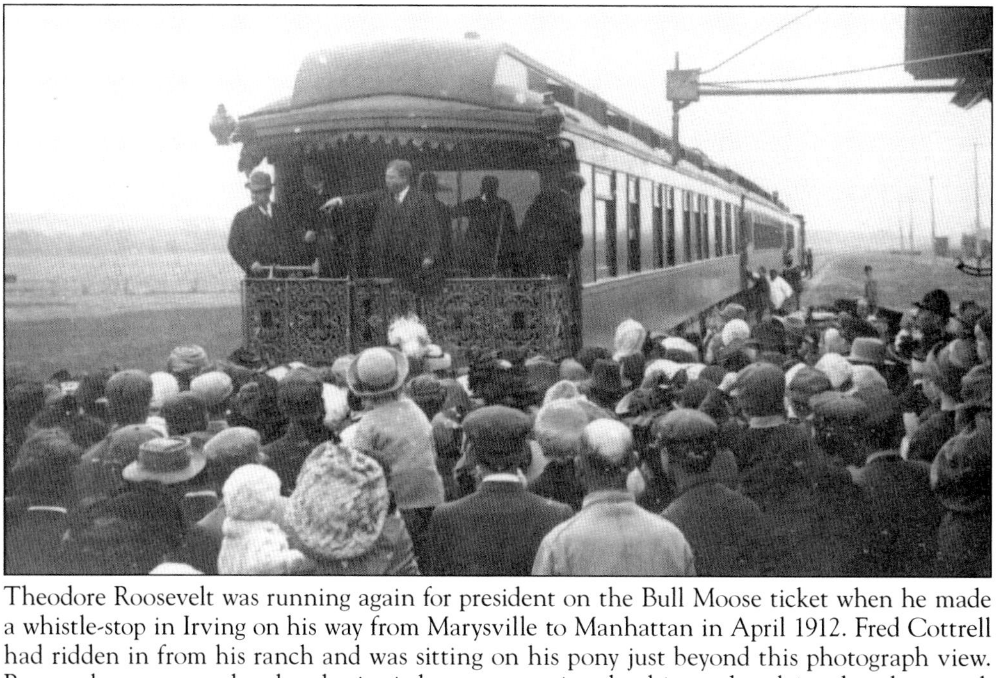

Theodore Roosevelt was running again for president on the Bull Moose ticket when he made a whistle-stop in Irving on his way from Marysville to Manhattan in April 1912. Fred Cottrell had ridden in from his ranch and was sitting on his pony just beyond this photograph view. Roosevelt, a renowned and enthusiastic horseman, pointed at him and exclaimed to the crowd, "That looks good to me!"

John Crome was born in Herkimer in 1887. He was a rural mail carrier and a dowser. In this 1940s photograph, he is holding a Y-shaped divining rod, probably from a local willow or peach tree. Sinking a well was very costly and many early homesteaders and farmers would not consider drilling without first consulting a dowser.

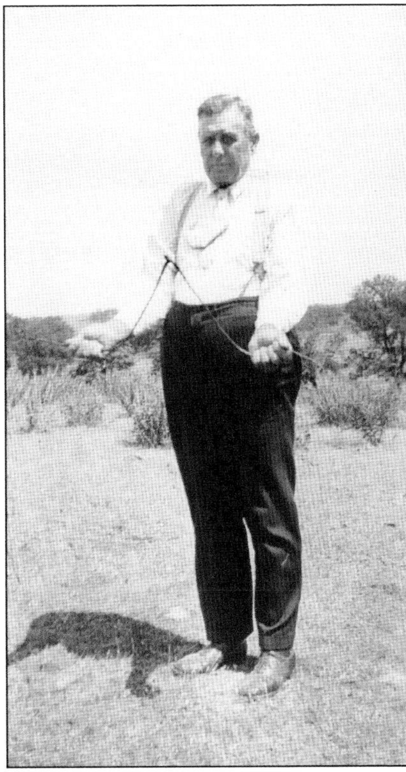

The Pecenka Orchestra, which provided music in Marshall County for three generations, is onstage in November 1931, probably at Bremen City Hall. The Pecenkas were the first Czech family to homestead in Marshall County, settling in the Bremen area in 1869, first in a dugout, later in a log cabin. In time, both a school district and cemetery were named for the family. Over the cemetery archway is the inscription, in Czech, "We were what you are: What we are you will be."

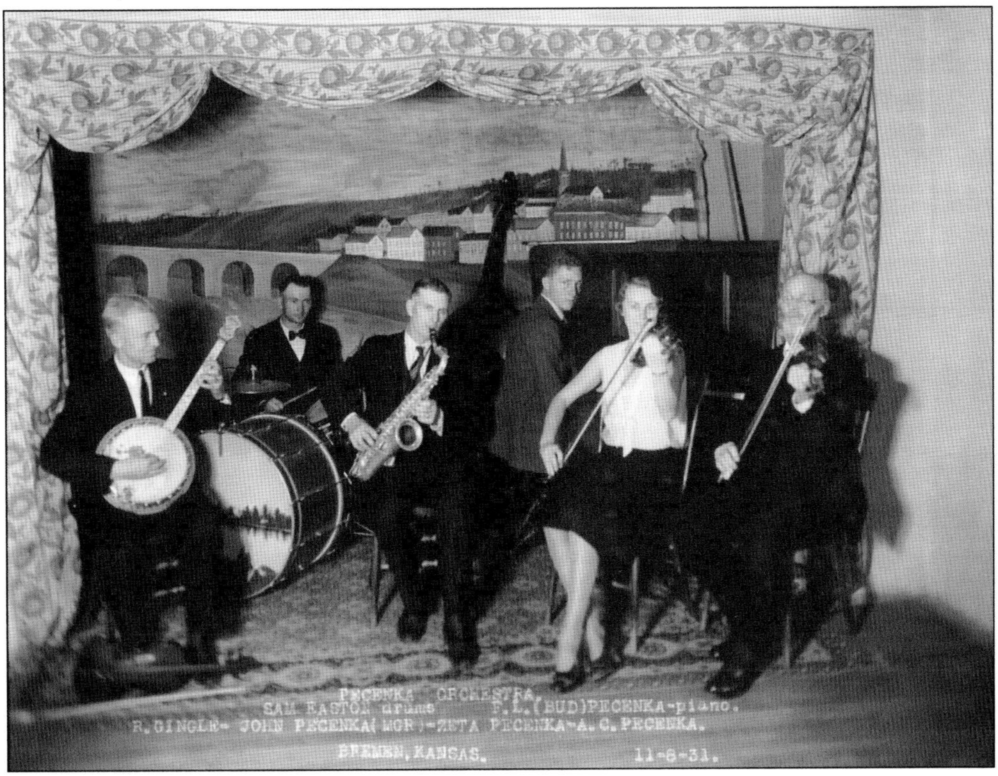

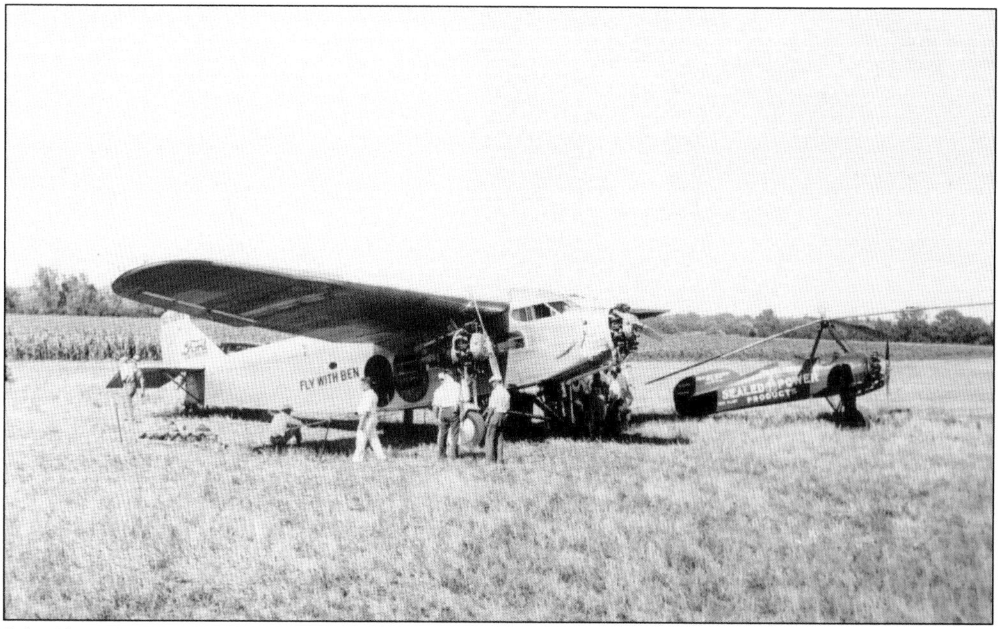


July 13, 1932, was Auto Gyro Day in Marshall County. The gyroplane, right, was a forerunner of the helicopter. It took off like a helicopter, but flew like an airplane. The airplane is a Ford Trimotor, also known as the "Tin Goose." Ford built 199 of the Trimotors, which were 50 feet in length and made of corrugated metal; they sold for $50,000. The event was held at a temporary airport on a Scully lease on the west side of the Big Blue River, just west of Marysville.

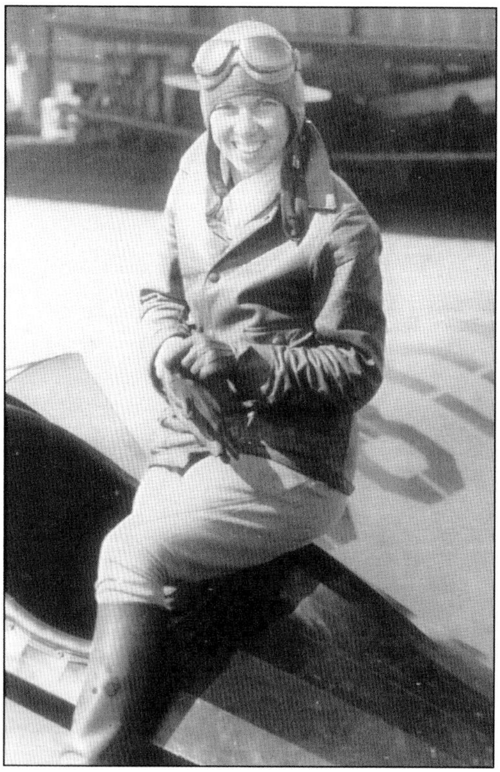

Ruth Blaney, a female aviation pioneer, was born in Irving in 1905. She took her first airplane flight near Irving in the summer of 1928 and began flying lessons in San Diego, California, in September 1929. She received her license on November 17, 1929, the 65th licensed woman pilot in the United States. Blaney received a second-class glider license in California in February 1930, and that spring became the first American woman to be a glider instructor. On July 11, 1930, she established a new light plane world record (for both men and women) of 26,600 feet. She died September 18, 1930, when her plane struck a hillside at Point Loma shortly after takeoff from Lindbergh Field, San Diego. She was returned to Irving and buried in Greenwood Cemetery.

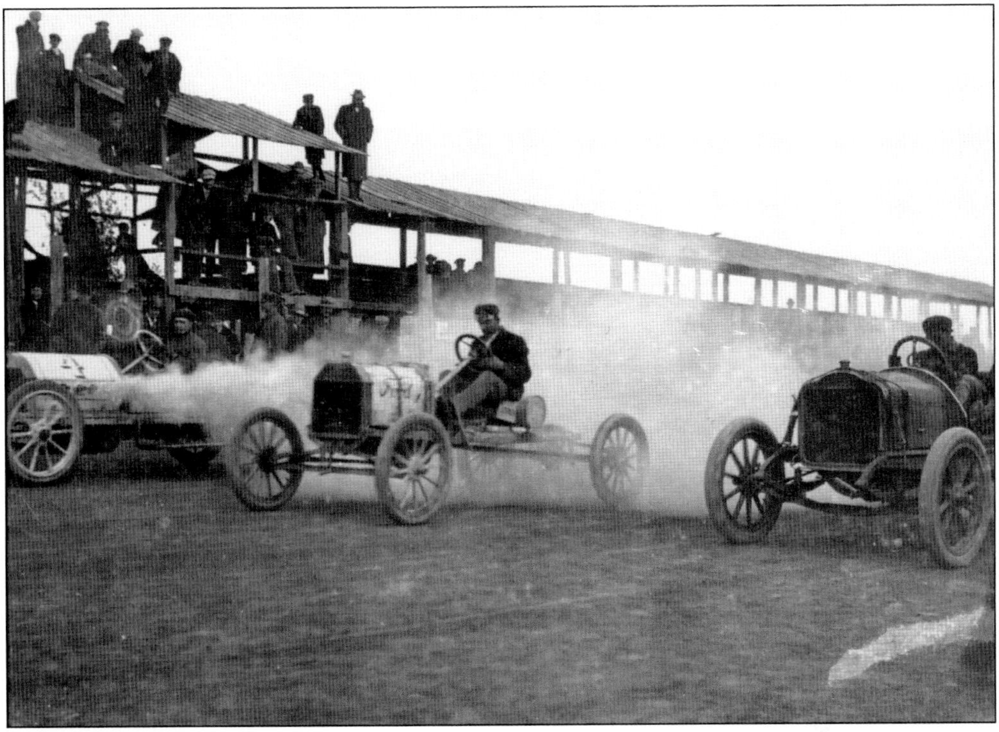

This automobile race was held in 1910 at the racetrack in Blue Rapids. The track was located in the same area where the county fairgrounds buildings were built in 1916. The grandstand pictured was on the north side of the racetrack, near the river. The racetrack is clearly identified on the 1904 plat map of Blue Rapids.

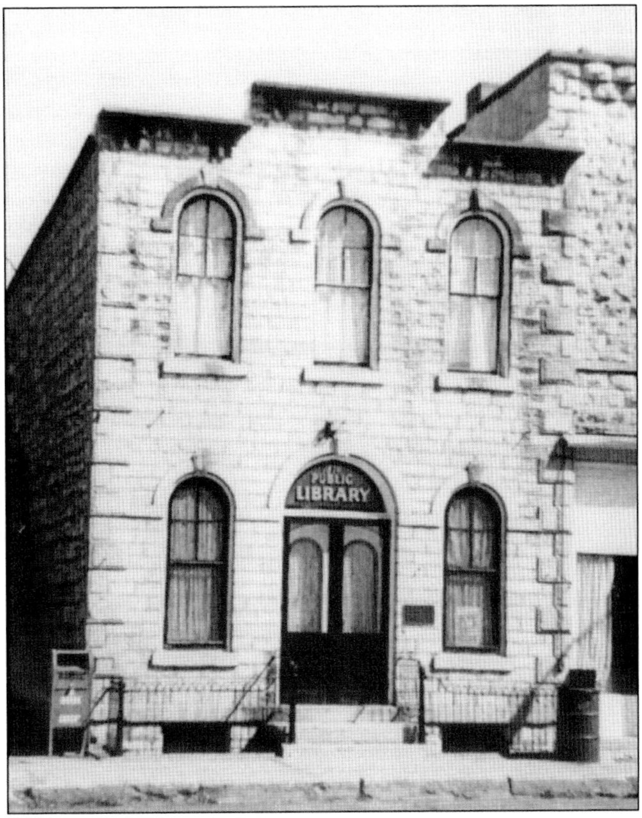


The Blue Rapids Public Library was founded in 1874. This building, erected in 1877, is the oldest library in continuous use in Kansas. It was placed in the National Register of Historic Places in 1972. In 2014, the library received a grant and other funding to construct a children's library expansion to the left of the current building.

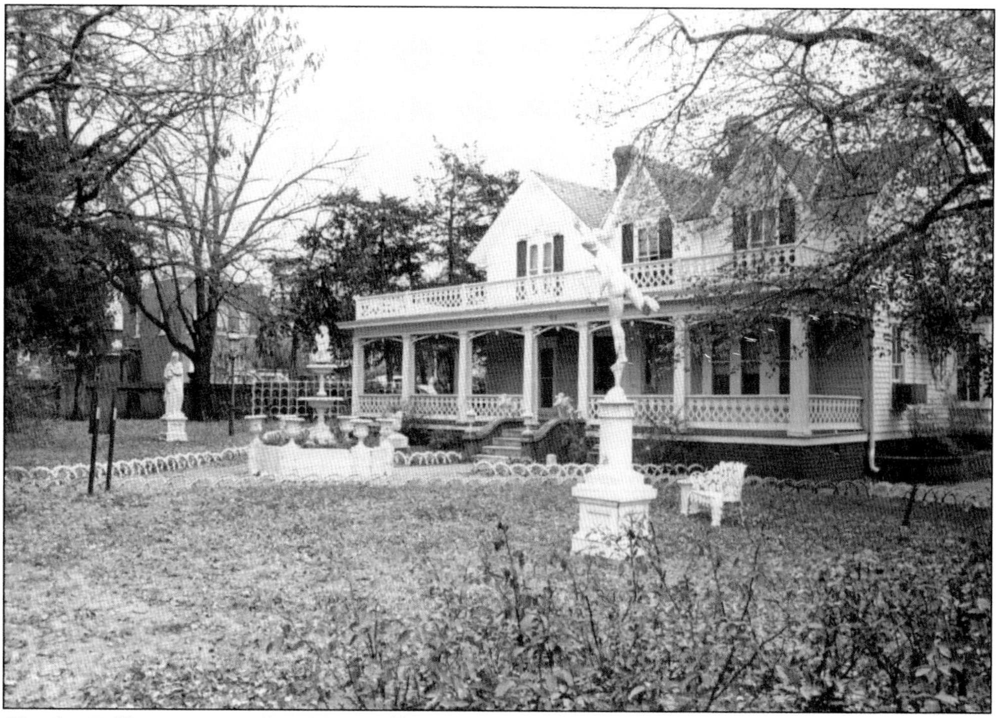

Charles F. Koester arrived in Marysville in 1860. He joined the banking firm of his brother-in-law Frank Schmidt in 1874, and in 1876 completed construction on his home at the corner of Broadway and Tenth Street. Laura Ingalls Wilder mentions this house and its cast-iron guardian lions in an 1894 journal entry. The Koester house gardens have the largest collection of zinc statues in the United States. The house was placed in the National Register of Historic Places in 1975. The home is open for tours and special events throughout the year.

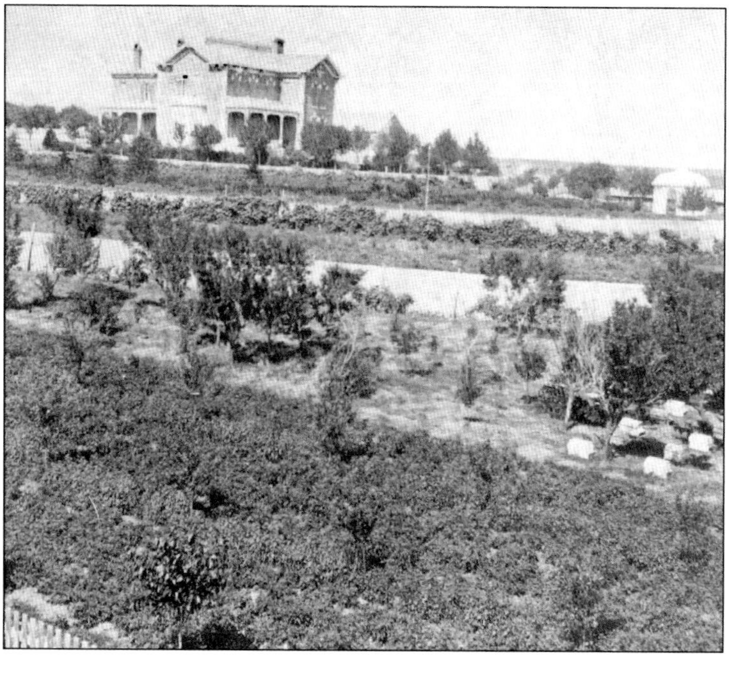

This is a view from around 1889 of the Schmidt mansion, home of Frank Schmidt and his family. The property included beehives, vineyards, and orchards to the south of the house. Schmidt and his brother-in-law, Charles F. Koester, were partners in the Exchange Bank of Schmidt and Koester. This house, located at the eastern end of Broadway, is now the Marysville First Baptist Church.

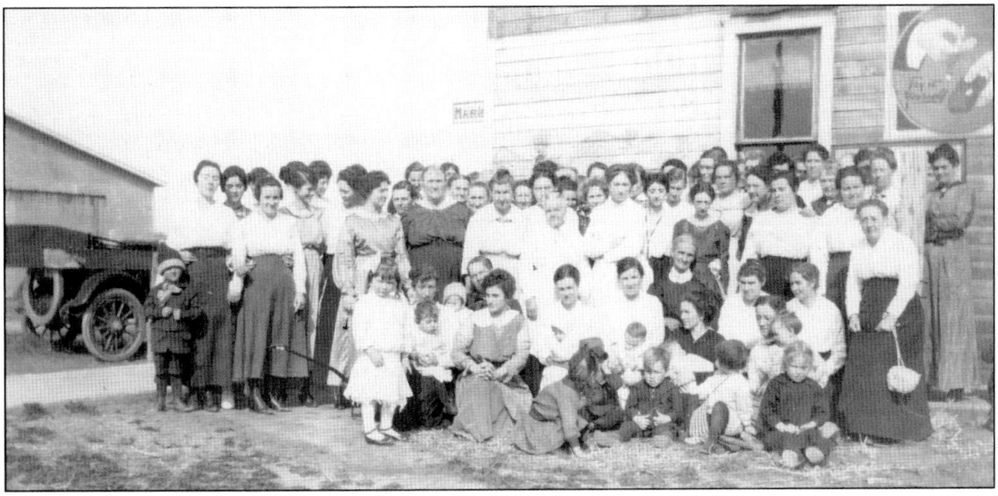

Women's days were long in early Marshall County. They were filled with joys, concerns, and a certain predictable tedium as each major chore had its designated day of the week. In the early 1900s, women's clubs were strictly social occasions, but they soon evolved to be opportunities for service to one another and to their communities. The hostess provided a meal for guests who might have come to wallpaper or paint a room, or make a quilt or clothing for needy families. One such club was the Marietta Needlecraft Club, shown here around 1910.

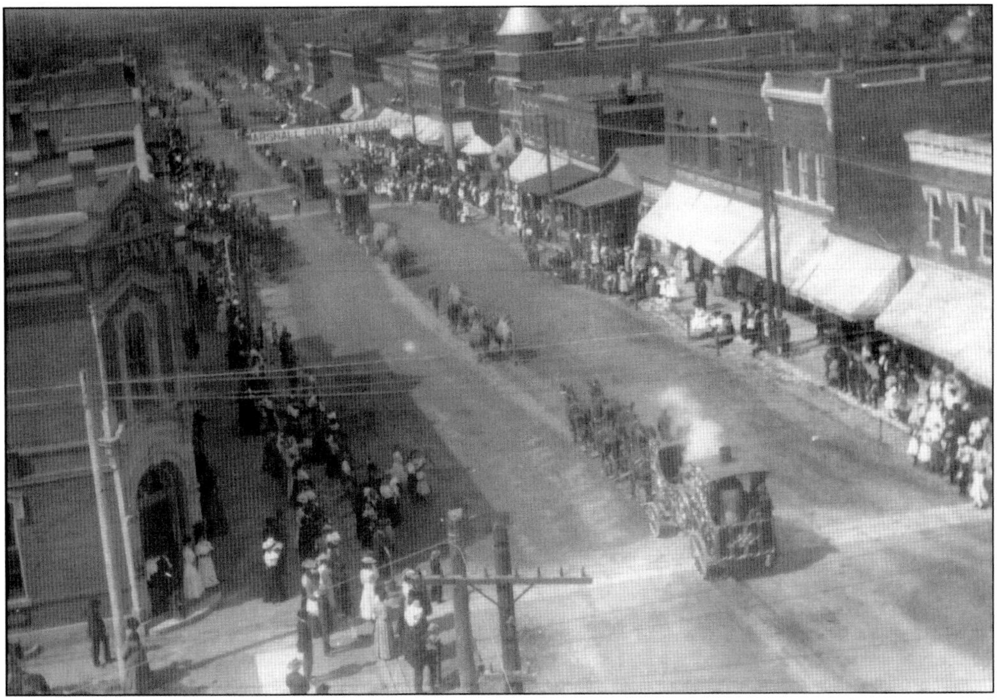

A Marshall County Fair circus parade is moving west on Broadway around 1900. The first annual county fair was held in September 1873. Between then and 1916, when the fair moved to Blue Rapids, the fairgrounds were located at the northwest edge of Marysville. Floral Hall was a "half-acre" tent, and spectators could watch outdoor events under a roofed viewing stand. Early county fairs often included concerts, ball games, and horse races, as well as exhibits of quilts, embroidery, other needlecrafts, paintings, baked goods, preserves, farm produce, and animals.

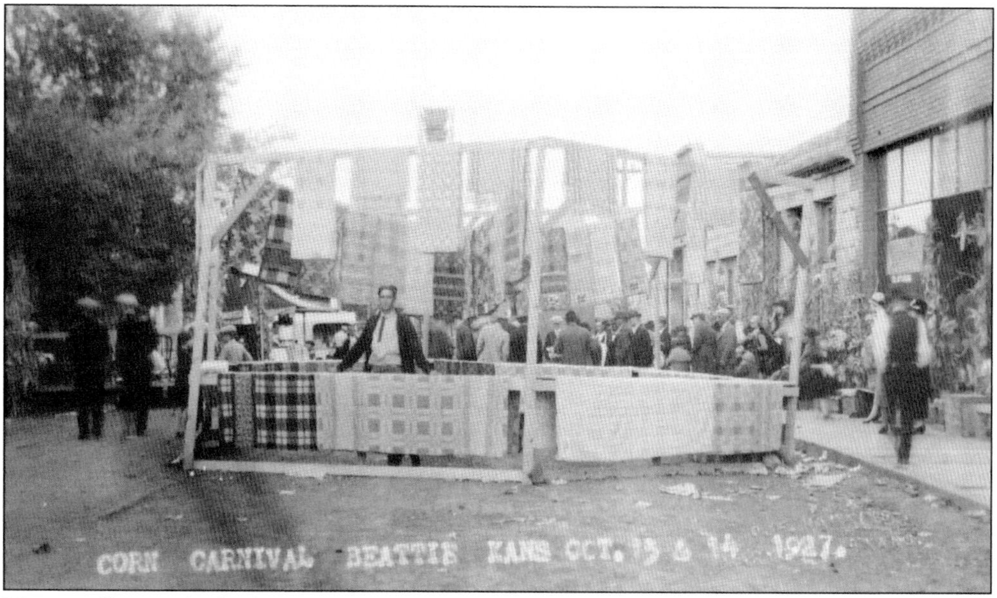


Most small towns had at least one celebration annually, and as in many rural counties, crops were often the focus, but dancing, food and handicrafts were added attractions. This booth at the 1927 Beattie Corn Carnival offers quilts made by local women.

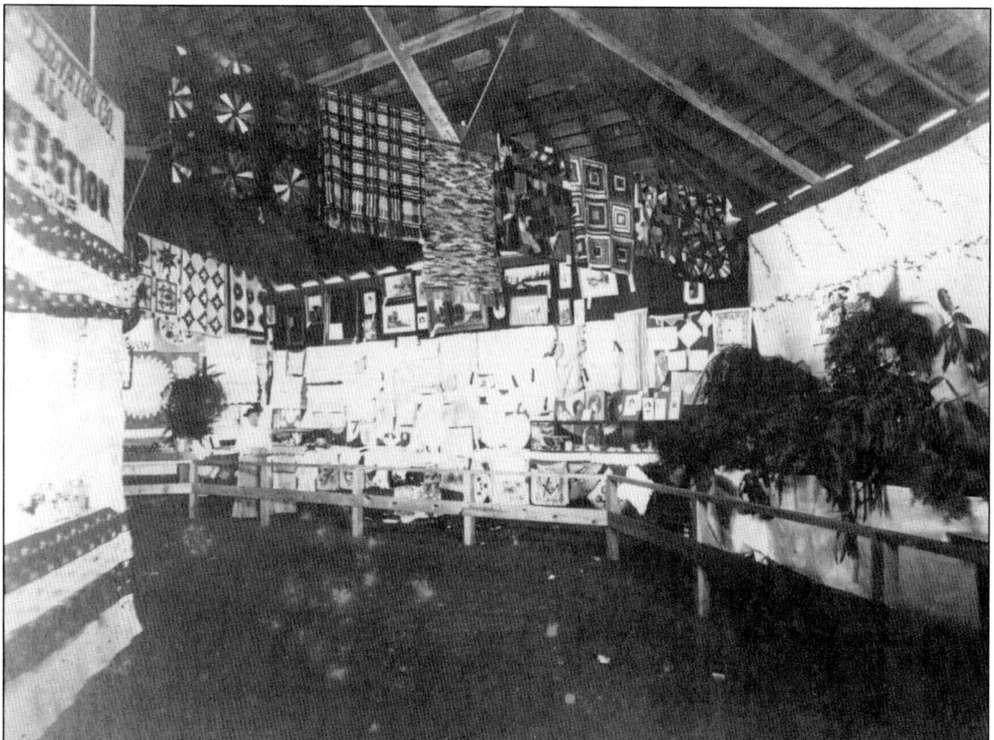

The Marshall County Fair was held in Blue Rapids for the first time in October 1916. In addition to buildings devoted to crops and animals, the fair had a Ferris wheel, horse races, concerts, business displays, and handicrafts.

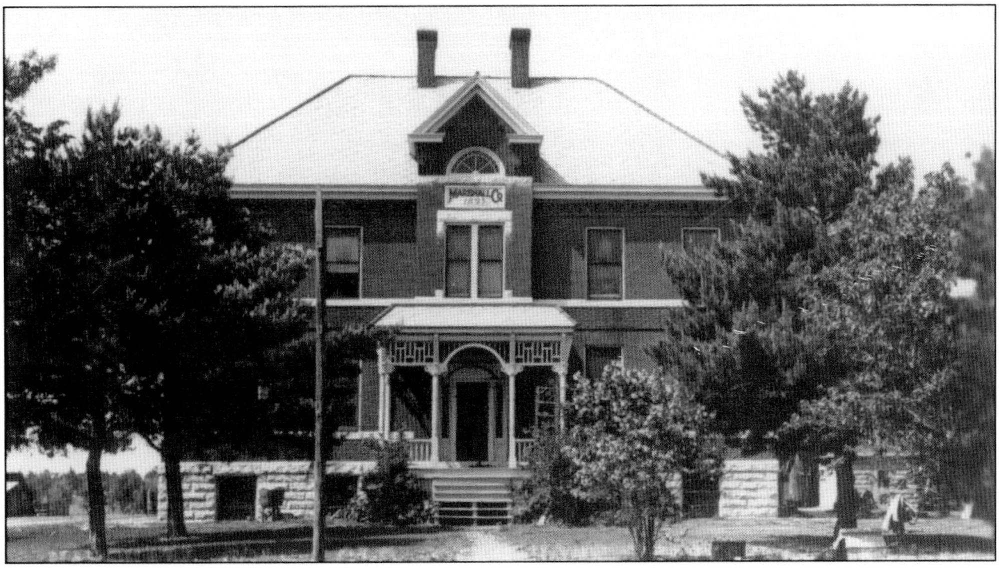

In the 1870s, the State of Kansas determined that counties were responsible for indigent residents. Marshall County commissioners established the Marshall County Poor Farm near Oketo for poor and elderly residents. In 1895, this Marshall County Home was built in Marysville. Limited understanding of aging and dementia resulted in the determination that many elderly residents were insane.

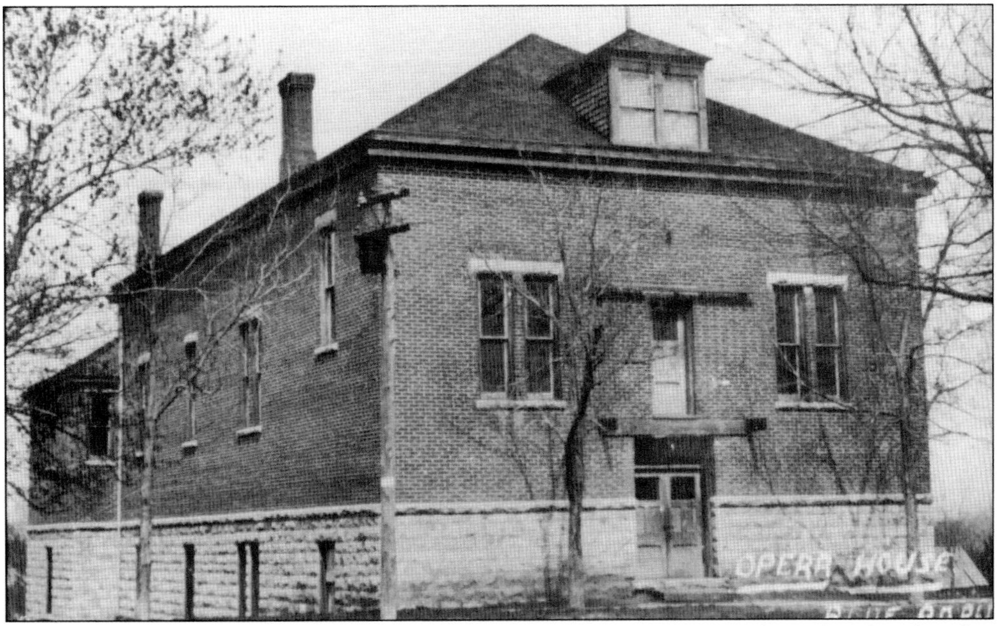


Between 1854 and the early 1930s, more than 200,000 children—most orphaned or abandoned—were taken from New York to other cities around the United States to be indentured or adopted. More than 5,000 of them came to Kansas. Between 1883 and 1909, some of those "Orphan Train" children arrived at Marshall County depots in Axtell, Beattie, Blue Rapids, Frankfort, Home, Marysville, Oketo, Reedsville, and Vermillion. The children who arrived in Blue Rapids in 1908 went from the depot to this opera house, where they met their new families. Built in 1893, it became a movie house in the mid-1900s and was razed in 1985.

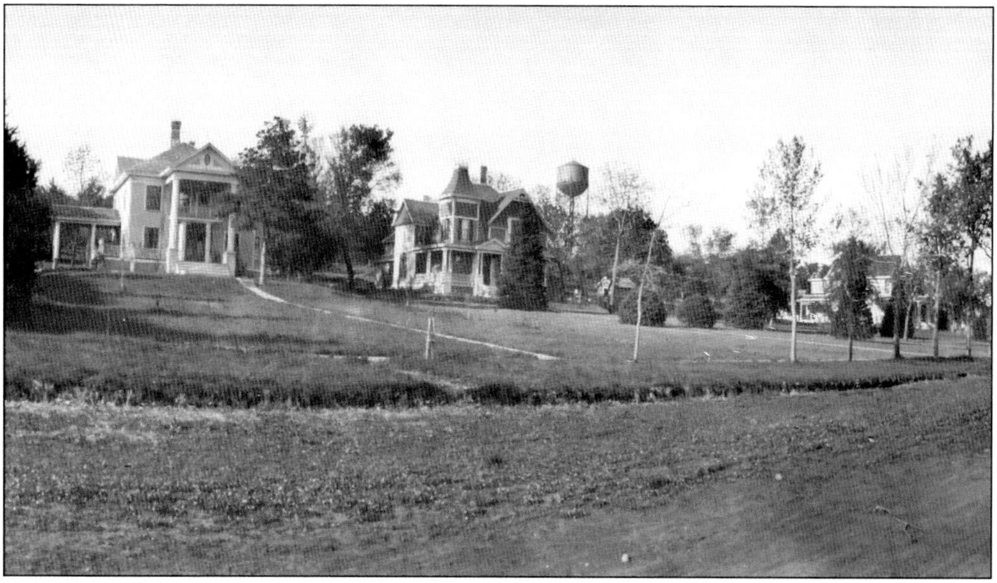

Known as Bankers Row, these three lovely Victorian houses on East Hazelwood Avenue were indeed all homes of Waterville bankers. From left to right, the homes were owned by Chester and Mary Thomas (built in 1910), Frank Thorne (1880), and George and Laura Hall (around 1900). (Courtesy of LaVerna Arganbright.)

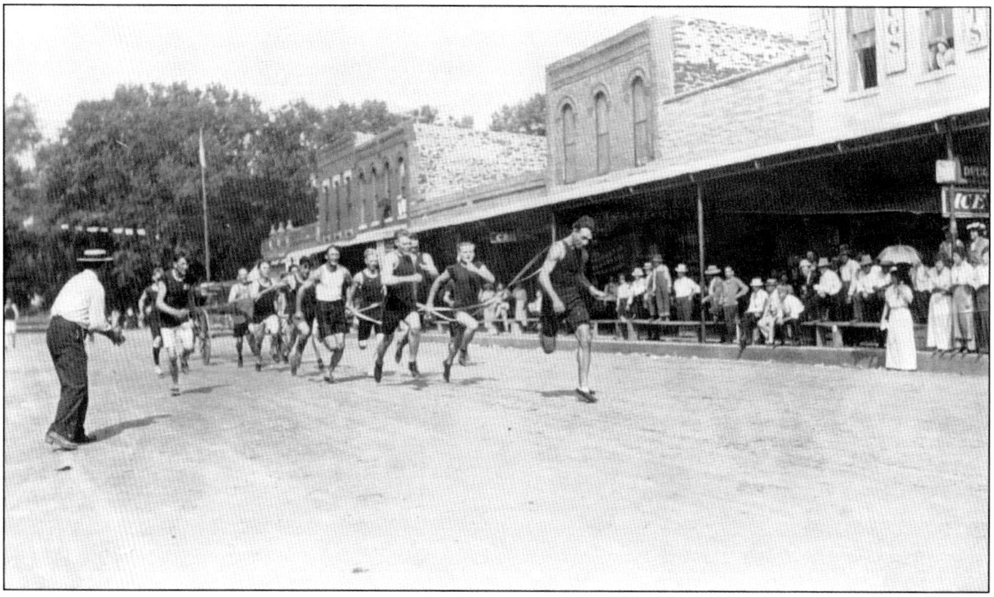

Members of the Marysville Fire Department are shown here pulling a hose cart at the Kansas State Firemen's Tournament in Ellsworth, Kansas, on June 3, 1914. The Marysville men took home the combined race trophy. Early fire wagons were pulled by the men rather than by horses because by the time horses were retrieved from livery, harnessed and attached to the wagons, it was almost invariably too late to combat a fire.

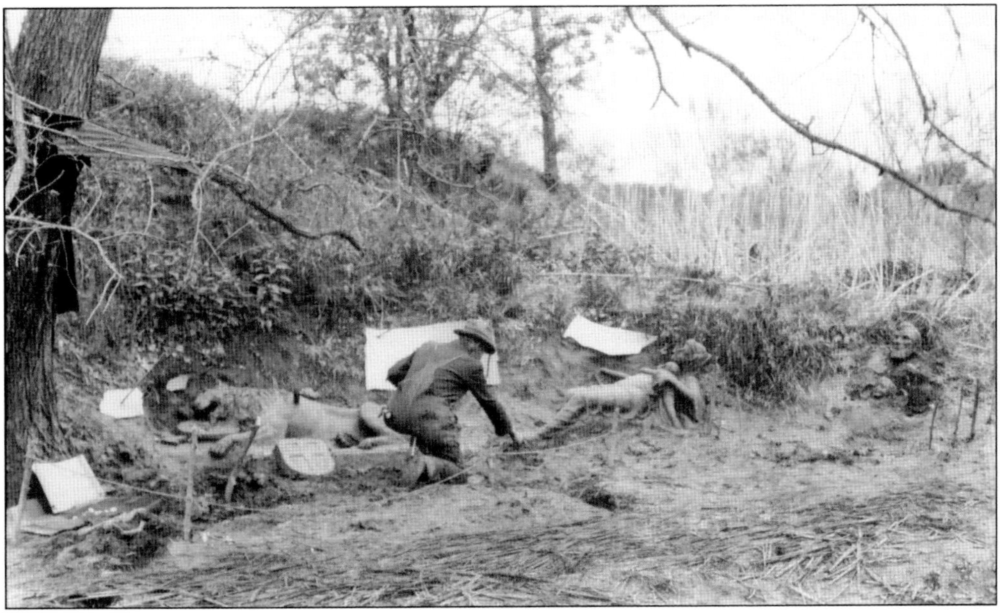

The photographer noted on this scene from April 29, 1930, "Mud sculptures on Blue River bank [Marysville] by J.B. McCord and Dan Nolan, St. Joseph [Missouri]." The sculptures appear to relate to the Civil War. The figure at left may be the *Lion of Atlanta*. The center figure is a dead woman with her arm wrapped around an infant. At the far right are a head of Abraham Lincoln and a small angel, possibly connoting his dead son Willie. (Courtesy of Dennis Richardson.)

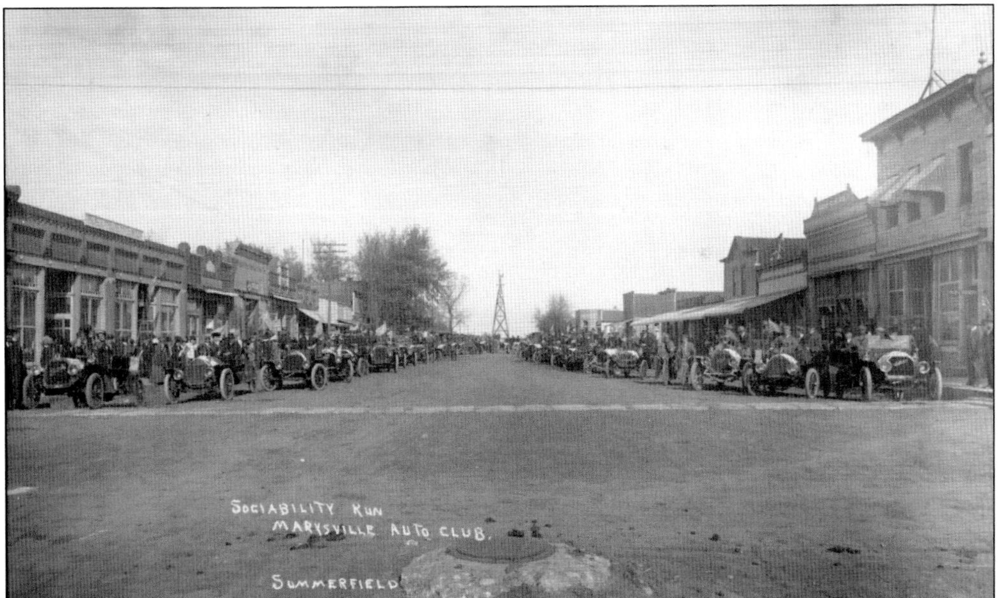


Automobiles were still a novelty in October 1909 when the Marysville Auto Club made a Sociability Run to Summerfield, a Marshall County community about 30 miles northeast of Marysville at the Nebraska state border. Given the road conditions of the era, it could have taken two to three hours to travel this distance on the country roads. A manhole is near the front edge of the photograph and the city windmill is at the end of the town's main street.

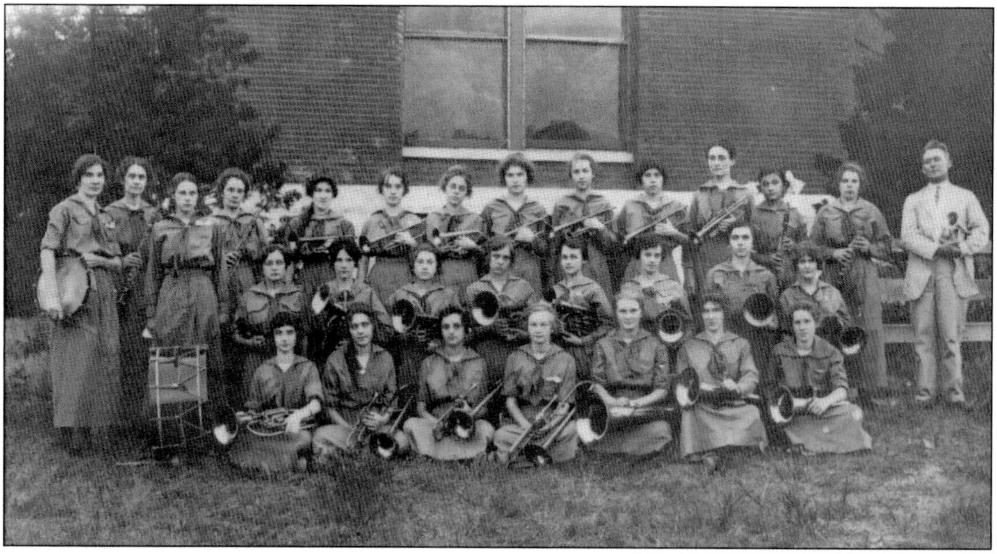

Forrest Warren, a Vermillion publisher, organized the town's all-girl band in the spring of 1914. With Warren as director and manager, the band played concerts in town and at neighboring community celebrations. It accompanied 1918 gubernatorial candidate Henry J. Allen on his swing through Marshall County.

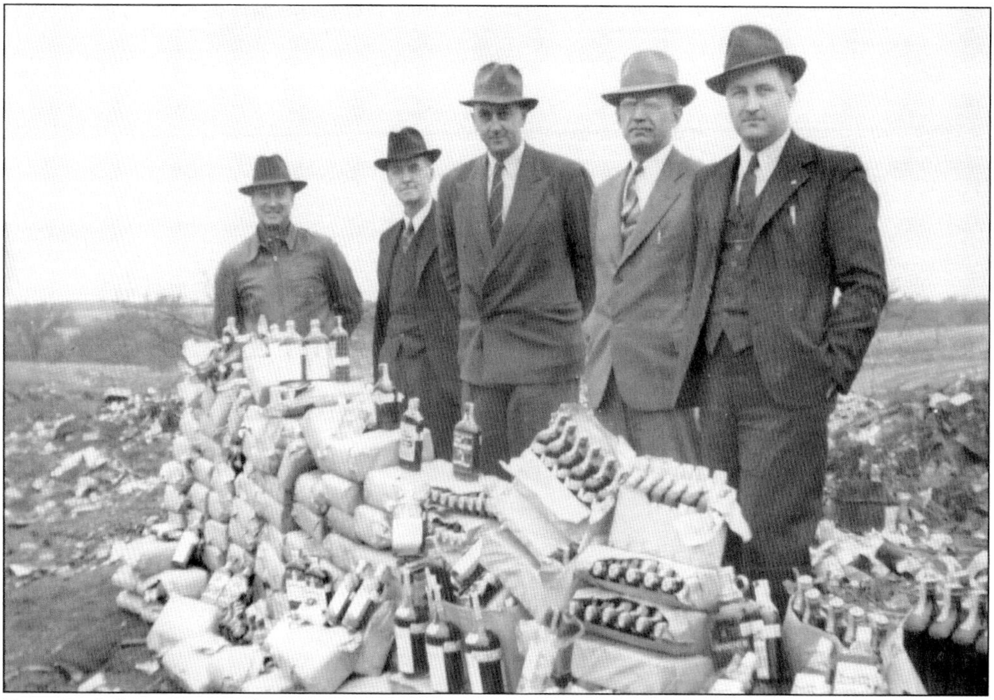

From Prohibition sprang bootlegging. Kansas was a dry state from 1881 to 1948, but it was difficult in some towns and impossible in others to enforce state liquor laws. The Eighteenth Amendment to the US Constitution, adopted in 1919, put federal law behind prohibition, but bootlegging continued. Marshall County lawmen are seen here at the Marysville city dump with confiscated liquor. Pictured, from left to right, are Howard Heleker, J. Sydney Johnson, Sheriff Harry Heleker, an unidentified man, and Judge Edgar Bennett.

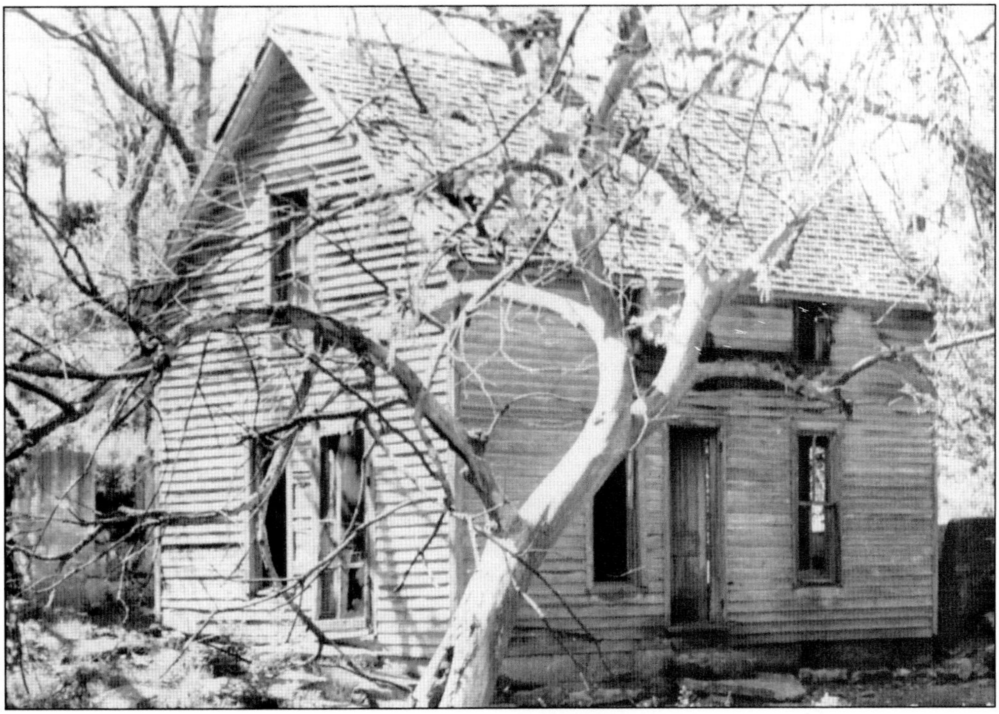

In 1898, James Dalton, cousin of the infamous Dalton Gang, and three other men escaped from the county jail, which stood where Marysville High School is now located. They hid out in this farmhouse, hidden by cliffs in a pasture known as Goodwin Holler, southwest of Marysville.

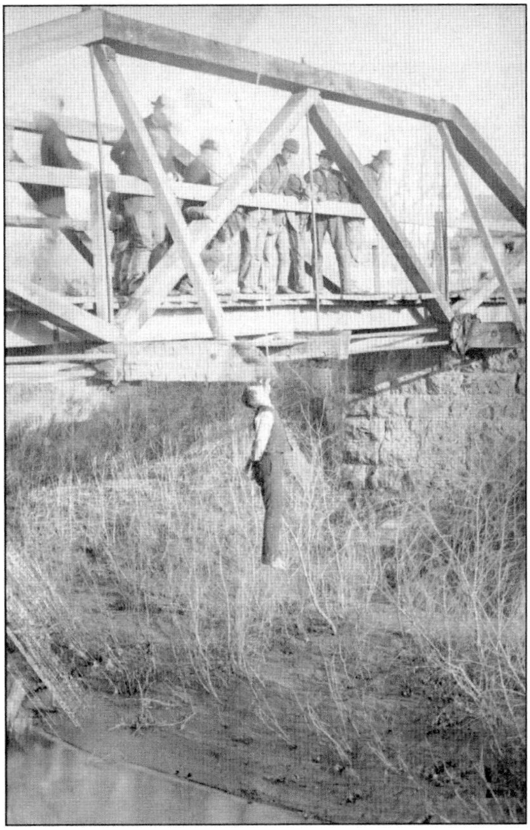

In February 1884, a Wells Township farm couple was murdered in their home. Samuel Frayer, an itinerant farmhand, was captured in Nebraska and returned to the Marshall County Courthouse to stand trial. He was found guilty and that night, while he was awaiting sentencing, a mob took him from the jail and lynched him at the Spring Creek bridge just south of Marysville.

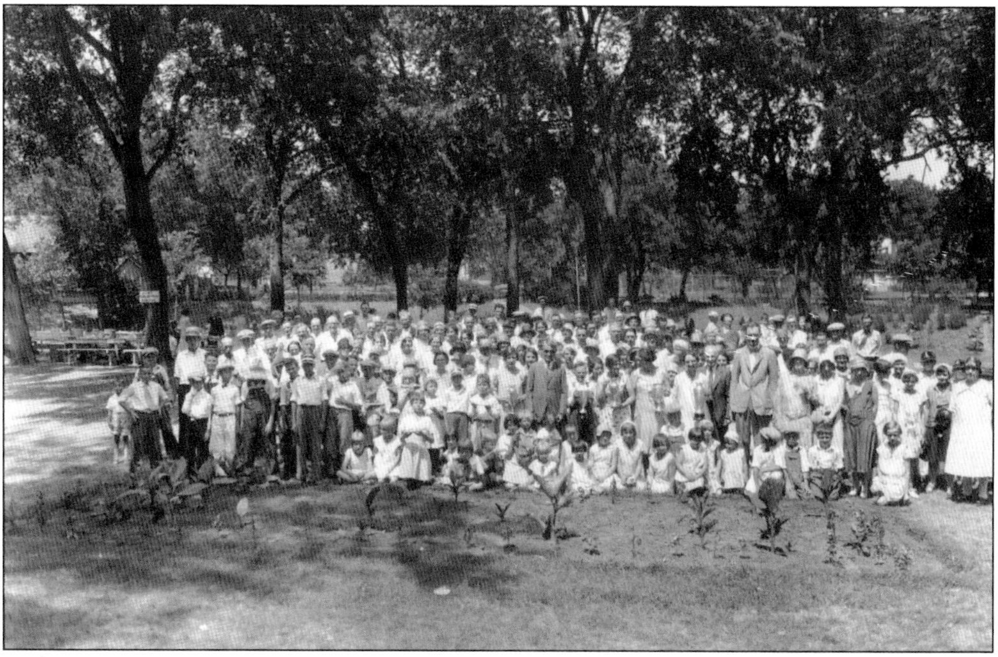

Arthur Capper was governor of Kansas from 1915 to 1919 and a five-term senator from 1919 to 1949. He created Capper clubs to support agricultural youth. On August 2, 1930, Senator Capper delivered an address at a picnic sponsored by Capper and 4-H club members of Marshall County.

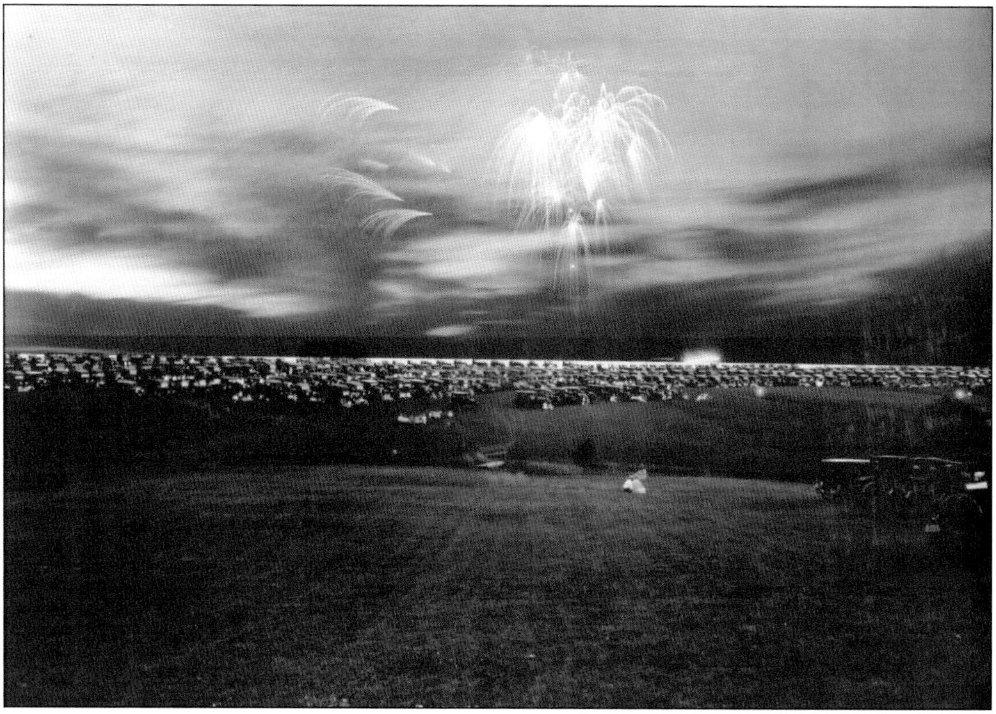

The county often celebrated Independence Day with parades and picnics, and communities held fireworks displays to cap the day. Here, a display lights the night sky on July 4, 1927, at the new Marysville Country Club.

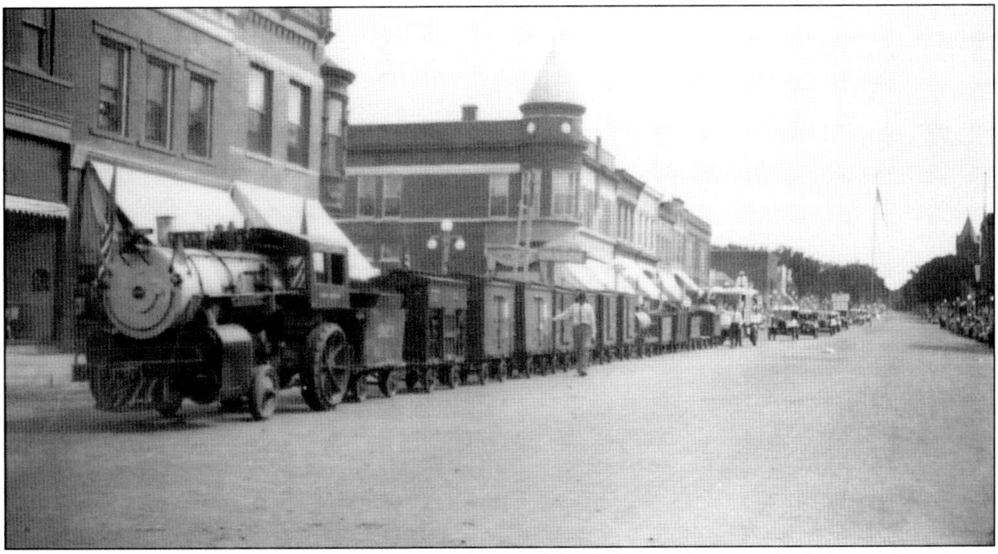

This parade train, built in 1923, was one of several built by workers at the Marysville Union Pacific train yards. It is leading a parade in 1925 westbound on the 800 block of Broadway. The flag erected in the center of the street at Tenth Street and Broadway is visible in the distance. One of the float entries following the train is a truck with a small house on the flatbed. Two men, either employees or retirees, are in rockers on the house porch. A banner on the truck reads, "Contented Employees of the Union Pacific."

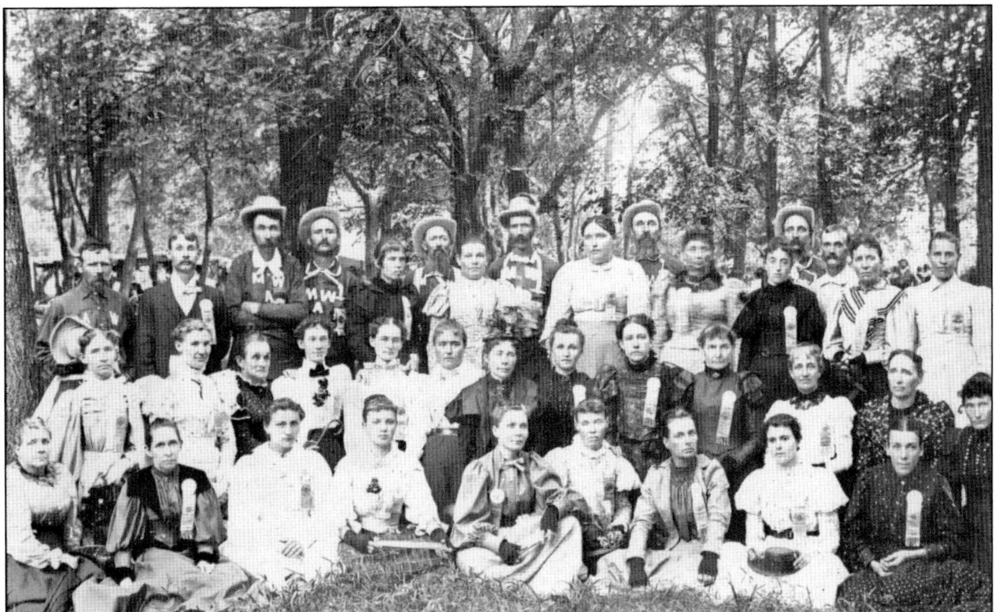

The Waterville chapters of Royal Neighbors of America and Modern Woodmen of America are holding their summer picnic at the city park in 1900. By 1911, there were 11 fraternal organizations in Waterville: Masons, Order of Eastern Star, Independent Order of Odd Fellows, Rebekahs, Modern Woodmen of America, Royal Neighbors of America, Triple Tie Benefit Society, Grand Army of the Republic, Women's Relief Corps, Ancient Order of United Workers, and the Knights and Ladies of Security.

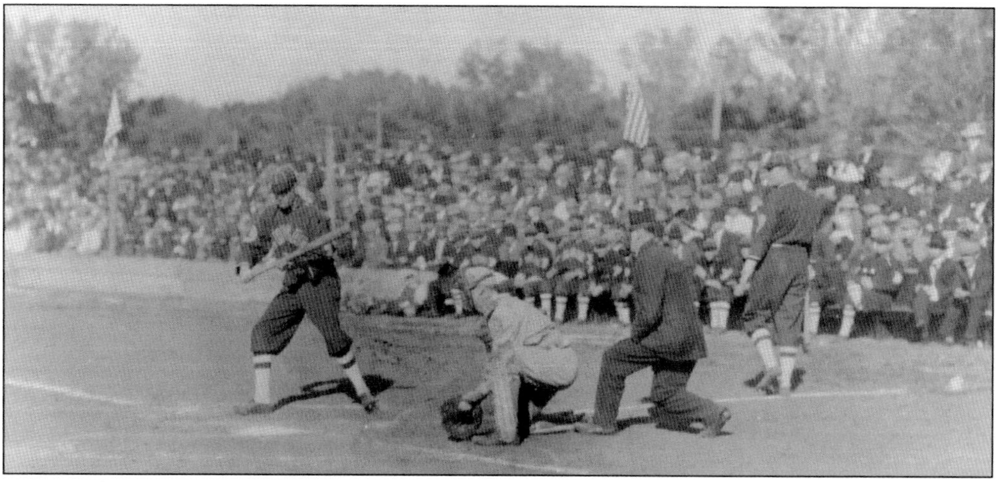

In 1910, the population of Blue Rapids was a little over 1,700 people. On October 24, 1913, more than 3,000 people crowded around the ball diamond at the city park to see the Major League Baseball game between the New York Giants and the Chicago White Sox. Jim Thorpe and Christy Mathewson were among the players. With no outfield fence, automobiles were used to mark the end of the field. Blue Rapids was the smallest town the teams played in during their 46-game world tour, and it has the only one of those baseball fields still in existence.

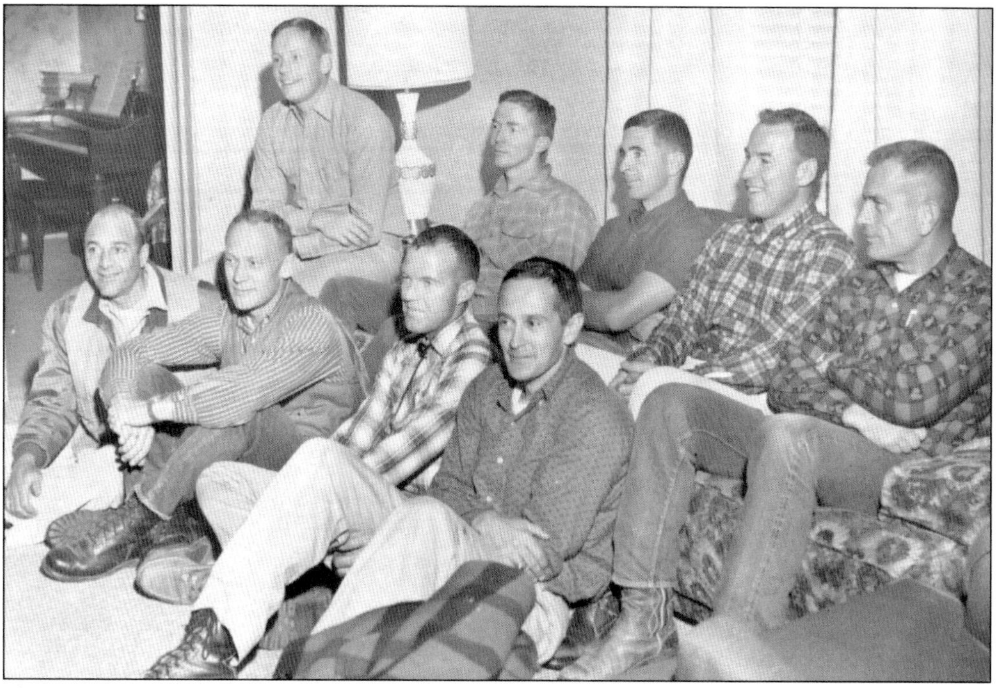

Eleven of NASA's early astronauts visited Marshall County in November 1967 to hunt quail on the farm of Dan Horigan, north of Frankfort. Nine of the astronauts are shown here relaxing in Horigan's home. They are, from left to right, (front row) Lt. Comdr. Ron Evans, Lt. Col. Edwin E. "Buzz" Aldrin Jr., Col. Gordon Cooper, and Charles Duke; (back row) Neil Armstrong, Maj. Stuart Rossa, Maj. William Anders, Capt. James Lovell, and D.K. Slayton. Air Force colonel Frank Borman and Air Force lieutenant colonel Michael Collins left for Topeka before the picture was taken.

# *Seven*

# School Days

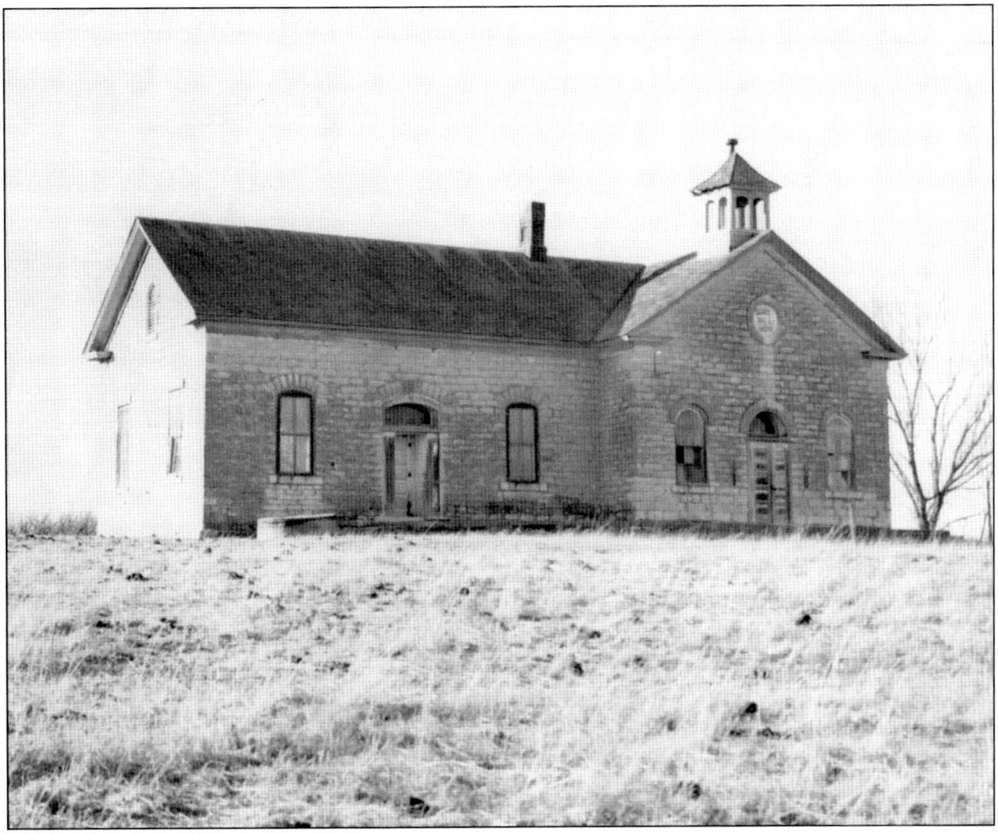

Barrett School, District 1, established in 1858, was the first school district in Marshall County. The original frame schoolhouse was replaced in 1870 by the right section of the stone building pictured here. The longer wing on the left was added in 1896. Elizabeth Mohrbacher of Marysville, the county's first paid teacher, rode horseback 21 miles to Barrett and boarded with a local family during the school week. The school closed in 1959. Known as Plains vernacular architectural style, this building was listed in the National Register of Historic Places in 1972.

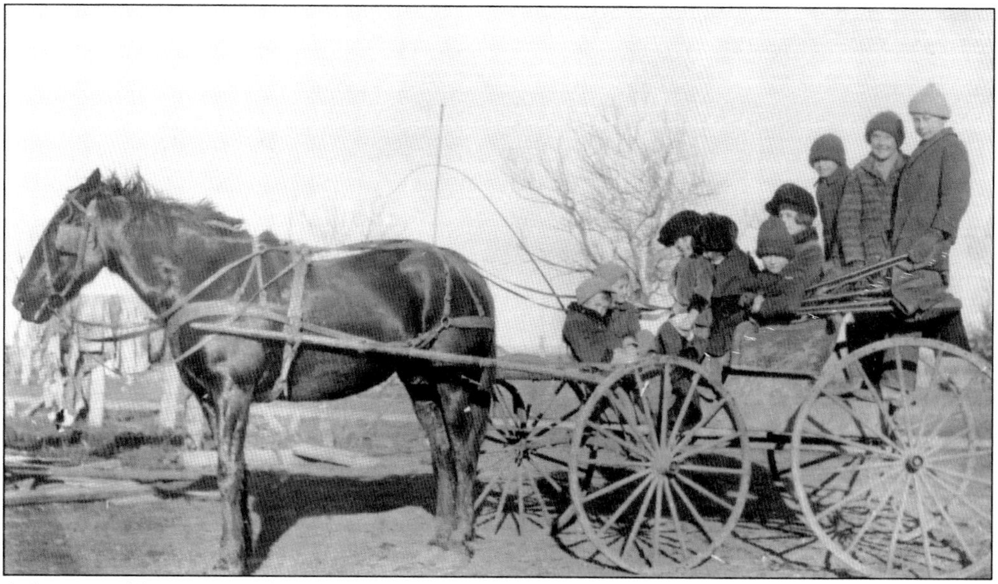

A horse and buggy was often the most practical way to transport students to the rural schools in the early 1920s, when this photograph was taken. These nine students are probably in the Cunningham school district, northwest of Marysville.

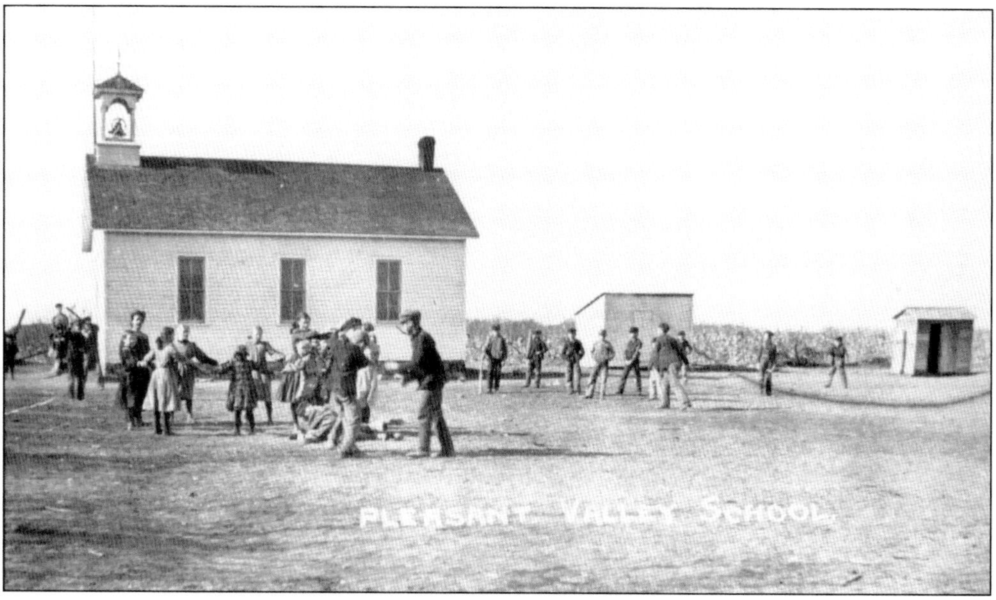


Recess was just as anticipated in early rural schools as it is today. Children are playing in the school yard at Pleasant Valley, District 49, in about 1910. The outhouse is the small building at the right edge. Between the outhouse and the school is the coal and cob house where fuel was kept for the classroom stove.

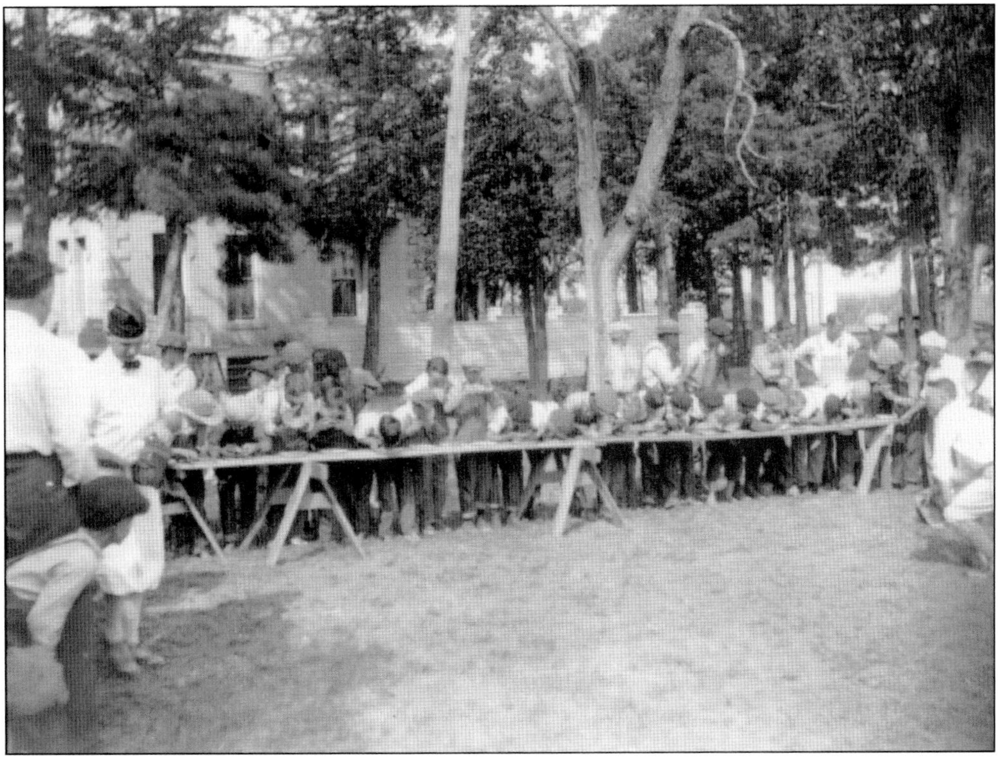

The boys in this August 1924 photograph are having a watermelon-eating contest during the annual back-to-school picnic that was held by the local Rotary Club for Marysville public school boys. This event was held at the old Marysville Country Club (originally the Perry Hutchinson house), northwest of town on US 77.

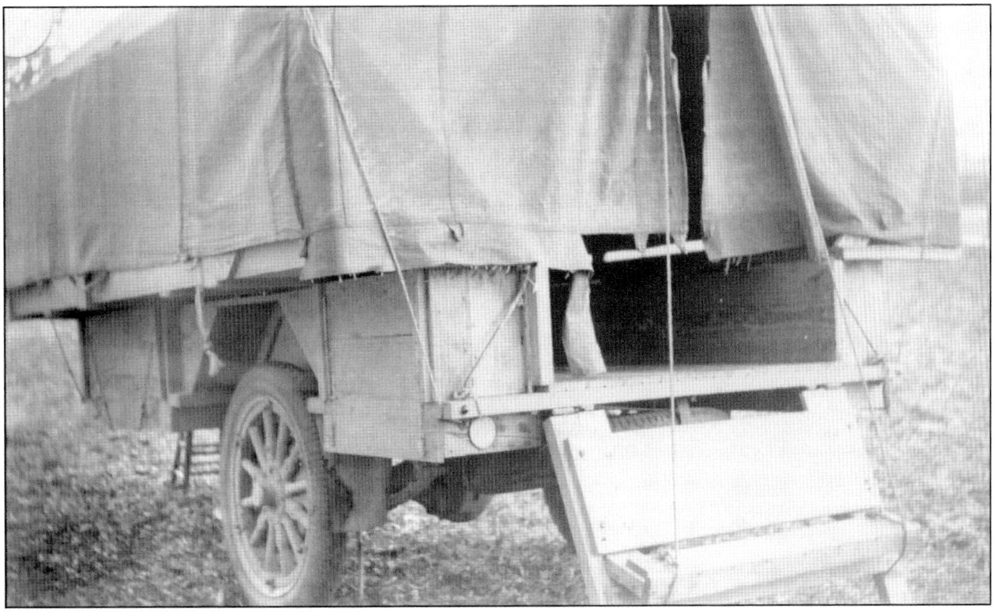

In the 1930s, music received heavy emphasis in Irving schools. This is the trailer that Supt. D. Donald Plumb used to transport both students and instruments to various festivals and contests.

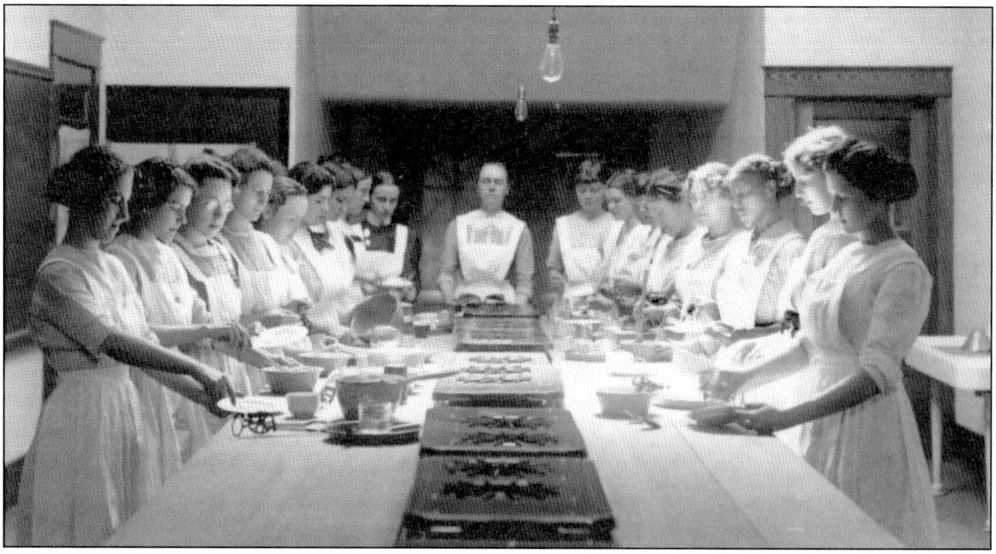

The girls in this 1912 home economics class at Frankfort High School would have studied the traditional home skills of the times: cooking, home management, and sewing. This school opened in 1903 with elementary classes on the first floor and high school on the second. In 1923, the high school moved to a new building and this became solely an elementary school until it closed in 1997. The building was listed in the National Register of Historic Places in 1972.

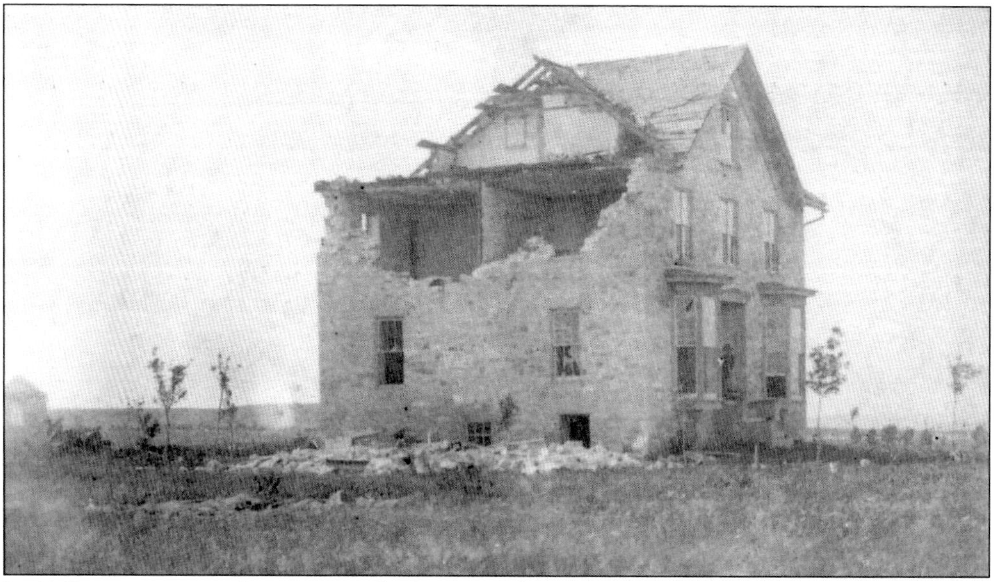

In 1862, twenty acres of prairie outside the town of Irving were purchased by three New Yorkers, and the dream of Wetmore Institute began. A building of locally quarried limestone and larger than its original three-story, 30-foot-by-40-foot plan was constructed about 1863. It was intended to be an exclusive academy to train young women to be teachers. Unfortunately, local families could not afford this school. Although records are sketchy, the school eventually became a boarding school, and apparently no classes were offered after the 1876–1877 school year. The school was sold at a sheriff's auction in August 1877. This dramatic photograph was one of a stereograph series shot in Irving after the tornadoes of May 30, 1879. To add further insult to this dream, the building suffered a massive fire in 1880. It was abandoned and the dream was over.

Between 1893 and 1904, John G. Ellenbecker of Marysville rented an 1866 stone school building attached to the high school for his Modern Normal College, a place to train young men and women who wished to teach. More than 300 students trained here during that time, and some of the graduates taught in the county's rural and town schools.

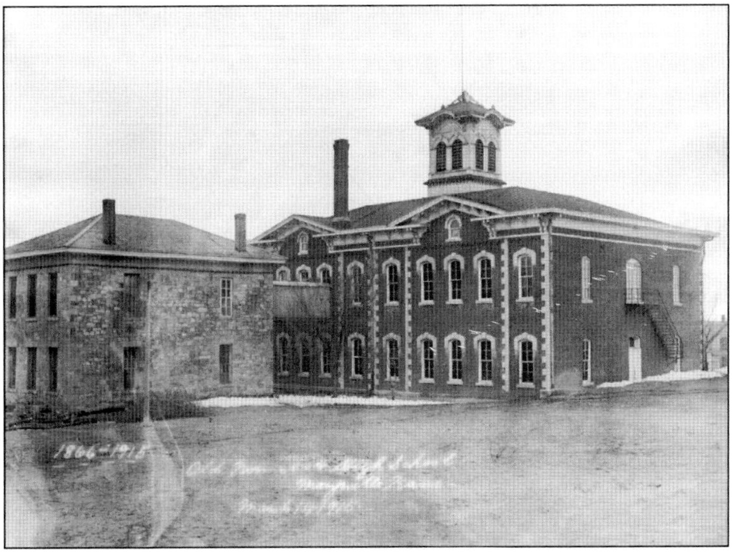


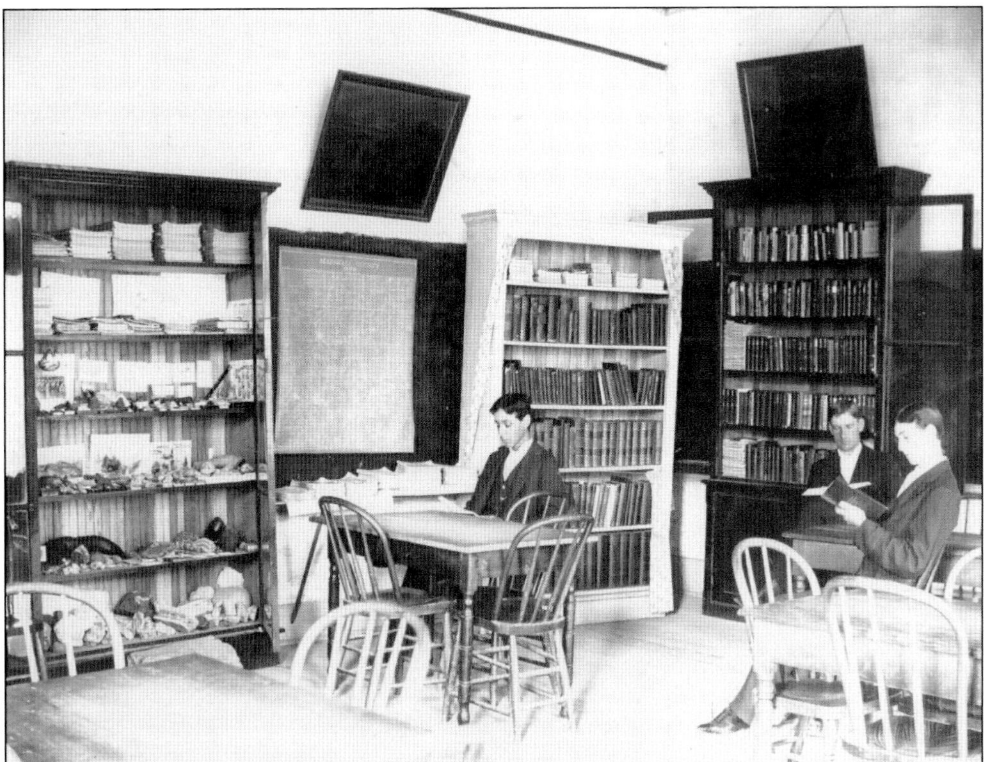

The Modern Normal College library in Marysville provided the usual quiet study space for students training to be teachers. In addition to books, the shelves hold artifacts and geological specimens, possibly to serve as teaching aids. An 1893 plat map of Marshall County hangs on the wall. These early teachers' colleges were designed to establish teaching standards, or "norms," both for what teachers learned and also for how they taught their students.

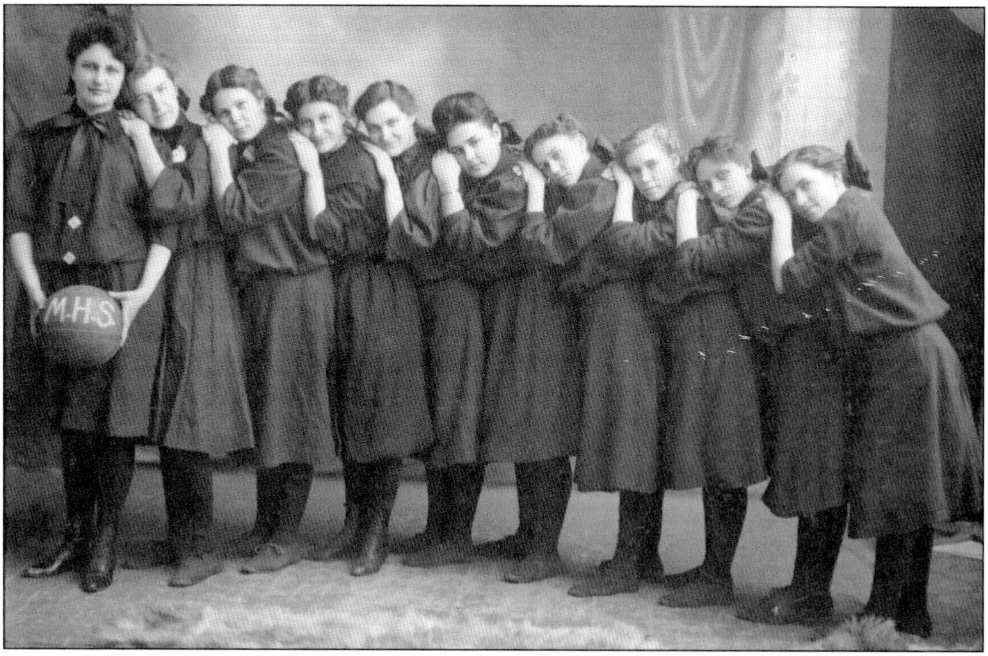


This is Marysville's first girls' basketball squad. Formed in 1905, it played two games in late December of that year, one in Barnes and the other in Irving. The team lost both games, but an article in the January 6, 1906, *Marysville Advocate-Democrat* reports that the girls had "a jolly time and say they were treated royally at each place."

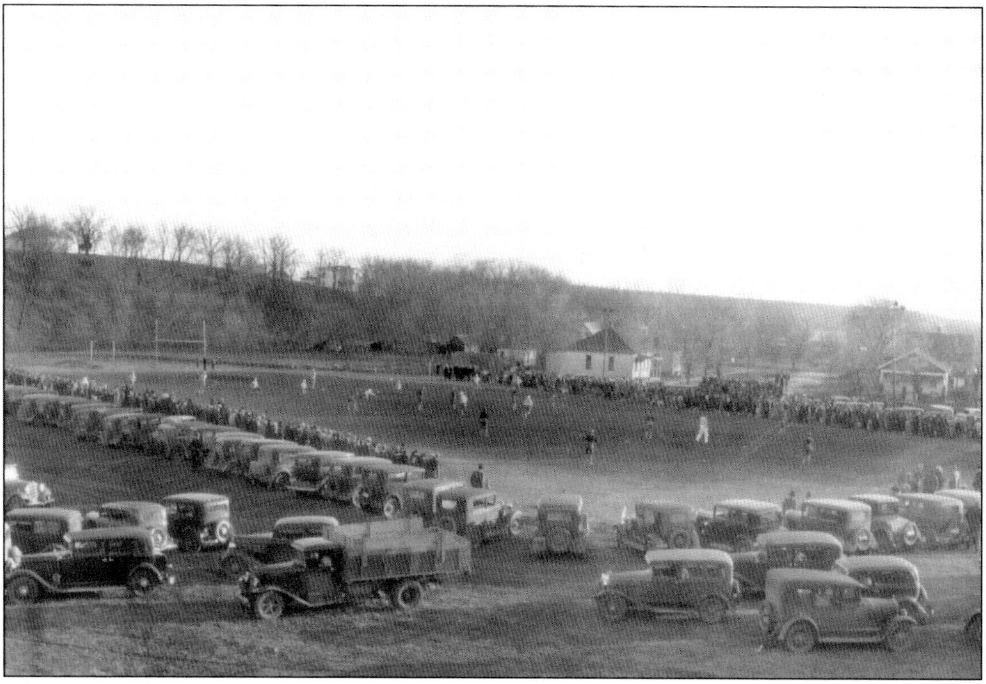

The annual Thanksgiving Day football game between Marysville and Waterville always attracted a large crowd. The teams alternated fields, and the game seen here is being played in Waterville on November 27, 1930.

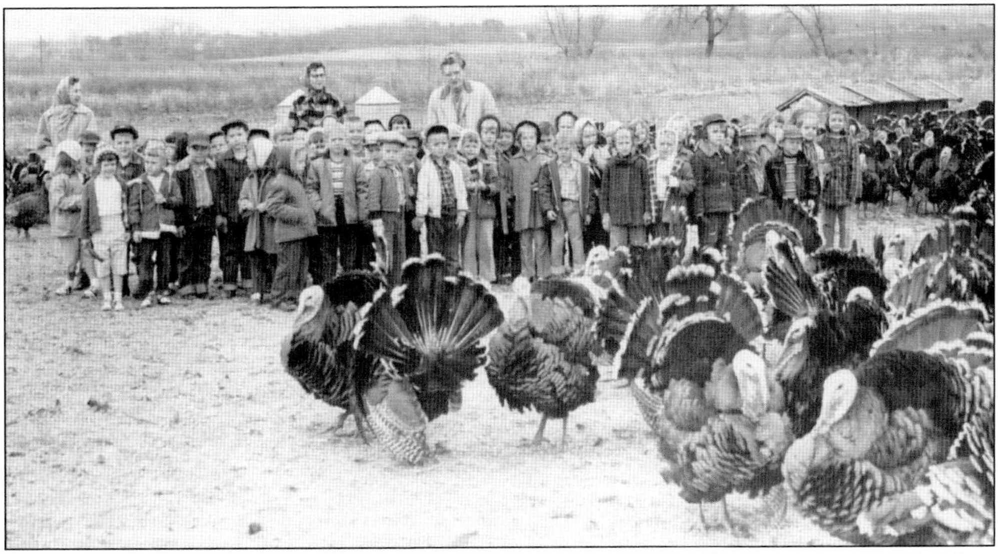

Fifty-four kindergarteners from Central Grade School in Marysville are visiting Lake's Silver Dollar turkey farm north of Marysville just before Thanksgiving in November 1958.

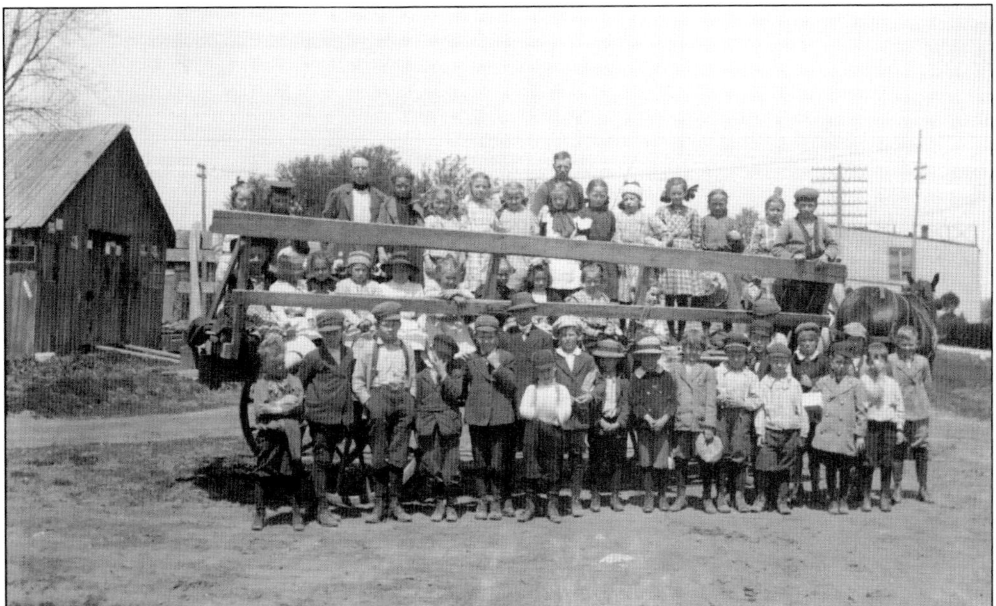

Teacher Augusta Carlson (third from left, back row) and her primary room students at Irving School pose for this photograph on April 21, 1911, at the beginning of their end-of-the-year celebration, which included a hay-rack ride to Bigelow and back. This trip of about four miles over country roads would have taken about two hours each direction.

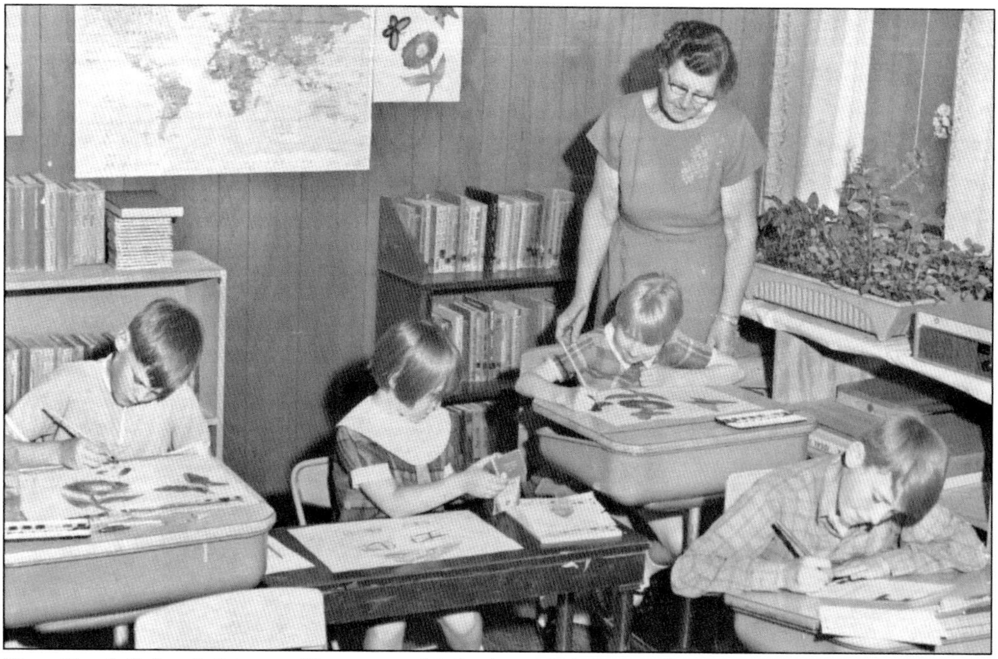

Deer Creek School, District 58, was established in 1882. Funerals were occasionally held at the school in the morning, and classes would resume in the afternoon. It was the last rural school open in the county. Marie Janssen Conard is shown here with her students on the school's last day. The students are, from left to right, Stuart Breeding, JoNell Breeding, Deneise Ehnen, and Brian Breeding. When Deer Creek closed in 1969, the era of the rural school in Marshall County was over.

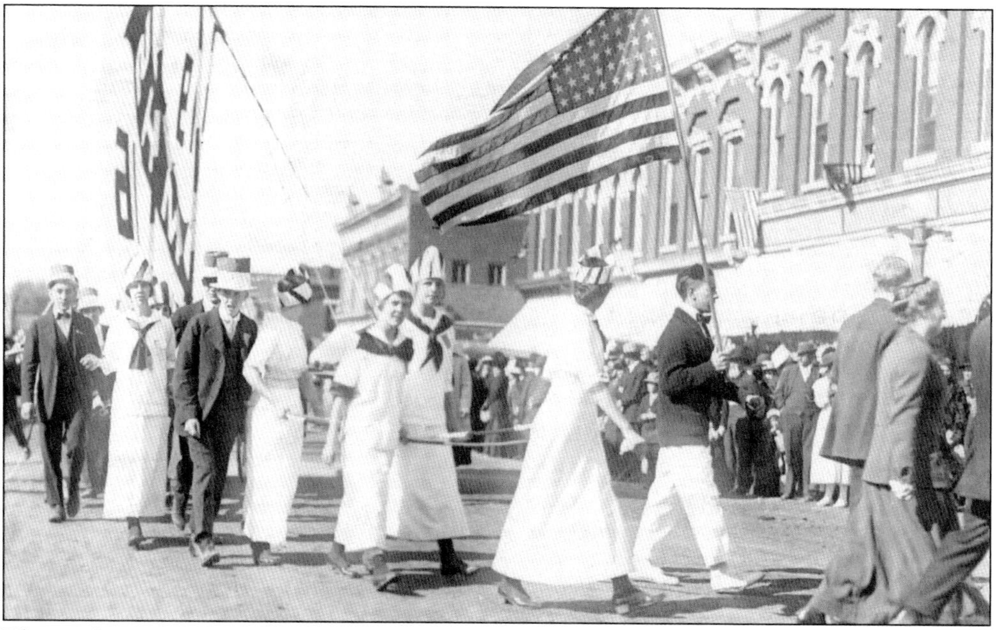

The graduating seniors of the Marysville High School class of 1916 are parading downtown. Although this tradition is a thing of the past, students now parade on Broadway before the prom each spring.

*Eight*

# THAT OLD-TIME RELIGION

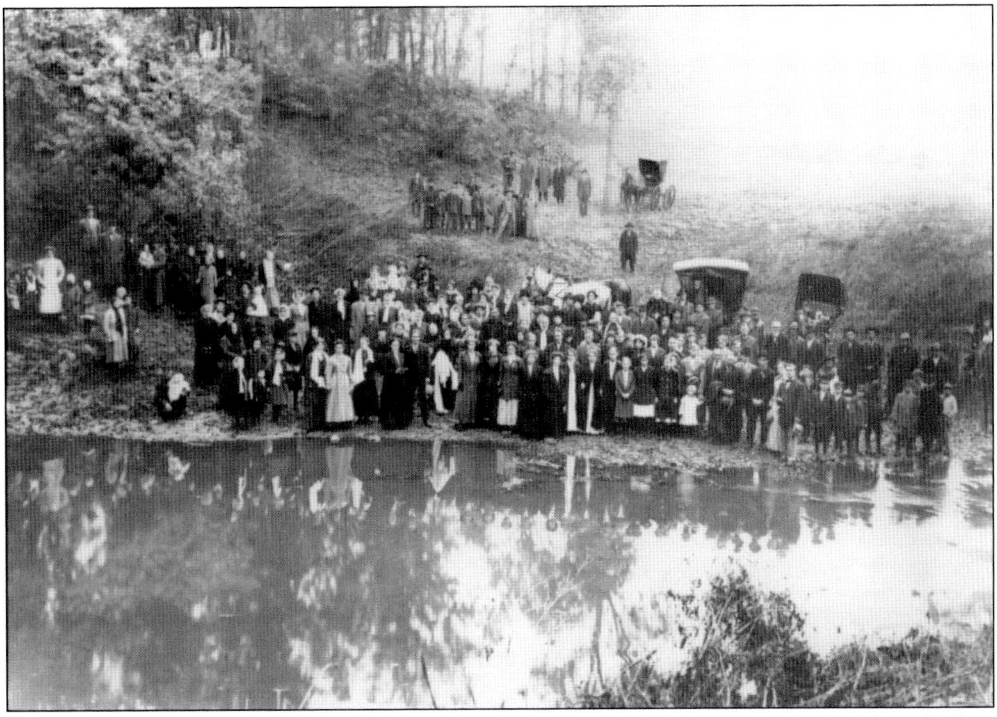

Immersion baptisms in Marshall County rivers, creeks, and ponds were not unusual in the late 1800s. The Bigelow Christian Church used a swimming hole in the Black Vermillion River west of town. People are shown here preparing for a baptism, probably of the woman in white in the first row.

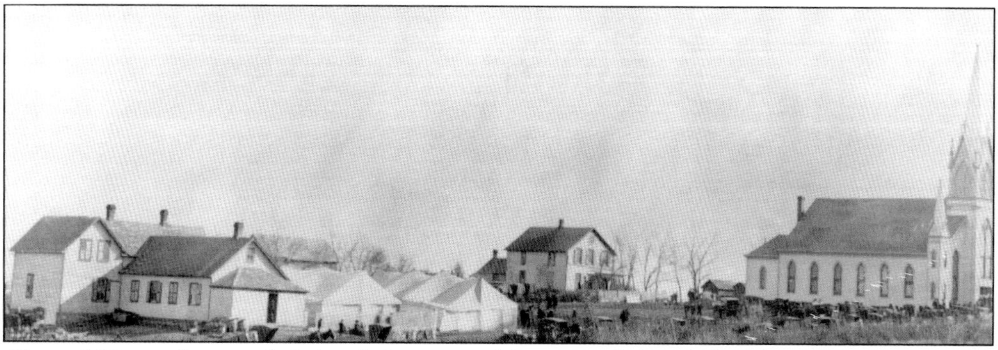

About 800 people attended the dedication of the second church building for Hermansberg Immanuel Lutheran Church, near Bremen, in November 1901. Pictured, from right to left, are the new church, the parsonage, tents for feeding the crowd, a barn behind the tents, and the school with an attached house for the teacher. Known as the teacherage, such housing was a rare luxury in the early days of rural schools.

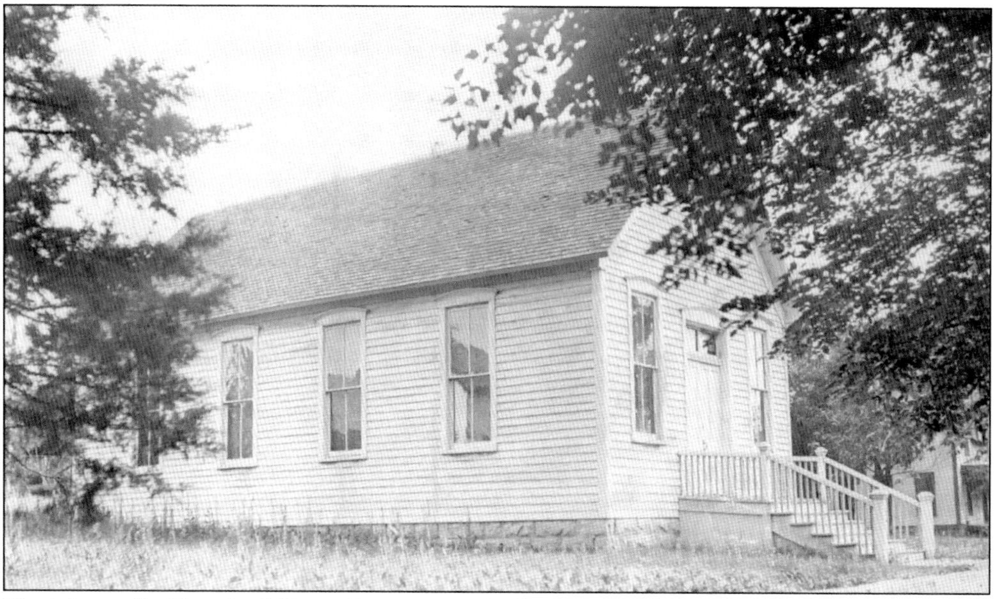

The Marysville Church of Christ, Scientist was built in 1893 at the northwest corner of Broadway at Fourteenth Street. It was said to be the second Christian Science church built in the world. A newer building was constructed on same site in 1923 and used until 1979. It was later used as the Berean Church and is now privately owned.

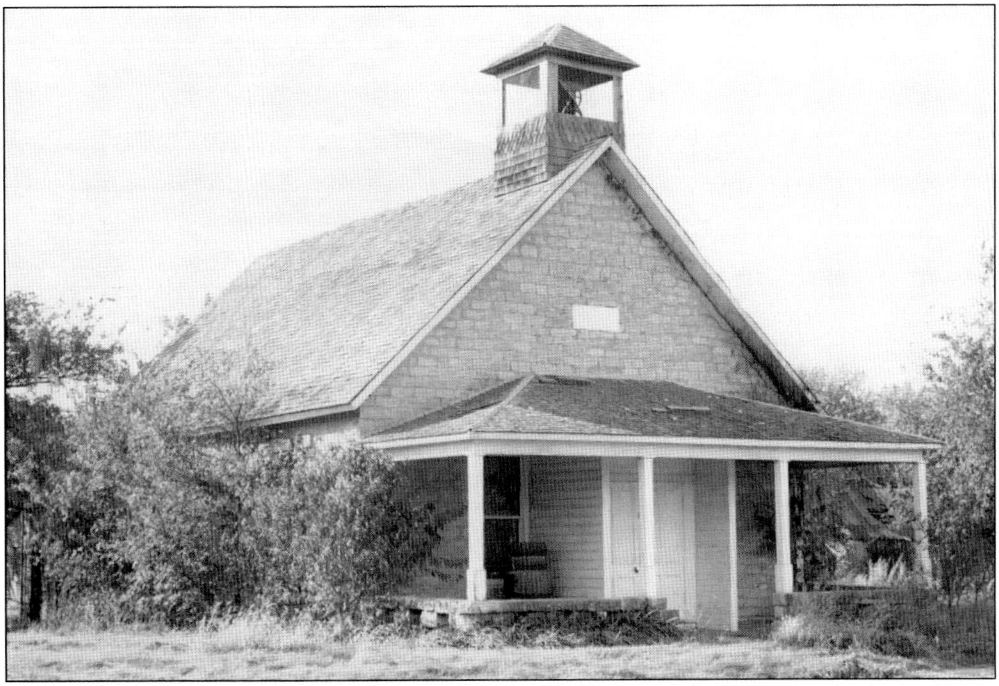

Bigelow Christian Church was the first Christian church in Marshall County. Built in 1884, it had a faithful congregation until imminent construction of the Tuttle Creek Dam forced the abandonment of the town. The final church service was held on Christmas Eve 1959.

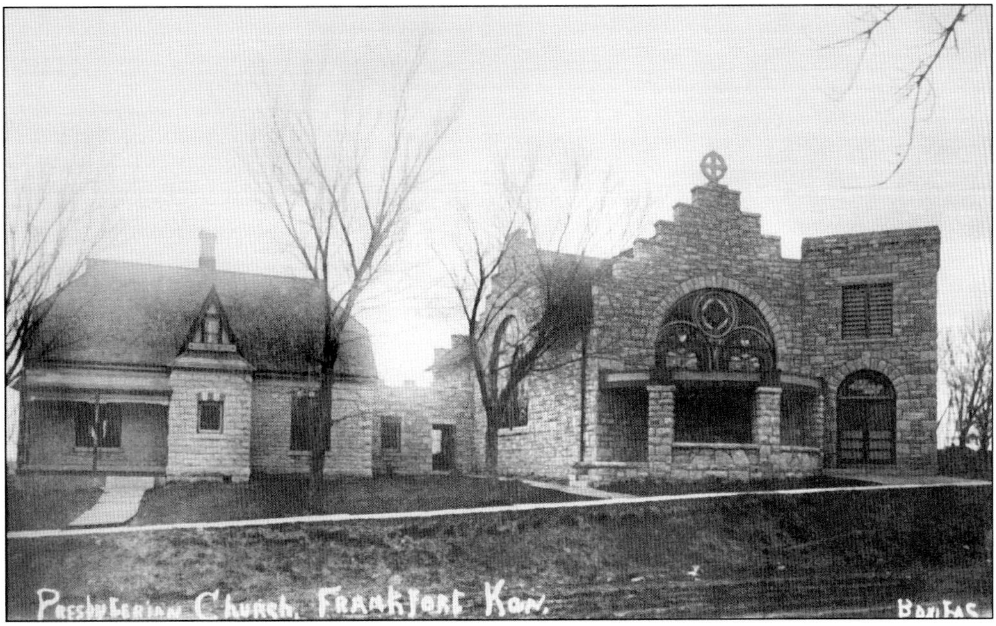


A Presbyterian congregation was formed in Frankfort in 1870 and the first church built in 1874. At the time of organization, there were 150 people in town. Since the Presbyterian was the first church, it held "union services," ecumenical services welcoming parishioners of all faiths. The church in the photograph was begun in 1903 and dedicated in 1904. According to carefully kept records, the cost of the church was $6,153.11.

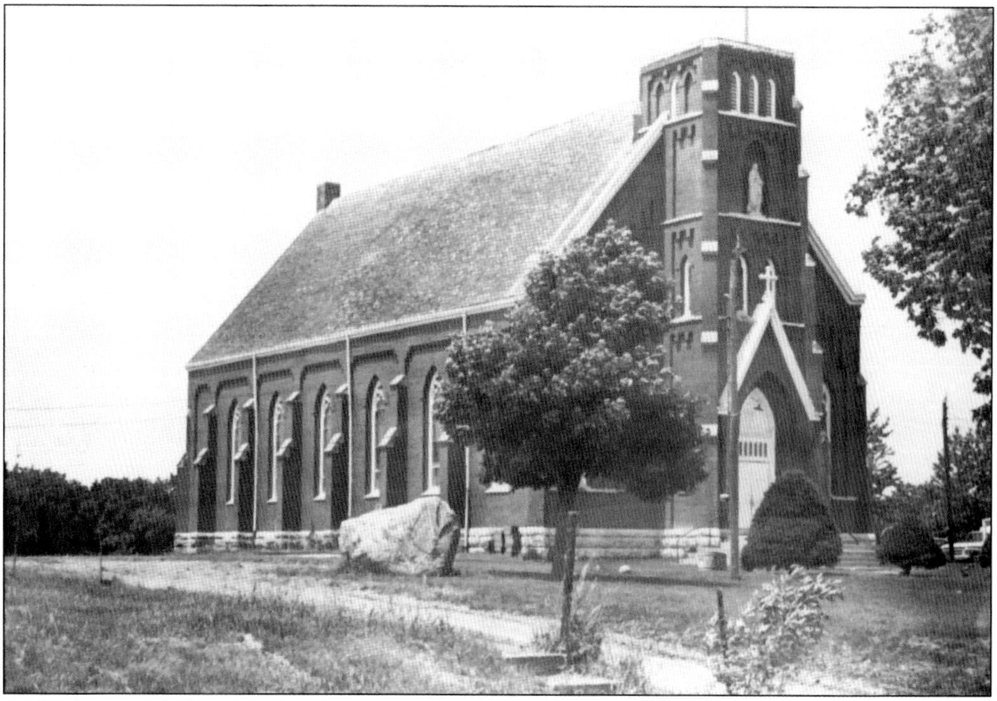

St. Bridget's Catholic Church is located in the country about six miles north of Axtell. A log church was built for this parish in 1862. This brick church, constructed between 1902 and 1908, was the fifth church built for the growing community. Between 1922 and 1932, the church sponsored a rodeo each August. The rodeo was started by the Reverend Jerome Twomey, an amateur Golden Gloves boxer and experienced horseman. The rodeo was the highlight of the season and featured horse races, baseball, band concerts, boxing and wrestling, a chicken supper, and a dance. The church was closed in 1967 and placed in the National Register of Historic Places in 1996.

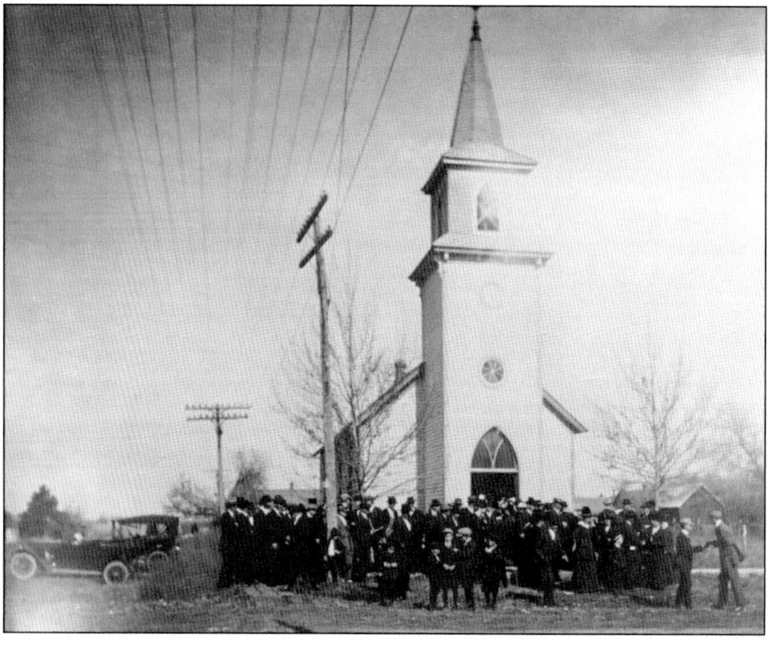

The Friedens Lutheran Church in Home City was built in 1885. The steeple, atop the church in this view around 1910, was added in about 1905. The church closed in 2010. It was remodeled, painted red, and became a gift shop in 2013.

The Czech Presbyterian Church was located southwest of Blue Rapids on the northwest corner of Cyclone Road and Eighth Road. The congregation was organized in September 1893 and its first church was nearly complete when it was struck by lightning and burned in May 1894. The members rebuilt the following year and then constructed a larger church in 1905 to accommodate the growing congregation. The last services were held in 1973 and the church was razed later in the 1970s.

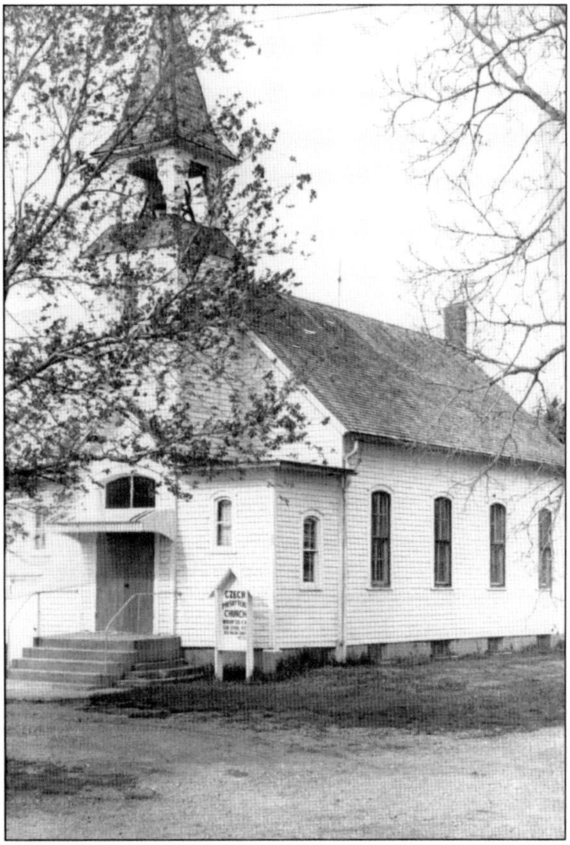


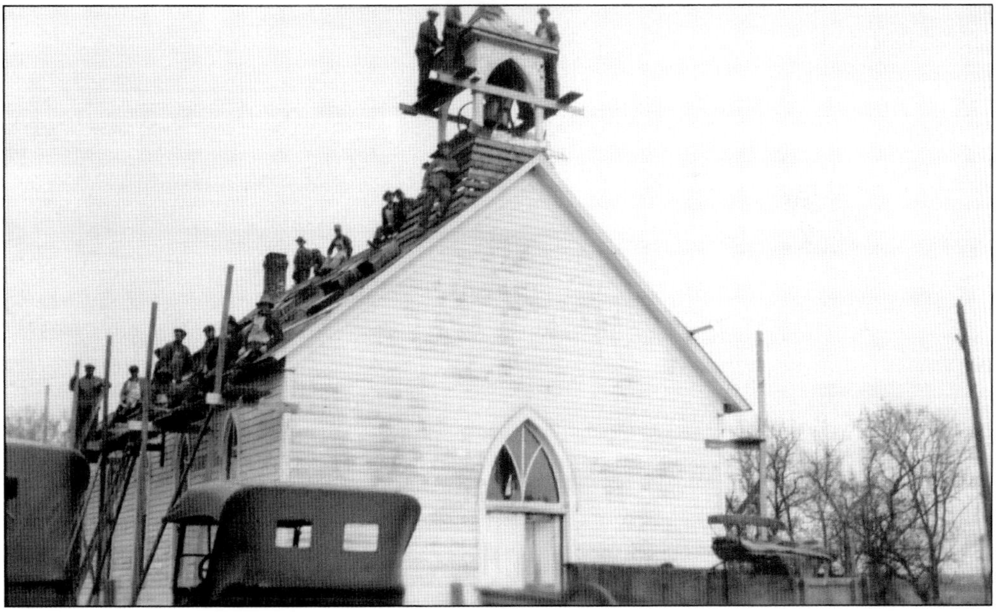

Built in 1902, North Elm Christian Church was located about three miles east of Marietta. In this 1926 photograph, workmen are beginning work on the east wing addition. The church closed in 1964 and the building was razed in 1965.

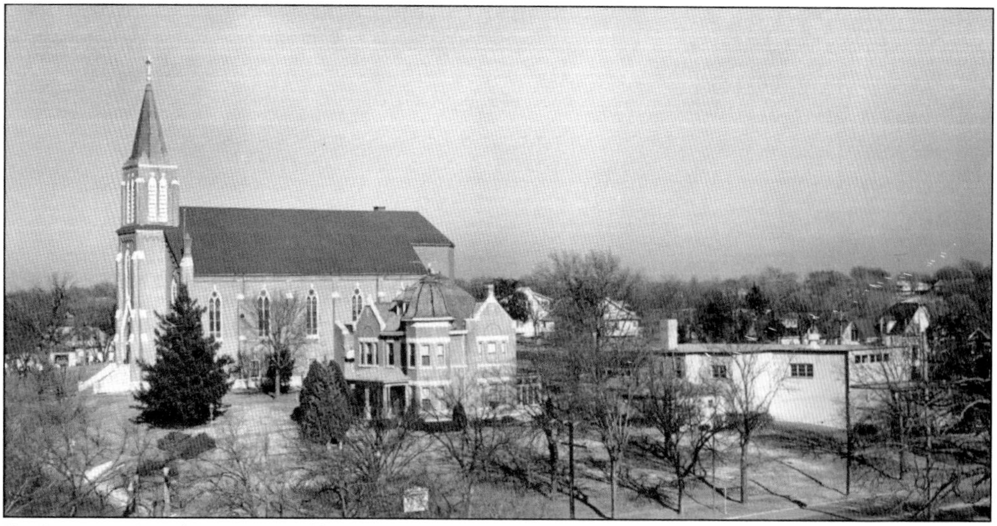

St. Gregory's Parish in Marysville was organized in 1861. Catholics began holding services in homes and buildings around town until a church was built. Land was donated and a cornerstone laid in 1886 for the building shown here. As the building progressed, services were held in the basement until the church was completed in 1894. The rectory, built in 1898, is seen in the center. A new school building, seen at right, was built in 1951. The lovely landmark church was demolished in July 1976 after construction of a new church in 1975. The rectory was razed in 2000 following a fire in December 1999.

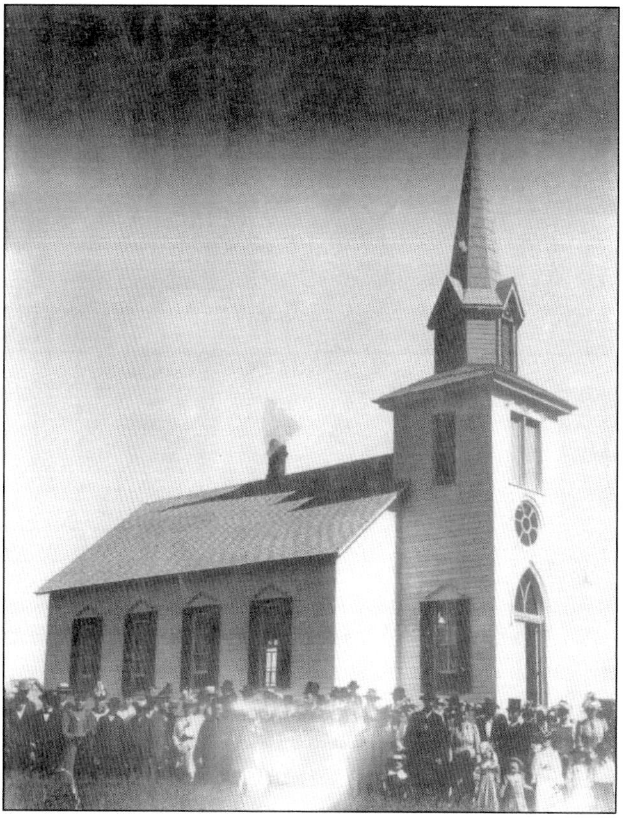

Gloria Dei Swedish Lutheran Church was organized in 1871, and members built their church in Cottage Hill Township in 1887. The church's cemetery is one of four in this small township. After being known as Gloria Dei Evangelical Lutheran Church of Waterville for 70 years, the name was changed in 1941 to Cottage Hill Evangelical Lutheran Church. In 1947, the church had 36 confirmed members and 12 children and still held one service in Swedish each month. The church closed in 1950 and was razed a year later.

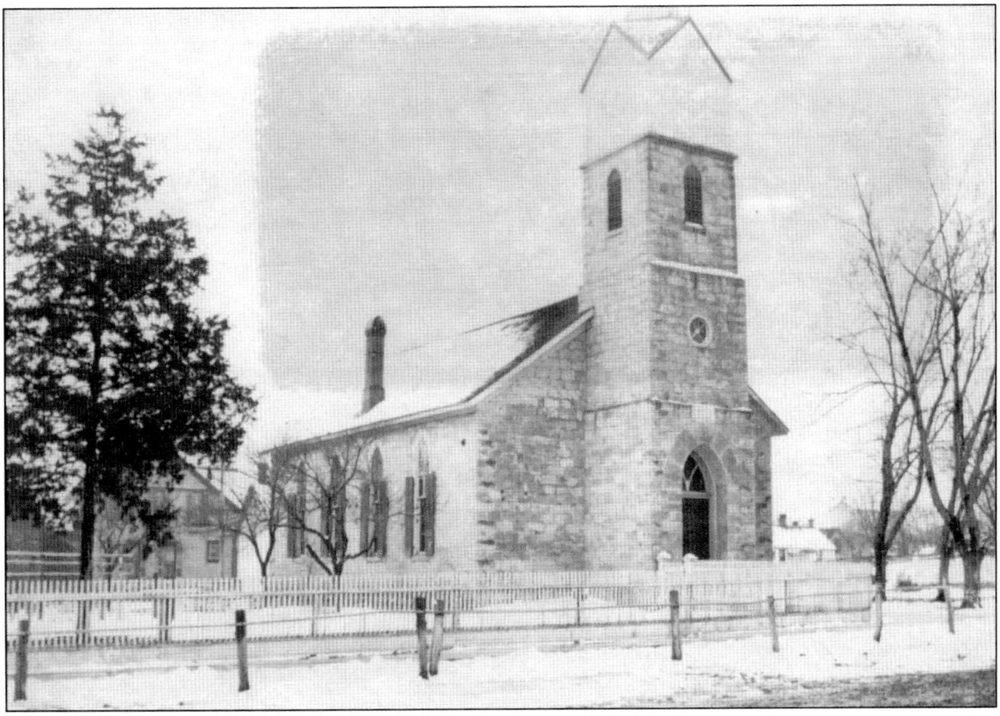

Marysville German Evangelical Church was founded in 1868. The lot on which the church stands, as well as a small frame building first used for services, were given to the congregation for the sum of 1¢ by local banker Charles F. Koester. This stone and brick church was built in 1874. The current brick building was erected in 1927. After several name changes, it is now the Evangelical United Church of Christ. As recently as the 1940s, some services were still conducted in German.

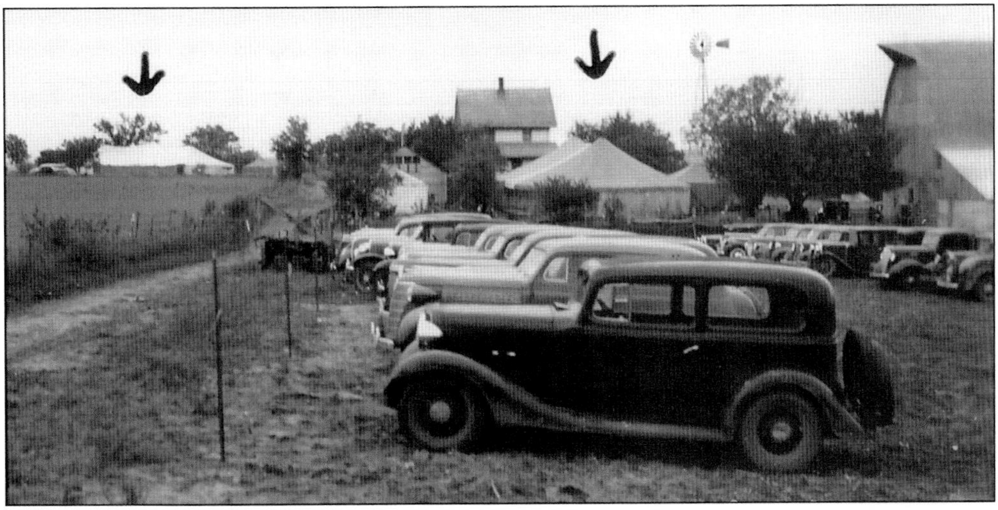

An annual nondenominational Christian fellowship convention has been held at the Grant Griffee farmstead southwest of Marysville each summer since 1941. The tents indicated by arrows in this 1940s photograph have been replaced by metal buildings. A nondenominational service was held in the large tent at left and meals were served in the tent at right. Several hundred people from Kansas and elsewhere in the Midwest crowded into the meeting tent for three meetings each day.

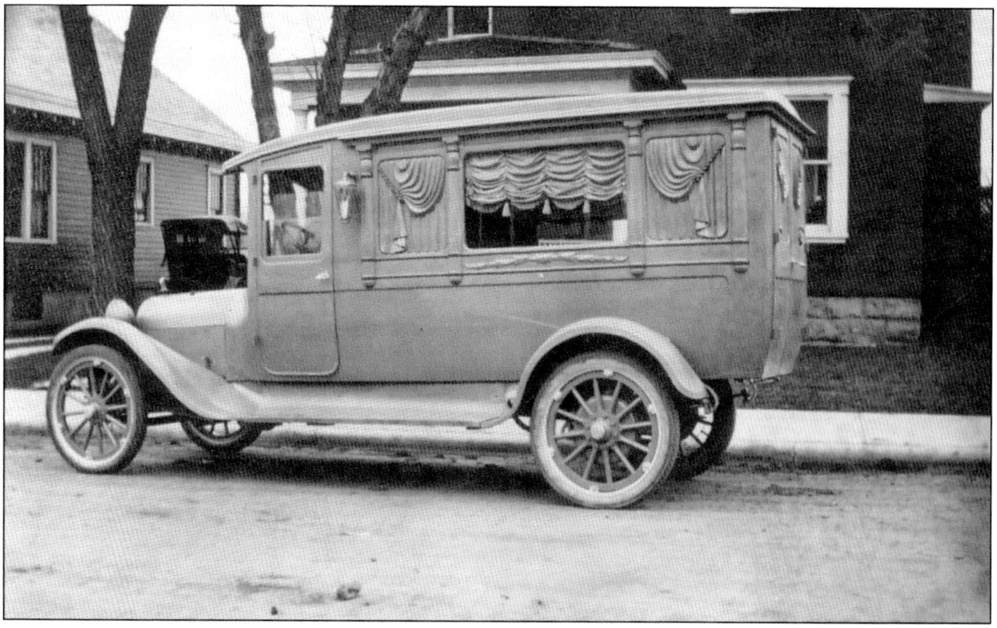

Born in Germany in 1857, William Kersten was the son and grandson of wagonmakers. He learned from them how to craft wagons by cutting the trees and then shaping the wood to form the wagon. He started a wagon shop in Marysville in 1889. As horses gave way to gasoline engines, Kersten built trucks, delivery vans, school buses, and hearses, including the one seen here. After his death, his sons maintained the shop until the last of them died in 1970.

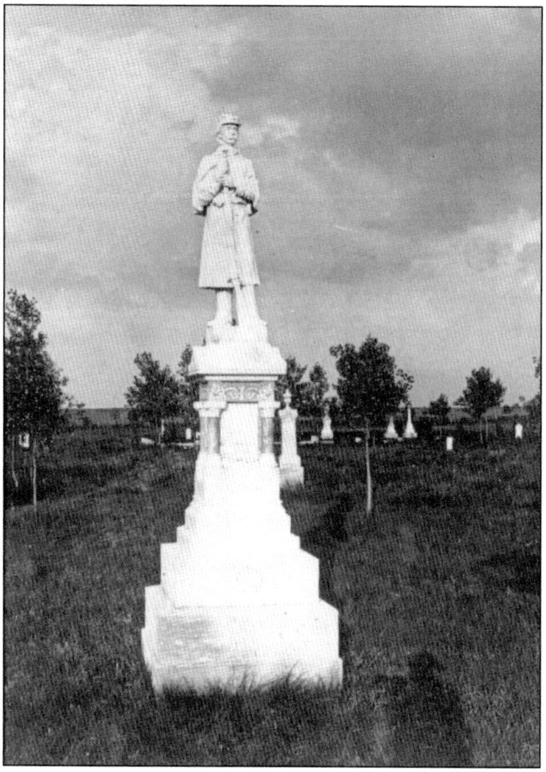

This life-size marble Civil War soldier in the Marysville City Cemetery was erected by the Grand Army of the Republic (GAR) in 1885. It was the first permanent Civil War monument in Kansas. A similar statue was erected in Frankfort later that year. Founded in 1866, the GAR was an organization open to Union veterans. Marshall County members included veterans of Gettysburg, Vicksburg, and other notable battles. The last county Civil War veteran, George Washington Springer of Axtell, died in 1939 at age 94. Springer volunteered for service with the Union army in 1861 at age 16 and was taken prisoner by Stonewall Jackson in 1863. Later paroled, he joined General Sherman on his March to the Sea. The GAR was dissolved nationally in 1956 when the last member died.

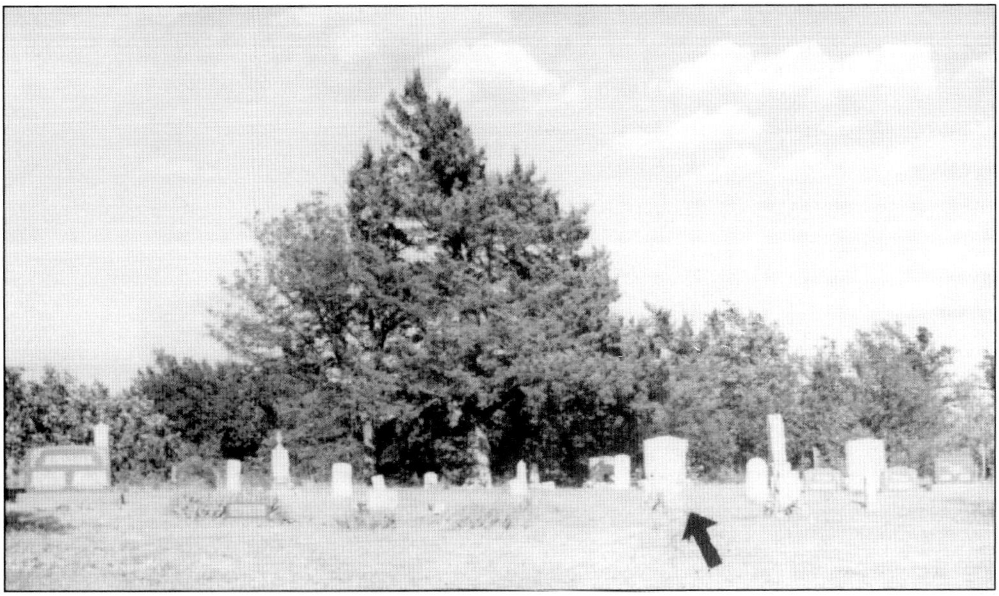

The arrow in this photograph points to the memorial in Wells Cemetery for John D. Wells, Civil War veteran, GAR member, and one of the first settlers in Marshall County. This was the first cemetery in Marshall County, and was located on "Congress Land" purchased by Wells in 1854. Congress Lands were tracts sold to the public through land offices in various cities by the General Land Office, which was created in 1812 to be responsible for public domain lands in the United States.

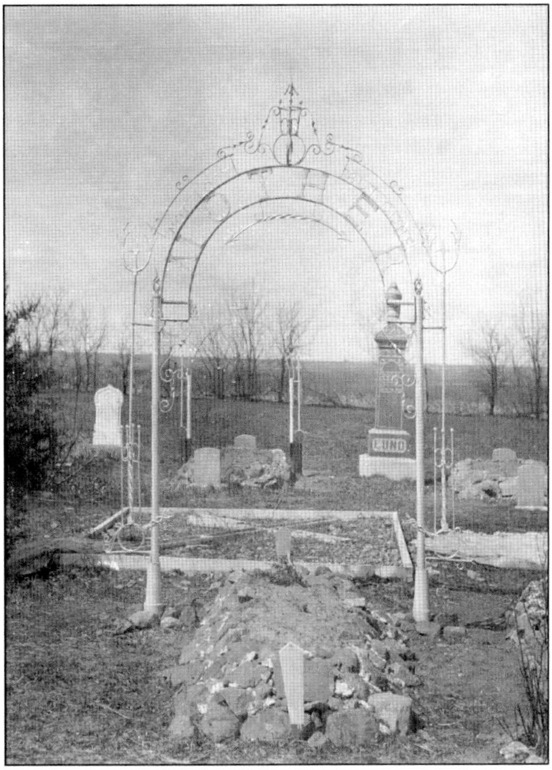



Unique memorial arches and gates were handcrafted of iron by Hans Hanson, a Marysville blacksmith and farmer. Many are in cemeteries throughout Marshall and Riley Counties. One of his prized creations was made for his mother in 1903. Among the tracery of scrolls and a cross is the name Mother. This and other family markers are in the cemetery adjacent to the Danish (English) Lutheran Church in Walnut Township. The final service at this church was held in 1955.

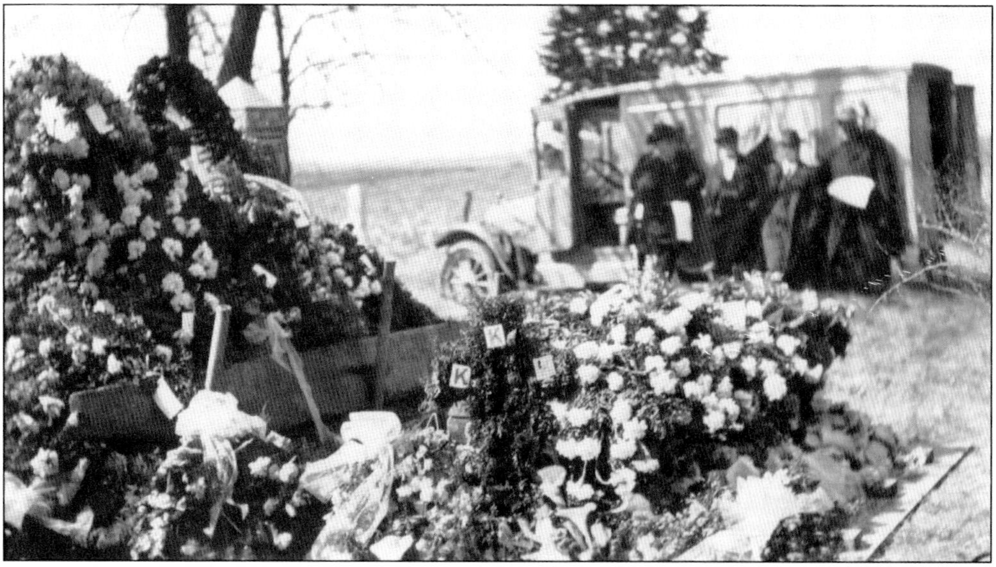

The Ku Klux Klan saw a resurgence in the early 1920s, and by 1924 had made inroads throughout Kansas, including in Marshall County. That year, the Klan applied for a charter to do business in Kansas. It was denied and the resulting lawsuit went all the way to the US Supreme Court, where the appeal was refused. On February 28, 1927, the Klan was legally ousted from Kansas. Although the decedent in this mid-1920s funeral is unidentified, it is likely he was a prominent citizen and a member of the local Ku Klux Klan because of the number and extravagance of the funerary flowers and the floral cross with KKK on it.

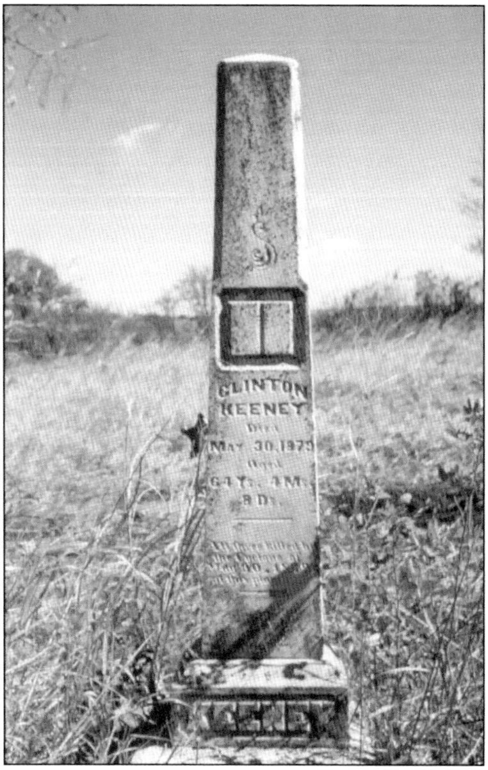


Clinton Keeney, who died in the tornadoes that devastated the town of Irving on May 30, 1879, was buried in Sylvan Shade cemetery at the east edge of Irving. The names of his son and daughter-in-law, also killed in the tornado, are on the sides of the tombstone. Keeney was visiting from Towanda, Pennsylvania. A letter of condolence was sent to Keeney's widow by the Reverend Charles Holmes, minister of the Irving Episcopal Church. It describes the injuries suffered by three surviving Keeney sons, the details of the communal funeral, and the burial of the dead.

# *Nine*

# Death of a Town

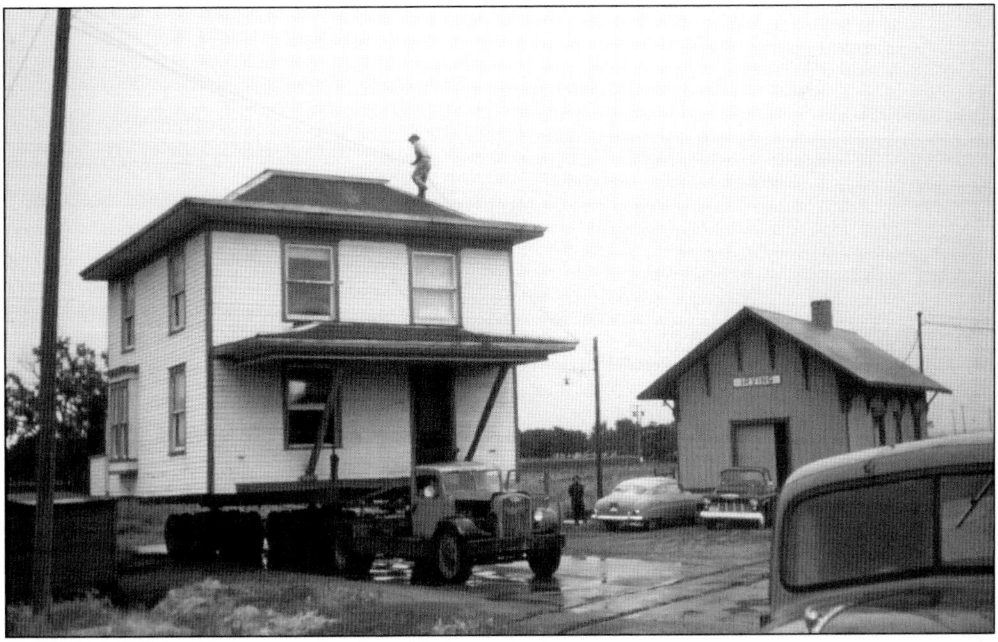


In the late 1950s, the town of Irving (population 300) and seven other communities in a 40-mile stretch of the Blue River valley were leveled to make way for the reservoir of the Tuttle Creek Dam. The dam was being built north of Manhattan, Kansas, by the US Army Corps of Engineers. First proposed in 1938, the project had been highly controversial, but by 1958 the campaign against it was over. In Irving, people were focused on selling or moving their property and beginning life elsewhere. Stone buildings in the town were bulldozed. Many frame buildings were moved. About 20 houses from the town and nine farmhouses in the area were moved five miles to Blue Rapids, and a few others were moved 15 miles to Marysville. Here, the house formerly owned by Fred Cottrell crosses the railroad tracks on its way to Blue Rapids.

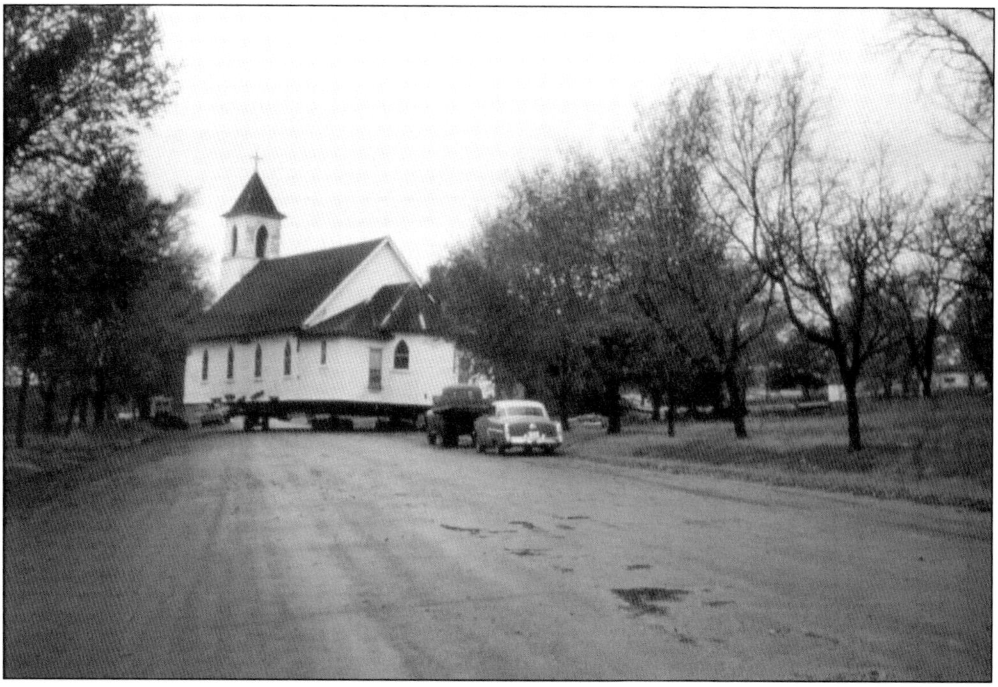

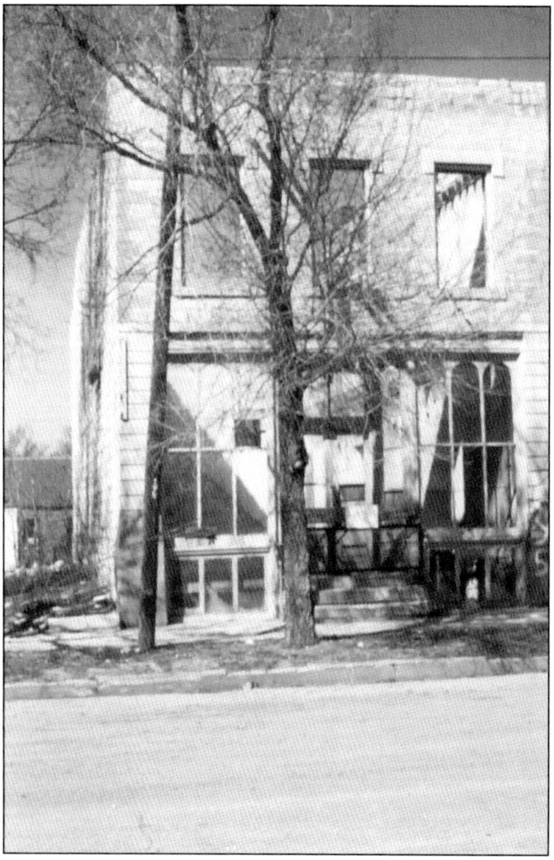

In fall 1958, St. Elizabeth's Catholic Church, built in 1913, begins its journey to the south edge of Blue Rapids, where it remains in use today. The headline in a local paper reads, "First People, Then Houses, Now Churches."

This 1876 stone building on the main street was originally a drugstore, then a general store, then for a time the post office, and finally a creamery. In the 1890s, a barber was located on the second floor. In March 1958, demolition was underway. Like the other stone buildings in Irving, the materials for this building came from limestone quarries located within a few miles of town.

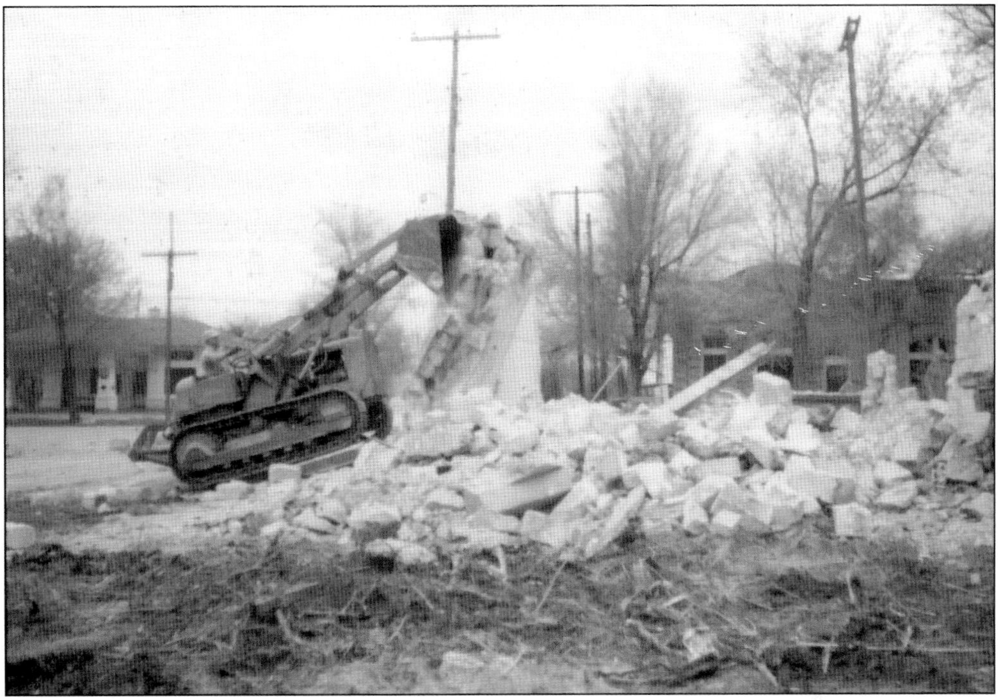

A month later, the bulldozer finishes its work on the back wall of the same building. Although the fate of these stones is not known, many of the stones from demolished buildings were used in construction of other buildings or for retaining walls in other parts of the county.

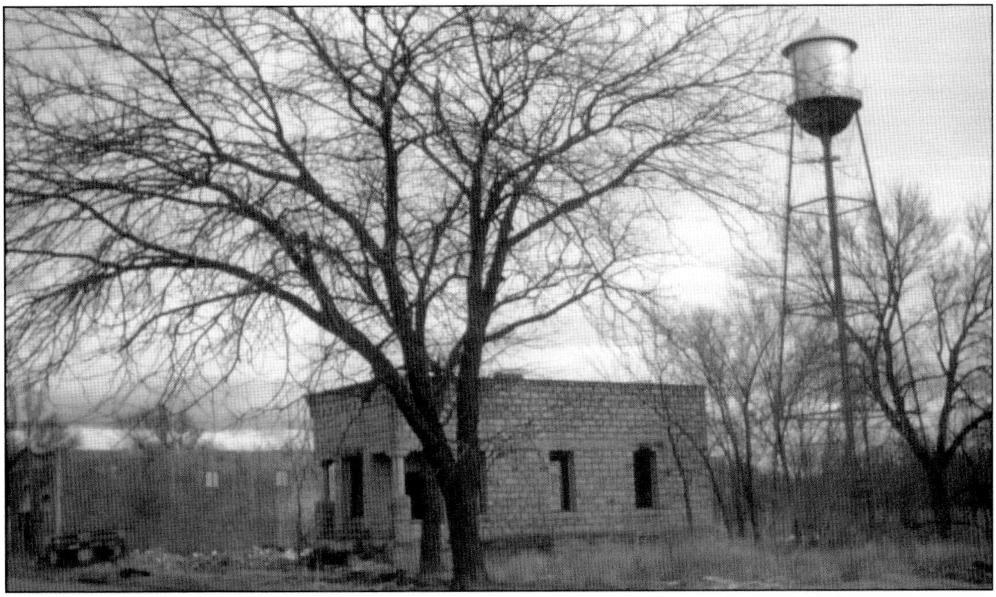

Frame buildings on either side of Irving's main street have been torn down. All that remains are the stone buildings, the most time-consuming to demolish. This building, a gift to the city by a wealthy local donor, was constructed in 1913 to serve as the city hall. Beginning in the 1940s, the town post office was located here. A limestone sign bearing the name Irving was saved from this building and was set up as a marker at the west edge of town.

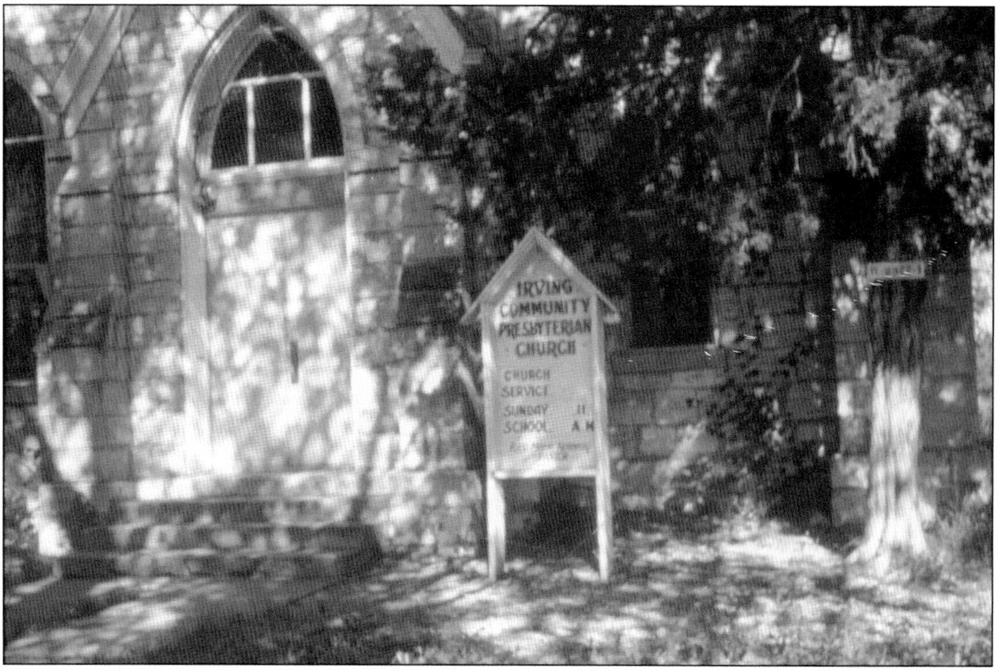


By September 1959, the US Army Corps of Engineers had placed a white marker on the tree at right, its designation that this church was slated for demolition. The oldest Presbyterian church in Marshall County, this congregation was organized in 1862 by Charles Parker, a well-known blind preacher. The first stone church building was destroyed by the tornado of 1879. The vestibule and belfry survived and were incorporated into this building, completed in 1882.

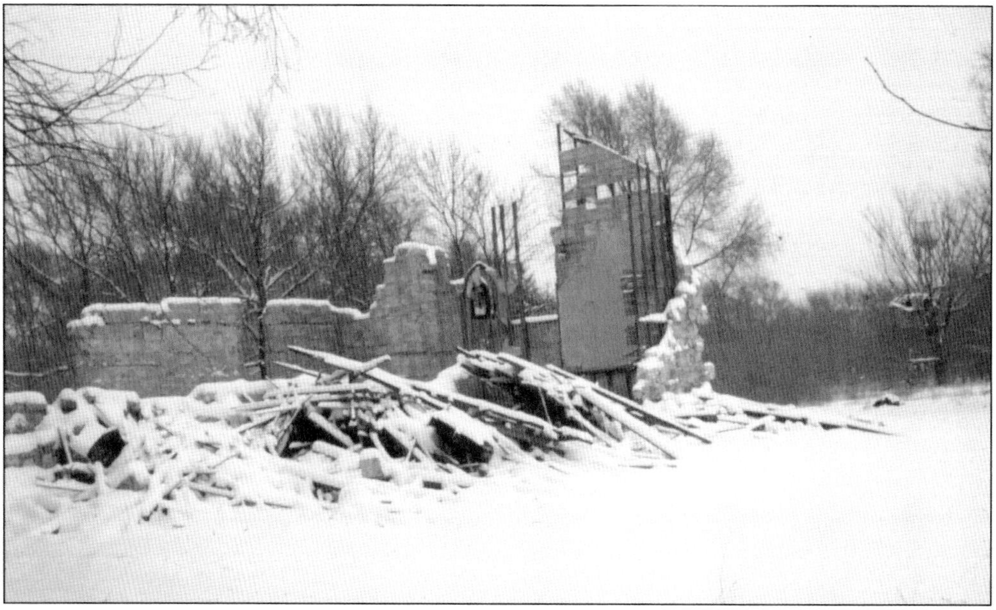

The ruins of the Presbyterian church stand in the snow in January 1961. Some windows and stone from the building had been saved and were later used in an addition to the Blue Rapids Presbyterian Church. The church bell was given to Trinity Presbyterian Church in Manhattan, Kansas, where it can be seen on display today.

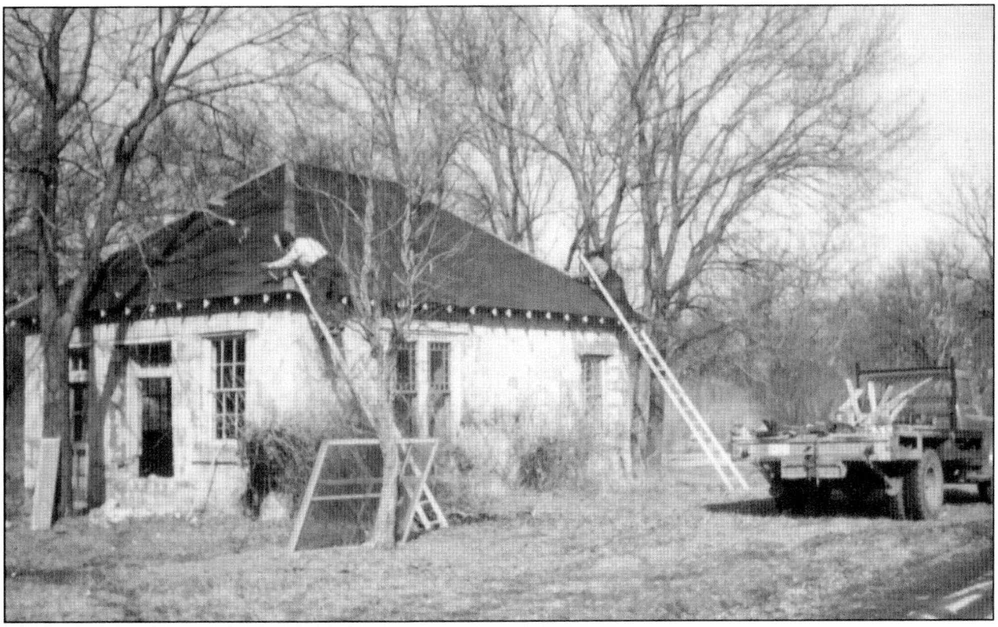

Workers remove shingles from the Irving Museum in January 1961. Built in the 1860s and believed to be the earliest permanent building in Irving, this was originally a blacksmith shop and later the Methodist church. It survived the tornadoes on May 30, 1879, and in the aftermath was used as a makeshift hospital or morgue. In 1941, after years of disuse, it reopened as the Irving Pioneer Museum, said to be the first museum in Marshall County.

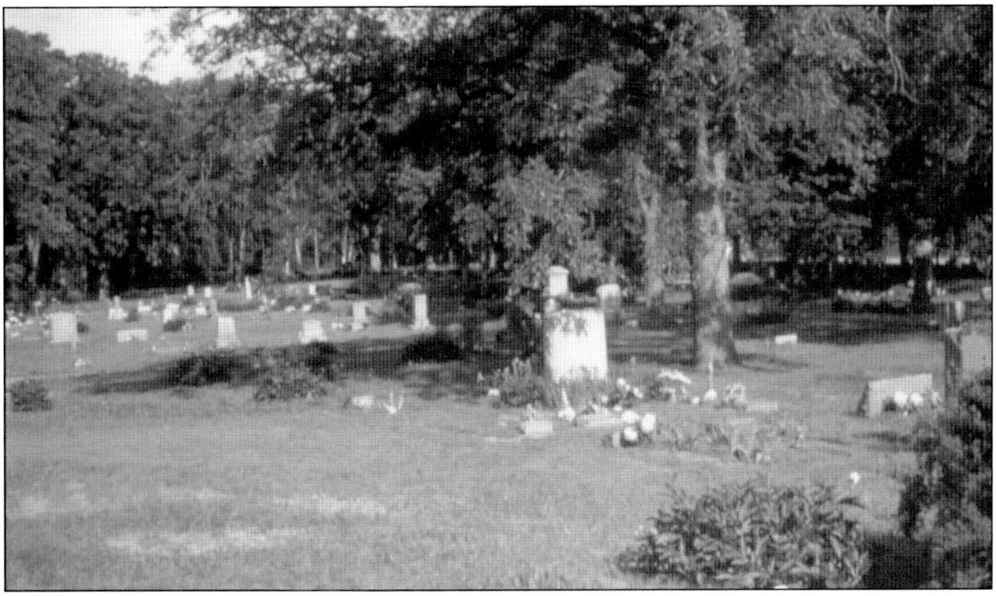

Greenwood Cemetery was established in 1876 across the Blue River from the Irving townsite. In the fall of 1959, nearly 900 graves were moved to a new Greenwood Cemetery that was south of Blue Rapids. The graves were moved by a crew from North Carolina hired by the US Army Corps of Engineers. The crew also moved the graves in Sylvan Shade, an earlier cemetery at the east edge of town. The victims of the 1879 tornadoes were buried there because the bridge between town and Greenwood Cemetery had been destroyed.

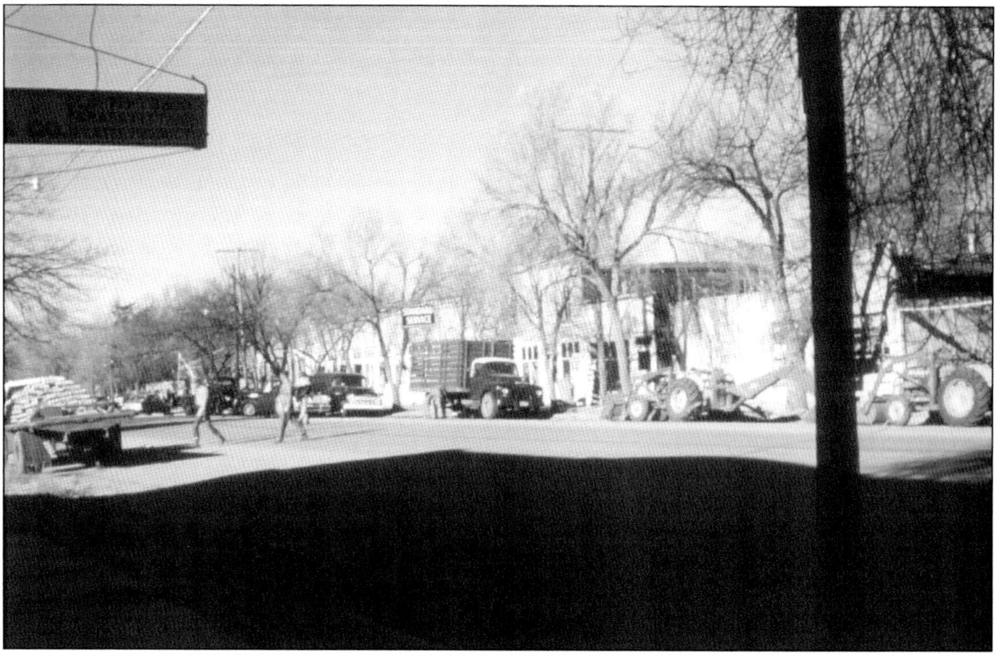

In late 1959, owners and renters along the north side of Main Street clear out their buildings. These people very likely differed in their views about the dam. While many adamantly opposed it, others welcomed the prospect of a chance to be bought out and to restart their businesses elsewhere. Decades later, newspaper interviews with former residents continued to reflect this divergence of views.

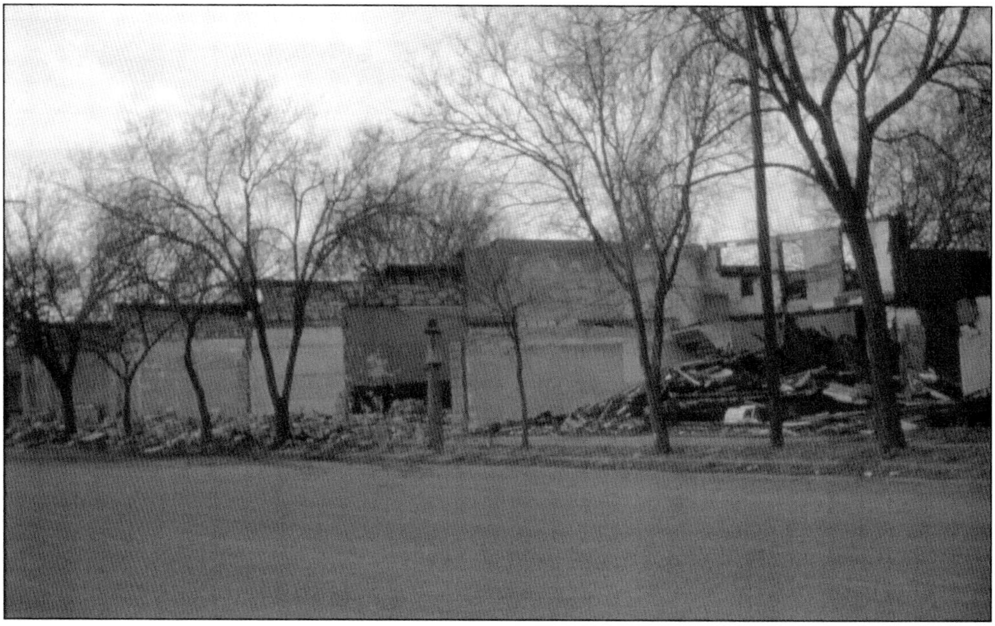

About a year later, demolition of the north side of Main Street is nearly complete. Rubble and common walls are all that remain of a garage and service station, blacksmith, grocery and dry goods store, barbershop, hardware store, restaurant, and a former ice cream parlor known as the Palace of Sweets.

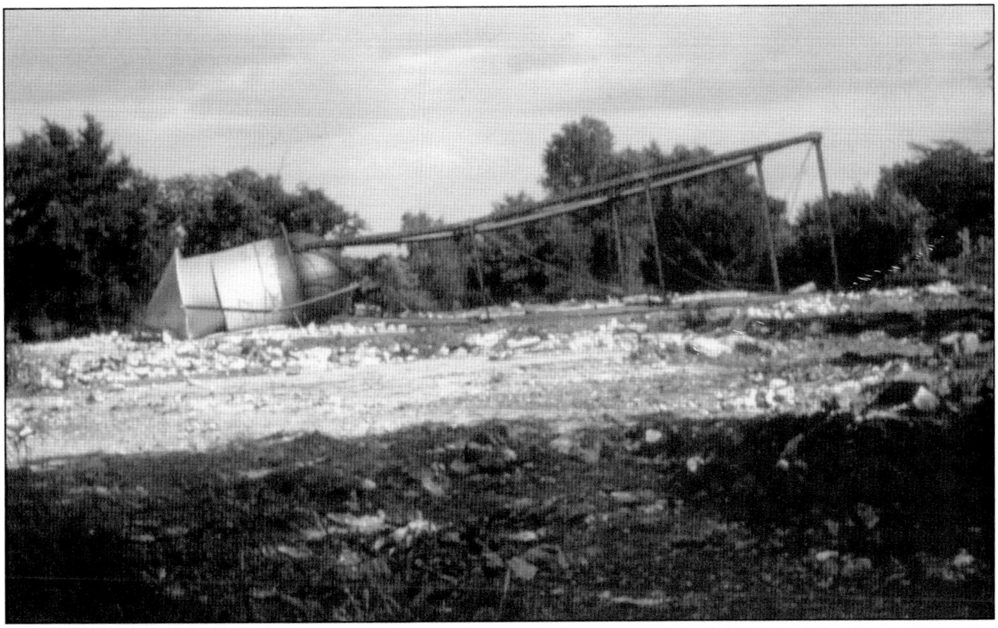

Among the last structures to be taken down was the water tower, in fall 1961. It had stood not far from the site of the "free picture show," a popular summer entertainment in the 1930s and 1940s that sometimes attracted more than 400 people. The town's noon/fire whistle was mounted on the first crossbar of the water tower. The whistle switch and central telephone switchboard were located in a nearby house. The owner of the Irving Telephone Company lived there with his family, who assisted in operating the telephone switchboard located in the front hall. His son recalls that as a child he accidentally bumped his head against the switch on several occasions, causing the switchboard to light up with calls to find out where the fire was.

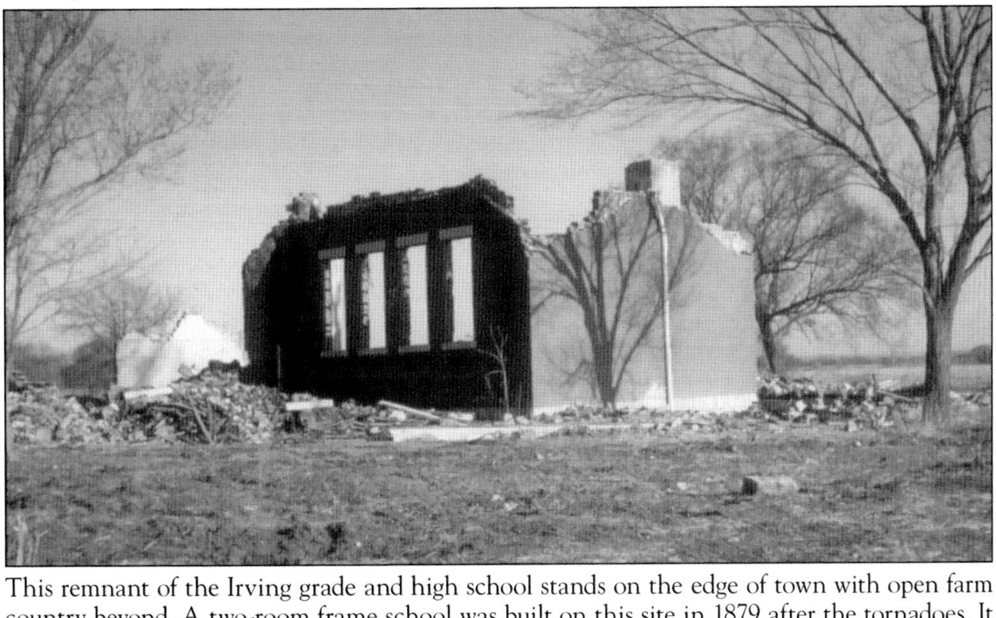

This remnant of the Irving grade and high school stands on the edge of town with open farm country beyond. A two-room frame school was built on this site in 1879 after the tornadoes. It was replaced in 1891, and a large brick addition was constructed in 1917. The last graduating class was in 1957.

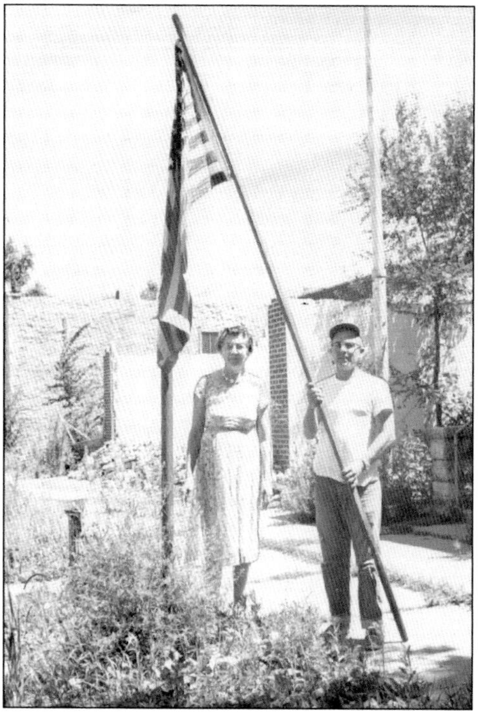

Flossie Harbin, postmaster, and Orville Lee Carter, mail carrier, lowered the flag at the post office for the last time on August 1, 1960. Established June 7, 1860, the post office was in service just over a century. Lillian Deibert wrote to her daughter, "Flossie tells me that she has a stack of letters a foot high sent in from every state in the Union asking for this last-day cancellation."

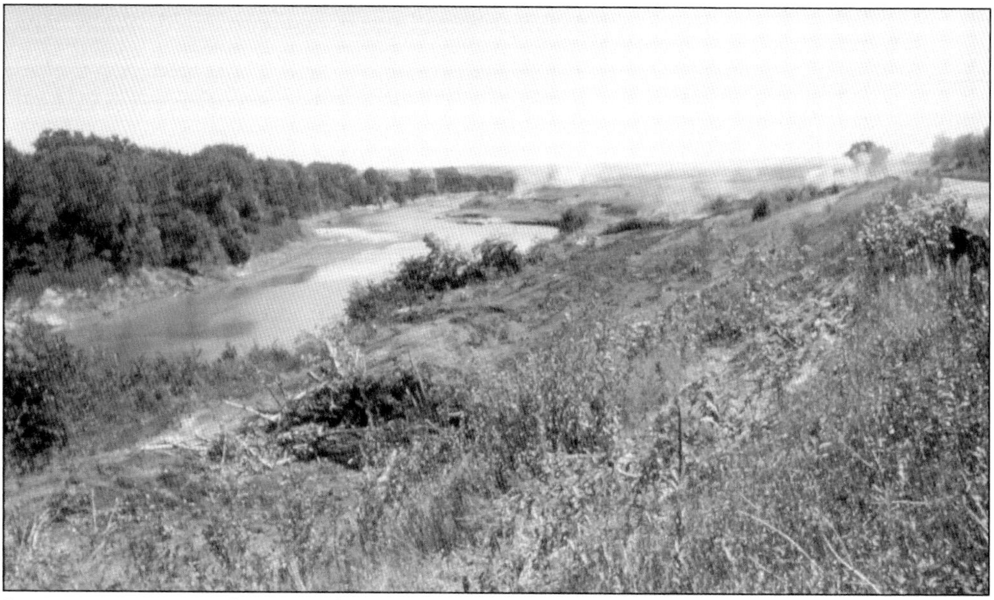

Large trees were cut down and burned throughout the valley to clear the floor of the future reservoir. Here, trees are burning along the Blue River southeast of Irving. In 1959, after a drive down the valley, town resident Lydia Cottrell wrote in her journal, "It makes me sick the way they are tearing up trees—abandoned farmsteads, great high weeds. Progress! Oh, my!" Because it was in that part of the reservoir reserved for flood control, the Irving townsite has been flooded only in times of high water. Farming on easement ground continues in the area and it is still possible to visit the townsite, although the side streets and building foundations have gradually disappeared as nature reclaims them.

# *Ten*

# But Not Forgotten

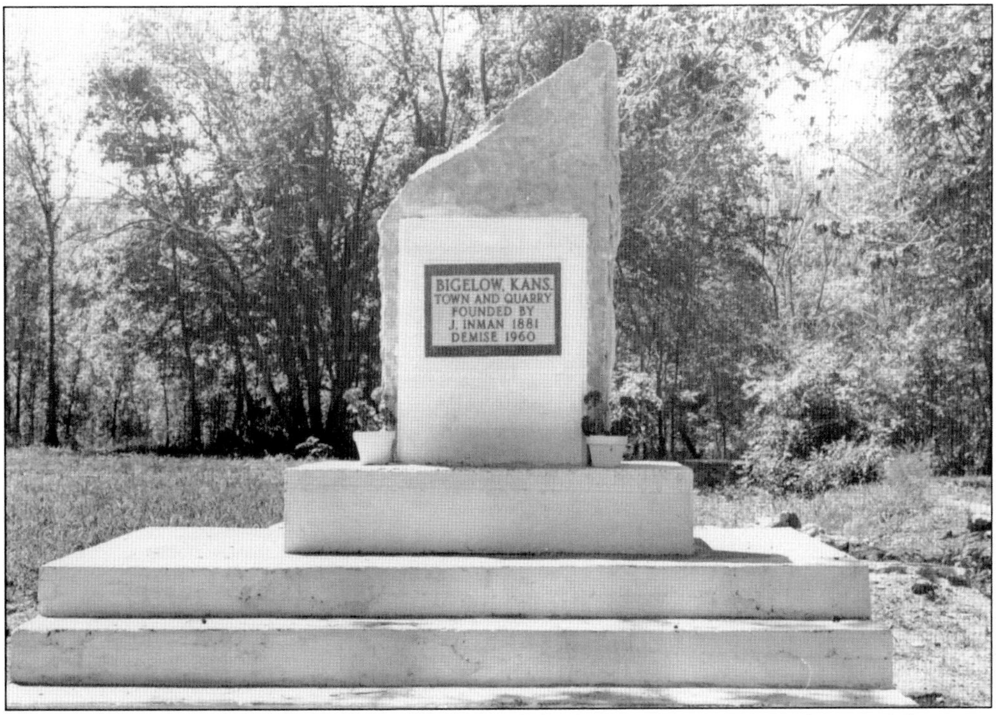


Bigelow was chartered in 1881 and grew up around the limestone quarries in the area. The stone was used for buildings and bridges, including railroad bridges on the local Central Branch line. Bigelow was one of three Marshall County towns that died for the Tuttle Creek Dam project. This marker was erected in 1975, fifteen years after the town was razed in 1960. The stone was quarried locally and was once in the abutment of a nearby bridge over the Black Vermillion River. The monument stands on the steps of the Methodist church, left behind when the church was demolished. More than 50 years later, former residents, their families, and friends continue to meet annually to reminisce and to renew friendships.

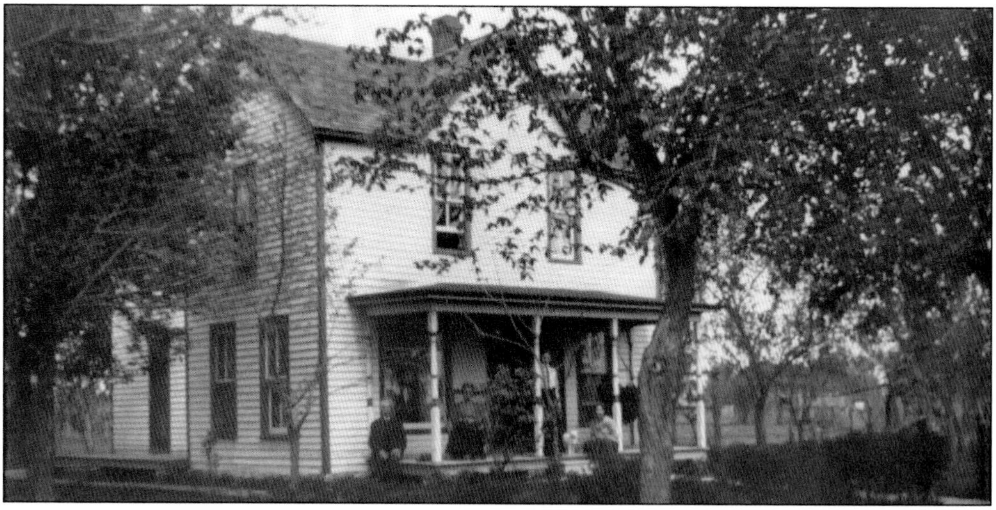

Barrett, like Bigelow and Irving, was claimed by the Tuttle Creek Dam project. A.G. Barrett was one of several men from the Ohio Colony Survey who visited the area in 1855 to choose land for a town. In a later trip, Barrett brought out equipment for a sawmill, hauling it by oxteam from Leavenworth. The Barrett home, shown here, was built in 1858 of native walnut sawed in the Barrett sawmill. Because of flooding from the Black Vermillion River, the house was moved to higher ground in the early 1900s. It was torn down in 1983. What remained of the town of Barrett was demolished to make way for the reservoir in the late 1950s.

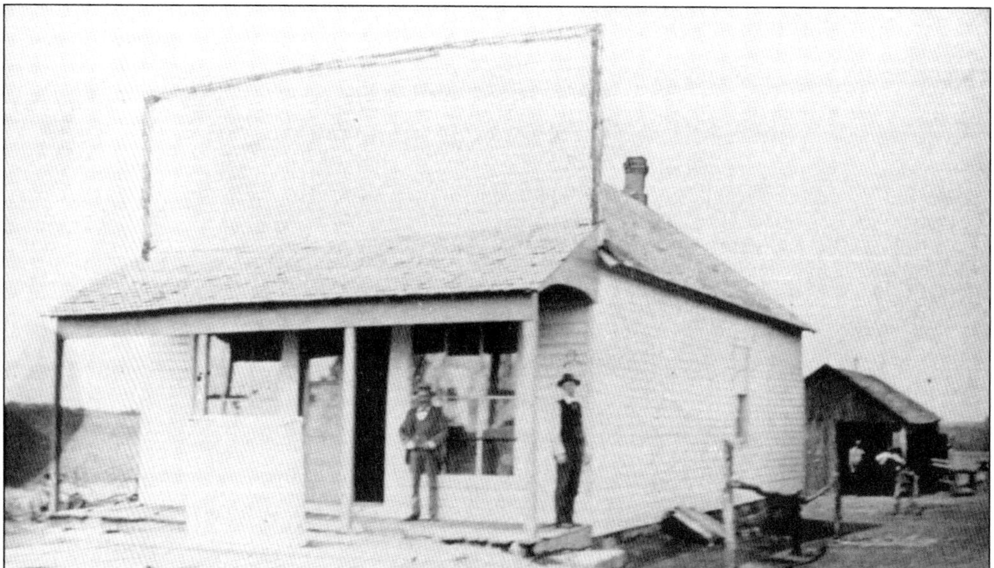

Wealthy Canadian Allen Reed arrived in Marshall County in 1869 and established Reedsville in 1870. When a county seat election was held in 1871, Reedsville was among the unsuccessful challengers to replace Marysville. Reed, at left, and his cousin Al Smith stand on the porch of his general store and post office. The Adamses' blacksmith shop, behind the store, is the only other structure in town. Although it was a convenient trading spot for farmers, it never grew as Reed envisioned. Reed was a state legislator in the 1870s and died in 1903; the town succumbed a year later. This grainy photograph is the only remaining record of this tiny town with lofty aspirations.

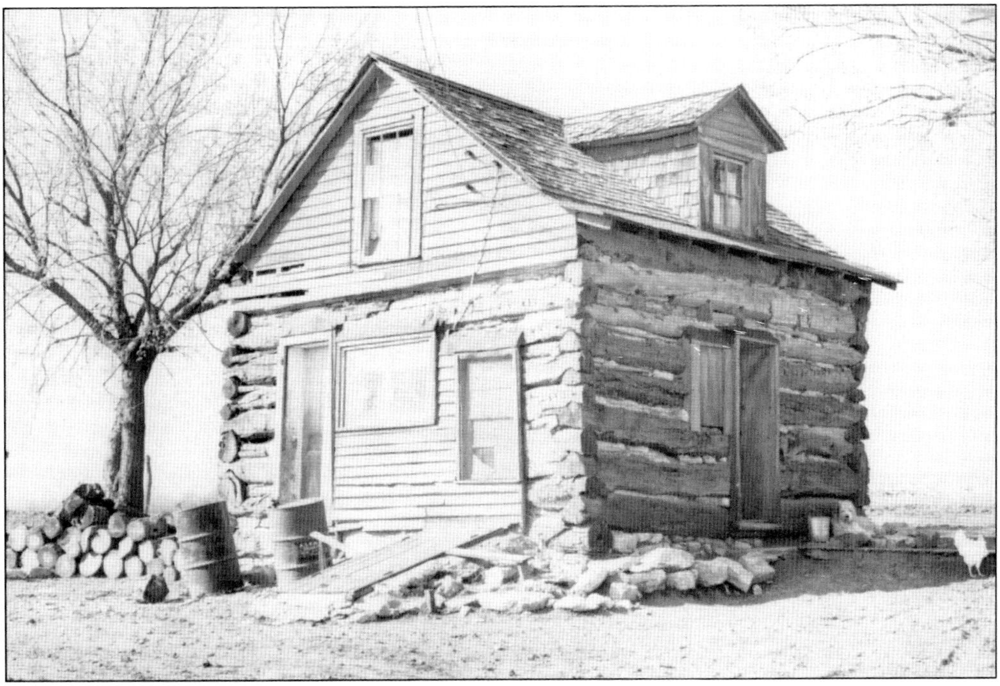

In 1857, New York native Edmund Jones arrived in Marshall County looking for land. He built this cabin south of Frankfort that same year. Legend says his French-born wife took one look and exclaimed, "La grange!" "The barn" is no name for a town, but the French equivalent had a certain rural beauty and so her home was named. La Grange became a post office on a star route in 1875. The name was changed to Lagrange in 1891; the post office closed in 1901.

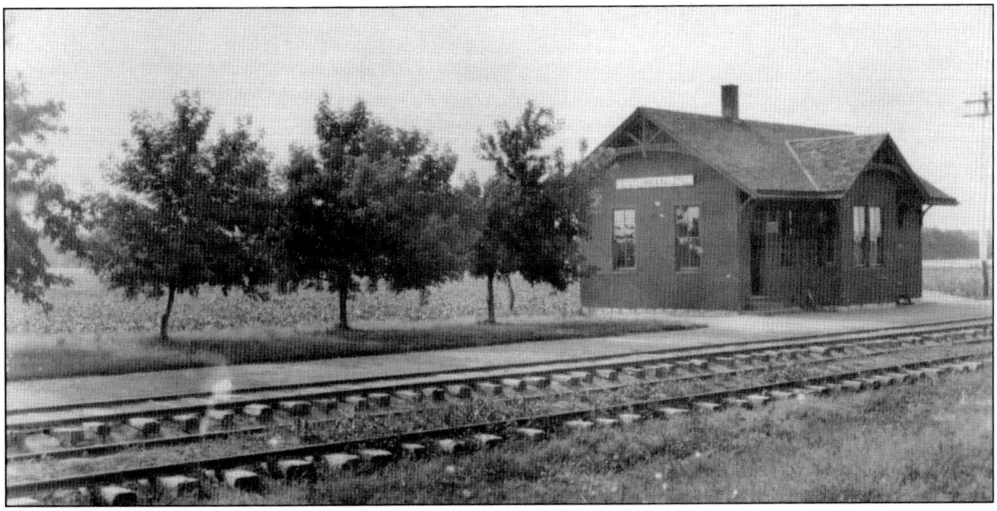

In 1884, the tiny community of Hull was a railroad switch track for the Blue Valley line of the Union Pacific. A post office was established in 1887 and a railroad station was finally built in 1898. The village had an elevator, a blacksmith, and a general store. In the 1920s, it even had a small business that created wood-chip egg crates. The post office was discontinued in 1921. After the elevator burned, the bridge was washed out in the countywide flood of 1941, and the railroad closed the depot, the community was kept alive by a single resident who lived alone in Hull for more than 25 years, finally moving in 1967.

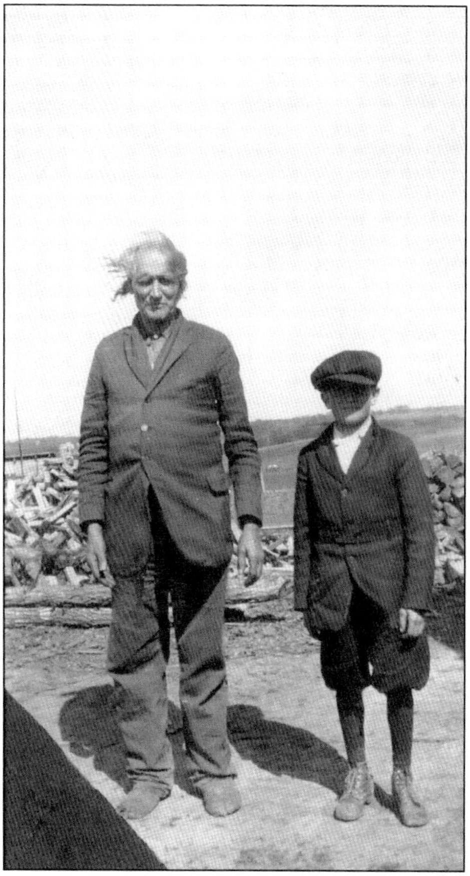

The Afton Store Company incorporated in 1893 and closed in 1921. The company, rather than the federal government, paid a postmaster from 1893 to 1898 and 1900 to 1901. Afton was big enough at one time to have a small town band. John Derringer, known in the county as Indian John, was a faith healer and herb doctor who lived near the Afton Store. He is shown here around 1920 with one of his foster sons, wards of the state, whom he kept in the summer to help gather the herbs and weeds he used to make tonics. He died at age 92 in 1924.

Mina had one of everything: one elevator, one depot, one store, one church, one school, and one street. It was platted in 1888 along Kansas City-Wyandotte-Northwestern tracks that had been laid in 1887. Abandoned by the railroad in 1925, it disappeared quickly into farm fields.

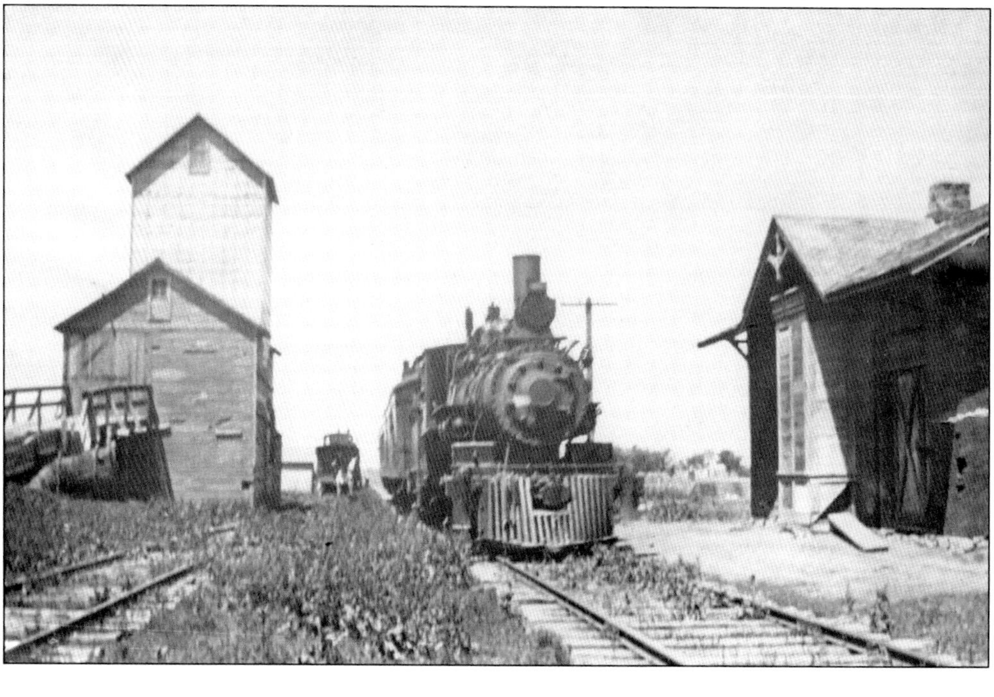

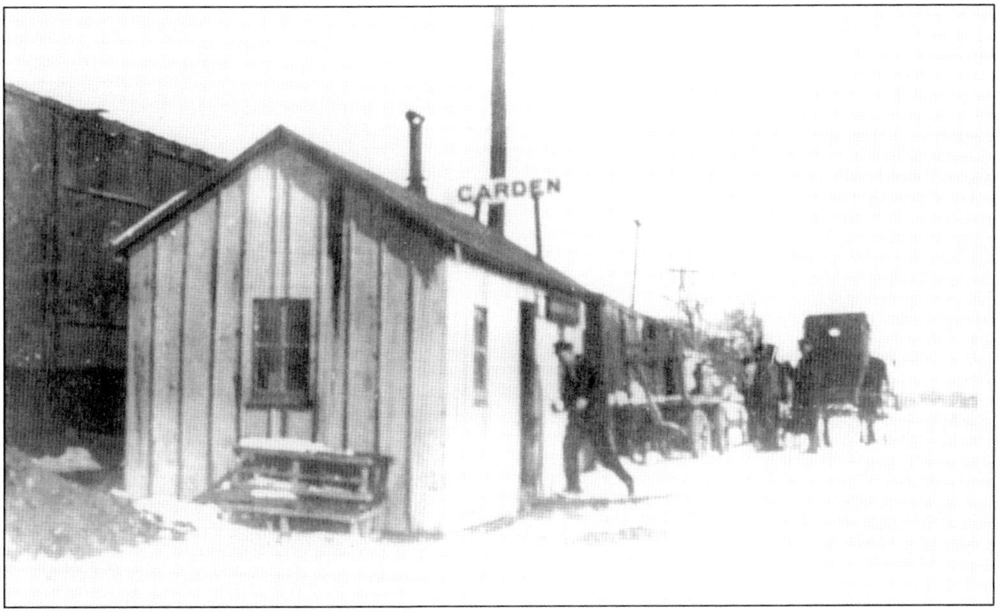


Carden was only one square block, barely large enough for this depot. Platted in 1901, the "town" was owned by Jake Andrews. Despite its size, Carden had an elevator, grocery store with post office, blacksmith shop, and the depot. The post office closed in 1923 and the town passed into history. This fading photograph is the only known picture of Carden.

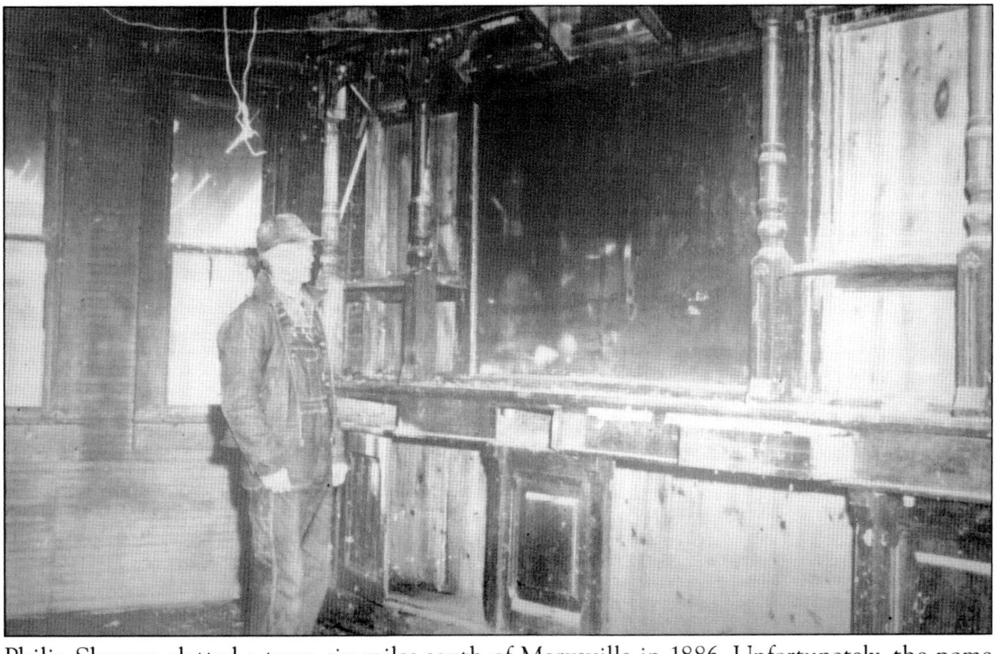

Philip Shroyer platted a town six miles south of Marysville in 1886. Unfortunately, the name was misspelled on the depot and the railroad said it would be too expensive to change it. Thus the town of Schroyer was born. In this photograph, Ralph Griffee, the last resident of the town, stands in front of the bar of the O.K. Saloon—the last remaining building of its type in Marshall County—around 1955. The bar was moved to Old Abilene Town in Abilene, Kansas, in 1960, and in 1967 the remainder of Schroyer was sold at auction. It is now farmland.

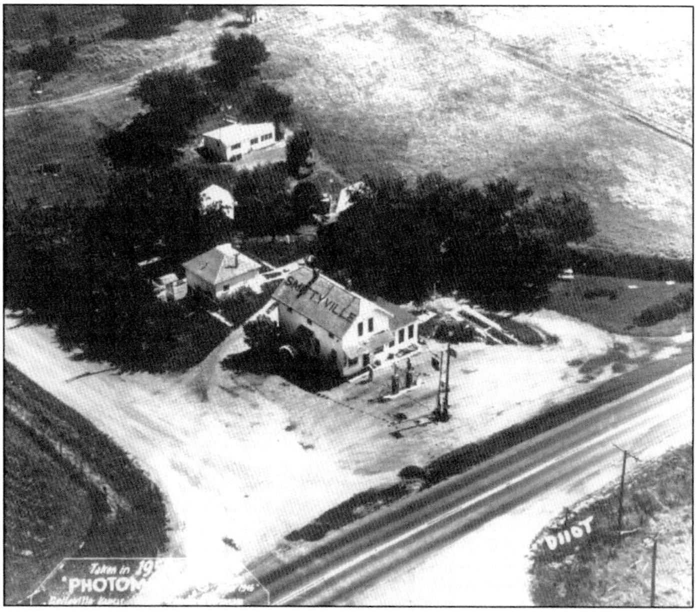

Smittyville was never really a town, but everyone knew this Highway 36 landmark. After selling his farm, Ed Schmidt built a gasoline station in 1935. Before long, he added cigarettes, soda pop, candy, honey from the family apiary, and other convenience items. During World War II, he bought and sold scrap. Schmidt died in 1949, but his wife continued the service station until 1956.

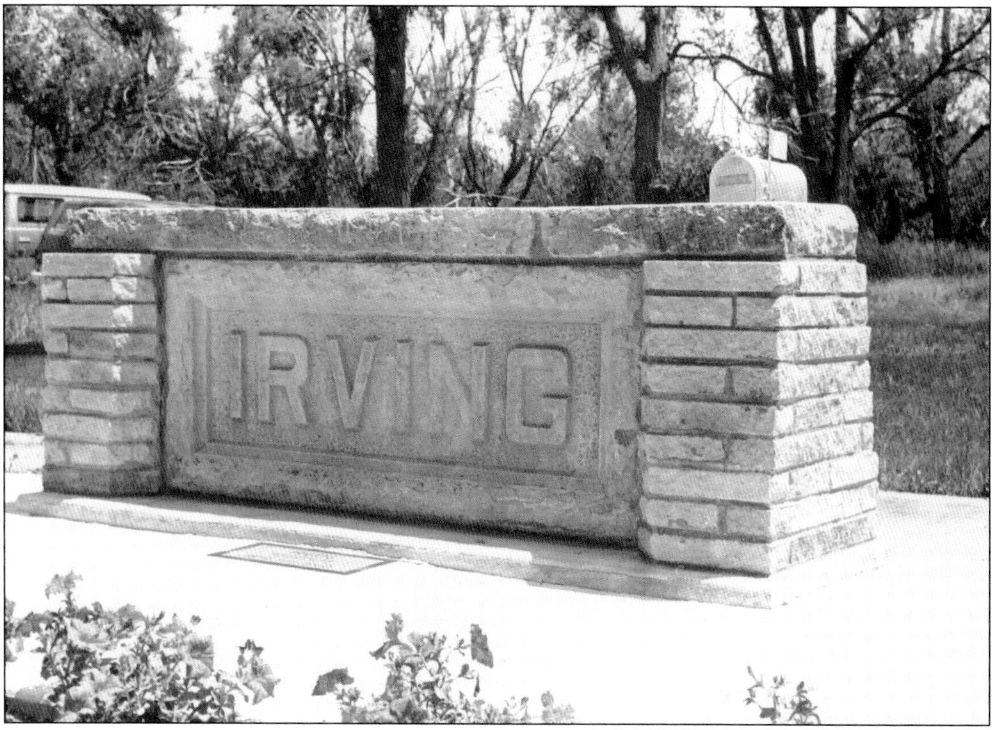


The Irving monument is located at a corner on the west side of the former town of Irving, five miles southeast of Blue Rapids. The mailbox is visible behind the monument in this 1988 photograph. Visitors are invited to leave a message in the notebook in the mailbox. Messages have included memories of Irving, love notes, accolades for friends and winning teams, and notes about visits to other vanished towns. With nearly 50 Marshall County towns and post offices that were the dreams of early settlers—some established, some never more than an elaborate plan—visitors to this monument have much county history to reflect on.

# About the Marshall County Historical Society

Despite Marshall County's rich pioneer history, it did not have a local historical society until 1971. The enthusiastic founders of the new organization were very soon swept up in a controversy over the future of the county courthouse, built in 1891 and deemed by some to be outmoded and possibly unsafe. The Marshall County Historical Society mounted a vigorous campaign to rally public support for preservation of the building. In 1979, when county government moved into a new building just 50 yards to the west, the historical society was given ownership and responsibility for the old courthouse. Since then, it has developed a county museum and a genealogical and historical research library in this majestic old building.

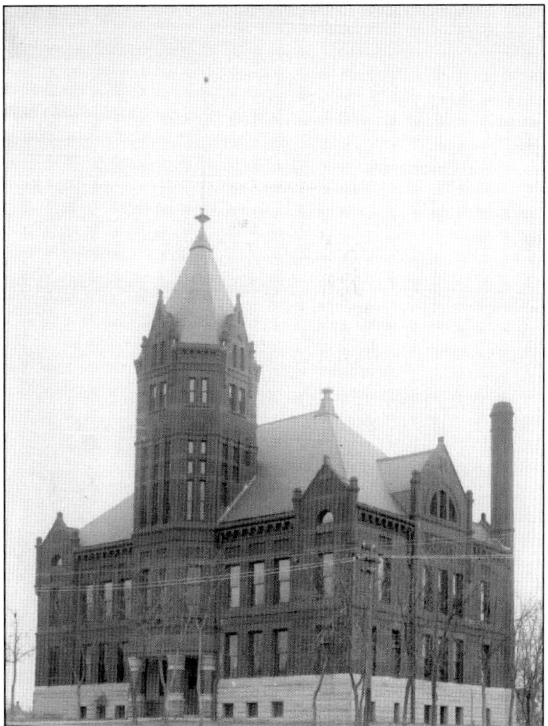

1207 Broadway
Marysville, KS, 66508
Phone: 785-562-5012
mchs@bluevalley.net
www.marysvillemuseumsks.org
Find us on Facebook at "Marshall County Historical Society Marysville"

Hours (April–October)
10:00 a.m.–4:00 p.m., Monday–Saturday
1:00 p.m.–4:00 p.m., Sunday
Hours (November–March)
1:00 p.m.–4:00 p.m., Monday–Friday